PSYCHOANALYSIS
AND
DEVELOPMENTAL THERAPY

Monograph Series of

The Psychoanalysis Unit of University College London
and
The Anna Freud Centre

Series Editors
Joseph Sandler & Peter Fonagy

PSYCHOANALYSIS AND DEVELOPMENTAL THERAPY

edited by

Anne Hurry

contributors

Tessa Baradon	*Maria Grazia Cassola*
Peter Fonagy	*Anat Gedulter-Trieman*
Viviane Green	*Adriana Grotta*
Anne Harrison	*Anne Hurry*
Mary Target	*Marie Zaphiriou Woods*

Foreword by

Anne-Marie Sandler

International Universities Press, Inc.
Madison   Connecticut

Excerpt on pp. 60–61 reprinted by permission from J. Hopkins, "From baby games to let's pretend: the achievement of playing." *Journal of the British Association of Psychotherapy, 31* (1, Part 2, 1996): 20–27.

First published in 1998 by
H. Karnac (Books) Ltd.
58 Gloucester Road
London SW7 4QY

Library of Congress Cataloging-in-Publication Data

Psychoanalysis and developmental therapy / edited by Anne Hurry ;
    contributors, Tessa Baradon . . . [et al.] ; foreword by Anne-Marie
    Sandler.
        p.   cm. — (Monograph series of the Psychoanalysis Unit of
    University College London and the Anna Freud Centre ; no. 3)
        Includes bibliographical references and index.
        ISBN 0-8236-5150-9
        1. Child analysis Case studies.   2. Developmental therapy for
    children Case studies.   I. Hurry, Anne.   II. Series: Monograph
    series of the Psychoanalysis Unit of University College, London and
    the Anna Freud Centre, London ; no. 3.
    RJ504.2.P794   1999
    618.92'8917—dc21   99-25799
                                                                             CIP

Manufactured in the United States of America

THE PSYCHOANALYSIS UNIT AT UNIVERSITY COLLEGE LONDON was founded by Joseph Sandler in 1984, when he was appointed to the Freud Memorial Chair of Psychoanalysis in the University of London (which replaced the annual Freud Memorial Visiting Professorship at UCL). The Unit is based in the Psychology Department, arguably the strongest, and certainly the broadest, department of psychology in the United Kingdom. The Unit quickly became a thriving centre for academic psychoanalysis and established a busy doctoral programme in psychoanalytic research. A weekly programme of lectures was organized, and several highly successful psychoanalytic conferences have been held each year. Through the Unit psychoanalysis began to occupy a central place in the intellectual life of University College London.

The Unit initiated close collaboration with the International Psychoanalytical Association. Major scientific meetings of the Association were held in conjunction with the Unit, including the annual IPA Conference in Psychoanalytic Research and an IPA Conference on Psychoanalysis and Literature. In addition to fostering these important links between international psychoanalysis and the British university, the Unit maintains close ties with the British Psycho-Analytical Society. It collaborates regularly with the major theoretical groups within the Society in offering an academic platform for presenting and discussing their views.

In 1992 Peter Fonagy succeeded Joseph Sandler in the Freud Chair, with Professor Sandler remaining as a Co-director of the Unit. The Unit's focus on post-graduate education has continued, with now over a dozen Ph.D. students at any one time. In collaboration with the British Psycho-Analytical Society, the Unit has created a Master of Science degree in Theoretical Psychoanalytic Studies (non-clinical). Over the years, the strength of the link between the Unit and other psychoanalytic organizations has increased, with academic members of the staff of The Anna Freud Centre becoming affiliated to the University via the Psychoanalysis Unit. The Unit's original links to the Psychology Department have been maintained and developed, with Professor Fonagy assuming the headship of the Sub-Department of Clinical Health Psychology on its inception in 1994. The international influence of the Unit continues to increase, and in 1995 it organized and hosted the first research training programme for psychoanalysts sponsored by the International Psycho-Analytical Association. As part of this development, leading psychoanalytic researchers became visiting professors of the Unit; these have included Professors Robert Emde, Horst Kächele, Wilma Bucci, Otto Kernberg, and Peter Hobson.

The mission of the Unit remains the integration of psychoanalytic ideas with academic pursuits across a range of disciplines—literature, medicine, the social sciences, the arts. The Unit frequently consults with leading academics from those disciplines who seek advice on psychoanalytic aspects of their work. It has become a national and international centre for psychoanalytic research and scholarship.

 THE ANNA FREUD CENTRE was founded by Anna Freud in 1940 as the Hampstead War Nurseries, which provided a home for children who had lost their own homes or were separated from their parents in some other way in the Blitz. After the war, Anna Freud responded to the urgent demand for greater expertise in child mental health and the childhood disorders by founding The Hampstead Child Therapy Course and the Clinic, which, after Anna Freud's death, was renamed in 1984 as The Anna Freud Centre.

Since its inception, The Hampstead Child Therapy Course has provided high-level, intensive training in all aspects of child psychoanalysis and psychotherapy. Training at the Centre has received formal accreditation from the International Association for Child Psychoanalysis, and many of the child psychoanalysts and psychotherapists trained at the Centre are currently practicing in the United Kingdom and elsewhere.

After the untimely death in 1992 of the Director, George Moran, Rose Edgcumbe functioned as Acting Director until 1993, when Anne-Marie Sandler was appointed to the Directorship. After her retirement in 1996, Julia Fabricius was appointed to the post. In addition to combining therapy, training, and research, the Centre provides a psychiatric assessment and advisory service for children and young adults, long-term therapy and young adults' consultation and preventive services, and an internationally recognized and highly esteemed programme of research. In an important collaboration with University College London, the Centre offers a Master of Science degree in Psychoanalytic Developmental Psychology. This unique course reflects the extension and accreditation of the Centre's well-established teaching programme.

amazon.ca™ **http://www.amazon.ca**

M

Amazon.com.ca, Inc.
c/o ACFSI
6363 Millcreek Drive
Mississauga, ON L5N 1L8
Canada

Gift From/De la part de:
Richard Bond
17 WEBSTER PL APT 301
EAST ORANGE, NJ 07018-1722
United States

Shipping Address/Adresse d'expédition:
Richard Bond
17 WEBSTER PL APT 301
EAST ORANGE, NJ 07018-1722
United States

Invoice for/Bon de livraison pour

Invoice number/N° bon de livraison Dc61nYmcR August 5, 2011

Your order of/Votre commande du:August 5, 2011
Order ID/N° commande: 702-5425023-3733020

Quantity/Quantité	Item/Article	Description/Description	Our Price/Notre prix	Total/Total
1	Psychoanalysis and Developmental Therapy **(** ** E-7 ** **) 0823651509**	Hardcover		

Thank You.

shipMessage4
shipMessageCa4

Amazon.com.ca,Inc. 410 Terry Avenue North Seattle, WA 98109-5210

CONTENTS

III

CLINICAL AND EDUCATIONAL INTERVENTIONS
IN WORK WITH CHILDREN

PREFACE

This book shows the child analyst at work; the clinical chapters give detailed accounts of the interaction between analyst and child. In presenting these case studies, we have been mindful of the need to preserve confidentiality. Patients, both adults and children, have the right for their privacy to be respected, and all the families in this book have been disguised.

A particular difficulty regarding confidentiality arises in the case of work with children, as concurrent work with the parents is usually an essential part of the treatment approach. But to publish details of work with parents alongside accounts of a child's treatment makes it more difficult to preserve patients' anonymity. We have therefore omitted any detailed account of work with parents, but we wish to acknowledge the commitment and courage of the parents of the children in this book, most of whom not only supported their child's treatment, but were also prepared to face their own difficulties where necessary.

It is not possible to disguise clinical material in such a way that it will be unrecognizable to the patient concerned. We share our work with others so that mutual learning may take place and our ability to help troubled children grow. Patrick Casement (1985) has thoughtfully explored the issues of confidentiality and publication, and we conclude with his words: "If patients . . . have gained as much from the clinical encounter as I have, I hope they may be glad that I have considered it to be worth sharing some of this with others" (p. 226).

* * *

Psychoanalytic work furthers the development of both patient and analyst. The authors would like to thank all those patients from whom they have learnt and with whom they have grown.

NOTE

For economy, in the general case, we refer to the child/patient as he and the main caregiver/analyst as she.

FOREWORD

Anne-Marie Sandler

Many books have recently appeared on a variety of psychoanalytic topics, but relatively few have dealt specifically with problems of technique and with the theory that informs those techniques. It is therefore particularly fortunate that this book does just that.

The central and greater part of the book consists of a series of detailed descriptions of clinical work with children. The authors have something in common, all having trained wholly or in part at the Anna Freud Centre. They have been guided in their understanding of their patients' problems by a fundamentally psychoanalytic orientation in which the role of internal conflicts, anxiety, guilt, love and hate, primitive as well as more sophisticated object relations, and a complex variety of defences take a central place. They have also been influenced by their knowledge of normal development and their awareness of the pathological consequences of uneven or faulty development. Their psychoanalytic technical approach has been influenced by recent advances in our understanding of development, in particular of the nature of infant attachment, of the vicissitudes of attunement between mother and baby and their consequences, and of the vital importance of the development of mentalization and the reflective function.

The book is divided into three parts, the first giving the theoretical background to the clinical descriptions that follow in Parts II and III. The first chapter, by Peter Fonagy and Mary Target, details some recent infant-observation research illustrating the interpersonal and interactional aspects of the parent–infant relationship and considers the implications of these findings for psychoanalytic practice. The second chapter, by Anne Hurry, distinguishes the developmental and the more classical "analytic" elements within the therapeutic process, giving the rationale for the various techniques that child analysts have found themselves using. It makes links between child and adult work, suggesting that the so-called developmental approach, which had been adopted by Anna Freud and extended by her followers, resembles in many ways the object relational approach found in the work of the Independent analysts in the United Kingdom, and Hans Loewald in the United States.

Central to this book is the view that developmental factors play a role in all analyses, alongside the analysis of neurosis. The authors show how the child uses the analyst both as a transference object and as a new developmental object, illustrating the mutually enabling and inextricably interwoven nature of developmental work and interpretation of conflict. They support the view that change comes about as the result of the child's internalization of new models of relating, gradually acquired and built up by the joint work of patient and analyst.

In the last section of the book, two chapters exemplify a special kind of application of psychoanalysis. The work undertaken with a young, traumatized girl beautifully illustrates how educational and therapeutic interventions can be used side by side to help certain types of children. In the final clinical case, the need for multiple interventions and thoughtful and sensitive collaboration between a number of professionals is described. In this case, no progress could have been achieved by psychoanalytic work alone, however sensitive and profound, without the support of a whole network of well-briefed colleagues.

CONTRIBUTORS

TESSA BARADON is a member of staff at the Anna Freud Centre, where she is Manager of the Parent and Infant Project—a consultative and therapeutic service for young children and their parents. She has been responsible for the planning and provision of services for parents and infants in local authority Social Services Departments and the NHS. She teaches therapists and allied professionals about normal and pathological child development.

MARIA GRAZIA CASSOLA is a Child Neuropsychiatrist, working at a NHS Mother–Child Clinic in Northern Italy. She co-ordinates and is in charge of the therapeutic programme.

PETER FONAGY is Freud Memorial Professor of Psychoanalysis and Director of the Sub-Department of Clinical Health Psychology at University College London. He is Director of Research at the Anna Freud Centre, London, and Director of the Child and Family Center at the Menninger Foundation, Kansas. He is a Clinical Psychologist and a Training and Supervising Analyst in the British Psycho-Analytical Society. His research interests include the study of the outcome of psychoanalytic psychotherapy and the impact of the early parent–child relationship on personality development. He is the author of over 170 chapters and papers, has co-authored and edited five books, and is a Fellow of the British Academy. He is a Vice-President of the International Psychoanalytical Association and is the current chair of its Standing Committee on Research. He serves on the Executive Council of the world association of Infant Mental Health.

ANAT GEDULTER-TRIEMAN is a member of staff at the Anna Freud Centre. Previously she worked with delinquent adolescents for almost a decade. As a senior supervisor in the Israeli Youth Protection Authority, she regularly trained and supervised social and residential workers. She was also involved in a special programme of family interventions within the YPA care facilities.

VIVIANE GREEN is a member of staff and Head of Clinical Training at the Anna Freud Centre London. She is a visiting lecturer at the University of Padua in Italy.

ADRIANA GROTTA is a clinical psychologist and psychoanalytically oriented child psychotherapist in private practice. She did part of her training at the Anna Freud Centre, where she attended the one year course on psychoanalytic theory, developmental psychoanalytic psychology, assessment, mother–infant observation and toddler observation. Subsequently her clinical work was supervised by A. Gavshon. She has a particular interest in assessment. In 1988 she developed a course on assessment utilizing the conceptualization of Anna Freud's diagnostic profile for the Department of Child Neuropsychiatry at the University of Milan.

ANNE HARRISON is a Member of the British Psychoanalytical Society. She has worked for a number of years in community mental health. She was a member of staff at the Portman Clinic for four years. She is currently completing training as a Child Analyst, and is a member of the editorial board of the Journal of Child Psychotherapy.

ANNE HURRY is a member of staff at the Anna Freud Centre where she is a clinical consultant and supervisor. She was the founding Chair of the Child Psychotherapy Training at the British Association of Psychotherapists where she is also a supervising and training therapist for the Adult Psychoanalytic Psychotherapy Section. She is a past editor of the Journal of Child Psychotherapy and has published widely on both clinical and theoretical topics.

MARY TARGET is an Associate Member of the British Psychoanalytical Society. She is a Senior Lecturer in Psychology at University

College London. She trained first in Experimental then in Clinical Psychology and worked for ten years in adult and child psychiatric units. Subsequently she has carried out research at the Anna Freud Centre on the outcome of child psychoanalysis, which has led to further innovative projects on the measurement of personality, emotional development, and attachment in childhood and adulthood, and the evaluation of psychotherapy process and outcomes. She has written with others on psychotherapy outcome, psychoanalytic theories of personality development, and child analytic technique, as well as on the relevance of findings from general psychology, including memory research, for psychotherapy theory and practice.

MARIE ZAPHIRIOU WOODS is a member of staff and a supervisor at the Anna Freud Centre where she was the Nursery School Consultant from 1986–1997. Currently she is consultant to the Toddler Group Staff. She is an Associate member of the British Psychoanalytical Society.

PART I

Theoretical background

CHAPTER ONE

An interpersonal view of the infant

Peter Fonagy & Mary Target

T his chapter aims to help extend ideas emanating from infant observational data into clinical work. Research on the social development of infants is probably the area of empirical science with most influence on psychoanalysis. The work of Stern (1985, 1994) as well as of Robert Emde (1980a, 1980b, 1981, 1988, 1992) established infant research as central to the further evolution of psychoanalytic theory. There have, however, been some cogent objections to the impact of infancy research on psychoanalysis. For example, Wolff (1996) warned of the epistemological dangers in extrapolating from infant research to the behaviour of adult patients. Others point to what such perspectives omit from the traditional psychoanalytic approach (e.g. Fajardo, 1993; Green, 1995). We welcome this dialogue and to an extent agree with these cautions, particularly that new ideas should not be felt to devalue the truth of the old—that the baby should always be taken safely out before dealing with the bathwater. Nevertheless, our sense is that many clinicians would join us in seeing the findings of psychoanalytically oriented empirical studies of early development as of clear relevance to clinical understanding and technique (see Lichtenberg, 1987).

Mental models and procedures

Developmental research has helped to revise some developmental propositions of psychoanalysis which turned out to be naïve. For instance, there has been a shift in emphasis in psychoanalytic practice from a focus on the retrieval of forgotten experience to one where the creation of a meaningful narrative is regarded as mutative (e.g. Spence, 1982, 1984). The interactional and interpersonal aspects of clinical work have become recognized as crucial, giving insight into the more primitive aspects of interaction seen in psychoanalysis. While we do not assume that formative experiences underlying these interactions have been retained in a way that allows them to be recalled, analogies continually emerge between the parent–infant and analyst–patient relationships.

Implicit in the understanding of these analogies is the idea that procedures, or patterns of actions rather than individual experiences, are retained from infant–caregiver interactions and that these procedures come to organize later behaviour. The procedures are themselves organized as mental models (Johnson-Laird & Byrne, 1991, 1993). They should not be conceived of as pictures and are better thought of as intricately interlinked sequences of events. Nevertheless, taken together, groups of procedures amount to a representation of a relationship, forever confined to the unconscious (phenomenologically rather than dynamically speaking) and observable only through an individual's manner or style of relating, rather than through the ideas or memories described. The goal of therapy for certain kinds of patient is, then, the observation of patterns of interaction, the identification of maladaptive models, and the correction of such models, principally through strengthening an overarching mental capacity to selectively activate alternative models of interaction; in language influenced by cognitive science, this capacity may be labelled metacognitive (e.g. Main, 1991) or reflective function (Fonagy & Target, 1997).

Attunement and its failure

It is not appropriate in this chapter to offer a comprehensive review of infant research pertinent to psychoanalysis. We can,
however, highlight some important findings. The original work of
Stern (1985) richly illustrated that the interaction between infant
and caregiver involved both self-regulation and a sensitivity to the
state of the other which has come to be known as attunement. This
interaction is supported by constitutional capacities such as the
capacity to imitate adult facial gestures from the earliest stages of
life (e.g. Meltzoff, 1993; Meltzoff & Moore, 1989).

Beatrice Beebe and her colleagues (Beebe, Lachmann, & Jaffe,
1997) have produced rich empirical evidence to illustrate how extremely rapid and complementary interaction occurs between
baby and mother. There is mutual reactivity to changes in facial
expression, which can be tracked and interpreted in terms of
the expectancies that each has about the reaction of the other. The
work of Tronick (1989; Tronick & Cohn, 1989) has demonstrated
that the contingencies between infant and mother are not perfect.
The breakdown of "attunement" is probably both inevitable and
developmentally desirable. Tronick's suggestion that the micro-
repair of misaligned interaction was probably at the heart of the
establishment of a viable human relationship naturally struck a
chord with many clinicians, who have observed that the reparation
of disrupted therapeutic alliance often has more long-term impact
than the mere presence of empathic understanding.

Beebe and her colleagues' challenging observation that the
degree of co-ordination of interaction between a stranger and a
baby of 4 months was more predictive of healthy emotional development at 1 year than was the degree of co-ordination between
mother and infant may also be understood in the context of
Tronick's findings. The young infant's awareness of another human being must be based on the range of responses that the
caregivers have offered. The "good-enough mother", in these
terms, is one who, while staying within tolerable limits, stretches
the infant's range of expectancies. The varieties of responses that
the infant can experience as attuned (as referring to him and recognizing of him as an individual) will be broader and more flexible

for the child whose mother and father were "reasonable" rather than perfect, sensitive rather than exactly mirroring.

Early interaction with the caregivers must prepare for all later interactions with other people. This preparation will be far more helpful if, rather than perfect attunement, it offers facilitation of the capacity within the child to elicit an adapted response from the other—a kind of primitive resilience relatively automatically performed yet deeply ingrained as a procedure in the child's mind. If, later on, we encounter narcissistic children and adults who feel that they "must" experience the world in exactly the way they anticipate, the clinician may in vain seek to find a rejecting or insensitive object. Paradoxically, the child's deficit may in fact have been rooted in interactions marked by too little insensitivity, too close or intense a tracking of the baby's expressions.

The teleological stance

Psychoanalysts can be tempted to go beyond the data, or to extrapolate too readily from experience of later childhood or adulthood, to make assumptions about what babies think or feel, without knowing that there is evidence that sets some limits on what is developmentally possible. They may, for example, assume that the infant of 4 months can attribute intentions to others (e.g. Klein, 1945), experiencing his own actions in terms of motivations (aggressive, sexual, and so on) and his parents' responses in terms of assumed feelings and ideas (anger, envy, etc.). Yet, studies of early infant–caregiver interaction seem to show that the baby is not at that stage able to respond to others' behaviour in terms of such states of mind. His behaviour is consistent with a combination of constitutional tendencies and an instrumental attitude: the infant behaves in ways that seem to be aimed at bringing about a particular state, but without treating others as motivated by goals also.

Awareness of such motivation then evolves gradually, probably on the basis of maturational processes that predominate at 6–12 months. At this time, infants appear to start thinking about things and people around them in terms of their "goals" (end states as opposed to intentions) and their actions as "rational" or "reasonable" in the light of such hypothesized aims. The work of two brilliant infant researchers, Gergely and Csibra (1996; Gergely, Nadasdy, Csibra, & Biro, 1995), has demonstrated that the principle of rational action is applied by infants to human and non-human objects alike. Infants of 9 months express surprise when various-sized discs in a computer-generated display appear to act irrationally. When a small circle chooses a longer than necessary path in order to reach a big circle (taking the same route that had previously been necessary to go around an obstacle), the infant's face reflects puzzlement. The same surprise is absent when the small circle finds the direct route, even though this route was a change from the earlier one that the infant had got used to.

These studies and several other versions of the same paradigm illustrate that infants overextend, to non-human moving objects, models of rational action that they have evolved to predict human behaviour. The enrichment of what Gergely and colleagues term the teleological stance into a mentalizing intentional stance (Dennett, 1983) is the business of the second year of life. How the infant comes to extend his model of rational action into a complex model in which he interprets his own behaviour and that of others around him in terms of beliefs, intentions, and desires is, we believe, deeply rooted in the emotional relationship with a primary caregiver. The teleological stance is the skeleton that is fleshed out by a gradually increasing awareness of at first emotional and then cognitive states in self and other. This must occur in the context of an attachment relationship. This view implies that the coherence and stability of the child's capacity to represent and experience his social world in terms of mental states will depend directly on the quality of his attachment relationship with his caregivers.

The theory of attachment

The nature of the attachment system

Attachment theory, developed by John Bowlby (1969, 1973, 1980), postulates a universal human need to form close affectional bonds. It is a normative theory of how the "attachment system" functions in all humans. Bowlby described attachment as a special type of social relationship, initially between a baby and his mother and father, involving an emotional bond. It may also be seen as the context within which the human infant learns to regulate emotion (Sroufe, 1990).

The stability of early childhood attachment patterns is well demonstrated. Mary Ainsworth and her colleagues (Ainsworth, Blehar, Waters, & Wall, 1978) developed a procedure commonly known as the "Strange Situation", which classifies infants and toddlers into one of four attachment categories, in relation to either parent. "Secure" babies explore readily in the presence of the parent, are anxious in the presence of the stranger, are distressed by the parent's departure and brief absence, rapidly seek contact with the parent following separation, and are reassured by renewed contact. The recovery from an over-aroused, distressed state is fairly rapid and smooth, and completed in that the infant returns to exploration and play.

Some babies, who usually seem less anxious during the separation, do not readily seek comfort and closeness to the mother or father on return and may show no preference for the caregiver over the stranger; these infants are designated "Anxious/Avoidant". The "Anxious/Resistant" infant shows impoverished exploration and play, tends to be highly distressed by separation from the parent, but has great difficulty in settling after reunion, showing struggling, stiffness, continued crying, or more passive fussing. The parent's presence or attempts at comforting fail to offer reassurance, and the baby's anxiety and anger appears to interfere with his attempts to gain comfort from closeness. Both of these insecure groups appear to be coping with arousal and ambivalence through attempts at precocious over-control of affect because they appear not to be certain that the parent will do his or her part to modulate the baby's emotional arousal (Main, 1991; Sroufe, 1990).

It is generally held that the patterning of attachment-related behaviour is underpinned by different strategies adopted by children to regulate their emotional reactions. As affect regulation is acquired with the help of the child's primary caregiver, the child's strategy will inevitably be a reflection of the caregiver's behaviour towards him. The secure infant's behaviour is based on the experience of sufficiently well coordinated, mainly positive interactions in which the caregiver is rarely over-arousing and is able to restabilize the child's spontaneously emerging disorganizing emotional responses. Therefore, the infant remains relatively organized in stressful situations.

By contrast, anxious/avoidantly attached children are presumed to have had repeated experiences when their emotional arousal was not restabilized by the parent because of personal or social pressures on her, and some degree of associated neglect or resentment of the child. The same expectations may arise in other children who have been over-aroused through intrusive parenting, who therefore *over-regulate* their affect and steer away from situations that are likely to be emotionally arousing. Anxious/resistantly attached children *under-regulate*, heightening their expression of distress possibly in an effort to elicit the normal response of the caregiver. These children have low thresholds for threat and may become preoccupied with having contact with the caregiver, but show frustration with this contact even when it is available.

A fourth group consists of infants who appear to exhibit a range of seemingly undirected responses giving the impression of disorganization and disorientation (Main & Solomon, 1990). Infants who show unusual or paradoxical behaviour such as freezing, handclapping, headbanging, and the wish to escape from the situation even in the presence of the parent are referred to as "Disorganized/Disoriented". It is generally held that for such infants the caregiver has served both as a source of fear and as a source of reassurance; thus, the arousal of the attachment behavioural system produces strong conflicting motivations. Not surprisingly, a history of neglect or some abuse is often associated with this pattern (Cicchetti & Beeghly, 1987; Main & Hesse, 1992).

Determinants of attachment security

It is beyond the scope of this chapter to consider in detail the rich literature on determinants of infant security. (One of the many excellent reviews available is Belsky, Rosenberger, & Crnic, 1995.) Clearly, genetic transmission may account for some component of the strong prediction from parental attachment status to the child's security of attachment (van IJzendoorn, Goldberg, Kroonenberg, & Frenkel, 1992). The influence of temperament on attachment security is controversial, but the balance of the evidence is now against a temperamental account (Kagan, 1982; Lamb, Thompson, Gardner, Charnov, & Estes, 1984).[1]

The quality of parental care has been shown repeatedly to be predictive of infant security. The sensitive responsiveness of the parent is traditionally regarded as the most important determinant of attachment security in the infant (Isabella, 1993; Isabella & Belsky, 1991). The parameters assessed include ratings of maternal sensitivity (e.g. Cox, Owen, Henderson, & Margand, 1992; Isabella, 1993), prompt responsiveness to distress (Del Carmen, Pedersen, Huffman, & Bryan, 1993), moderate stimulation (Belsky, Rovine, & Taylor, 1984), non-intrusiveness (Malatesta, Grigoryev, Lamb, Albin, & Culver, 1986), sufficient synchronizing of interaction (Isabella, Belsky, & von Eye, 1989), and warmth, involvement, and responsiveness (O'Connor, Sigman, & Kasasi, 1992). These associations have been strengthened by findings from experimental studies, in which the enhancement of maternal sensitivity has been shown to increase the proportion of secure infants in high-risk populations (van den Boom, 1995). Similar parameters have been predictive for fathers (Cox et al., 1992) and for professional caregivers (Goosens & van IJzendoorn, 1990).

These predictors of infant security are correlated to one another and are all likely to be unequally distributed across socioeconomic groups. It is known that lower social class and other indicators of social deprivation are linked to both infant and adult insecure classifications (e.g. Crittenden, Partridge, & Clausen, 1991; Ward & Carlson, 1995; Zeanah et al., 1993). Poor parenting skills and the maltreatment of children are more common in families suffering

---

[1] There is little evidence that distress-prone infants become anxious/resistant babies (van den Boom, 1990). Temperament changes in the first year of life (Belsky, Fish, & Isabella, 1991) and the attachment pattern of a child to his two parents is often inconsistent (Fox, Kimmerly, & Schafer, 1991) and appears to be dependent on the internal working model of each parent (Steele, Steele, & Fonagy, 1996).

economic hardship (Garbarino & Sherman, 1990). Maltreatment of children is most likely to be associated with the disorganized/disoriented pattern of infant attachment (Belsky, 1993).

The transgenerational transmission of attachment patterns

There is important evidence of transgenerational transmission of infant security. This evidence relies on studies using the Adult Attachment Interview (AAI: George, Kaplan, & Main, 1995). The AAI asks about childhood attachment relationships and the meaning that an individual currently gives to attachment experiences. The interview transcript is rated according to the scoring system developed by Main and Goldwyn (1994), which classifies individuals into *Secure/Autonomous*, *Insecure/Dismissing*, or *Insecure/Preoccupied*, or *Unresolved/Disorganized with respect to loss or trauma*, categories assigned according to the structural and linguistic qualities of their narratives of early experiences. (Whereas *autonomous* people clearly value attachment relationships, regard these as formative, and are able to describe them in a coherent and plausible way, *insecure* individuals are poor at integrating memories of experience with the meaning of that experience. Those *dismissing* of attachment may deny memory for early relationships but idealize them, or denigrate attachment. *Preoccupied* individuals tend to be confused and bogged down when discussing early relationships, and caught up in either angry diatribes or passive ruminations about their past or current relationships with their parents.) Two studies (Hamilton, 1994; Waters, Merrick, Albersheim, Treboux, & Crowell, 1995) have shown a 68–75% correspondence between attachment classifications in infancy and classifications in adulthood.

A parent categorized as secure is three or four times more likely to have a child who is securely attached than is an insecure parent (van IJzendoorn, 1995). This turns out to be true even in prospective studies in which parental attachment is assessed before the birth of the child (Benoit & Parker, 1994; Fonagy, Steele, Moran, Steele, & Higgitt, 1991; Radojevic, 1992; Steele et al., 1996; Ward & Carlson, 1995). It is very important to note that infants quite commonly have different patterns of attachment to different caregivers. In the London Parent–Child Project, initiated by Dr Miriam Steele, there was only a marginally significant association between the attachment classification with mother and that with father. However, each Strange Situation result was powerfully predicted by the attachment classification of the respective parent on the AAI (Steele et al., 1996). The results suggest that the infant develops independent models (self–other schemata) for his major attachment relations, based on his history of interactions with each of those individuals. In turn, these interaction experiences reflect each parent's representation of her or his own attachment history.

The continuity of patterns of attachment

Bowlby proposed that the quality of childhood relationships with the parents results in internal representations or working models of the self and others that provide prototypes for later social relations. Internal working models are mental schemata in which expectations about the behaviour of a particular individual towards the self are aggregated. The expectations are themselves abstractions based on repeated interactions of specific types with that individual. If any physical injury to the child is effectively dealt with, and sources of unhappiness are rapidly addressed, the child will develop the legitimate expectation that, with that person at least, his distress is likely to be met by reassurance and comforting. The internal working model is the result of a natural process of abstraction of the invariant features from diverse social situations with a particular individual (Stern, 1994).

Such internal models of attachment commonly remain relatively stable across the life span (Collins & Read, 1994). Secure children, with the benefit of well-regulated relationships with their parents behind them, are expected to evolve positive expectations about play and learning and to achieve a reliable capacity for modulation of arousal, a good capacity for communication within relationships, and, above all, confidence in the continuing availability of the parent. Early experiences of flexible access to feelings are regarded as formative by attachment theorists, enabling secure children both to maximize the opportunities presented to them by the environment and to draw on socially supportive relationships. The autonomous sense of self emerges fully from secure parent–infant relationships (Emde & Buchsbaum, 1990; Fonagy, Steele, et al., 1995; Lieberman & Pawl, 1990). The increased control of the secure child permits him to move towards the ownership of inner experience, to feel able to get help with regulating emotion, and later to achieve an understanding of self and others as people whose behaviour is organized by mental states—thoughts, feelings, beliefs, and desires (Fonagy, Steele, et al., 1995; Sroufe, 1990)—which makes the internal and the social worlds much more meaningful and predictable for the child. The importance and roots of this understanding, or reflective function, are further elaborated below.

The development of reflective function

Reflective function

"Theory of mind" is an interconnected set of beliefs and desires, attributed to explain people's behaviour. The value of a capacity to develop and use an explanatory framework like this has been increasingly recognized in developmental psychology and in the philosophy of mind, where Dennett's (1983) approach has been extended (Hopkins, 1992; Wollheim, 1995) to unconscious processes. These workers pointed out that one of Freud's most important contributions was to extend folk psychology to a theory of *unconscious* mind, thus making those aspects of behaviour meaningful which—using the ordinary constructs of intentionality—make little sense (e.g. dreams, neurotic symptoms, humour). These behaviours may be understood if we add unconscious beliefs, thoughts, and feelings to our everyday model of the mind.

Reflective function organizes the experience of one's own and others' behaviour in terms of mental state constructs. Individuals differ in the extent to which they go beyond observable phenomena to explain their own or others' actions in terms of beliefs, desires, plans, and so on. This intentional stance, in the broad sense considered here (i.e. including apparently irrational unconscious motives), explains one's own behaviour and therefore creates the continuity of self-experience which is the underpinning of a coherent self structure.

It is important that reflective function is not conflated with introspection. Introspection or self-reflection is quite different from reflective function, as the latter is an automatic procedure, *unconsciously* invoked in interpreting action. It can be seen as an overlearned skill, which may be systematically misleading in ways much more difficult to detect and correct than mistakes in conscious attributions would be. Reflective function lends a shape and coherence to self-organization which is outside awareness, in contrast to introspection which has a clear impact on experience of oneself.

Attachment and mentalizing

A number of authors, including Stern (1985), have distinguished between physical and psychological aspects of self-development. Neisser (1991), for example, suggested that two preconceptual aspects of self emerge in development: the ecological and the interpersonal. The latter is generated via the perception of one's own actions and related contingent actions of others. Approaches to infant development such as these have lent support to the interpersonalist psychoanalytic theoretical tradition (Lionells, 1995; Shafran, 1995; Sullivan, 1953). In brief, although formulated in a variety of ways, the idea is that psychological self-development is an intersubjective process whereby the infant's awareness of internal states is clarified and organized in terms of the reaction of the caregiver to the infant's expression. There is every reason to assume that the infant's experience of his emotional states is thoroughly confusing at first. How would an infant feeling aroused physiologically, and expressing avoidance behaviourally, know that this experience is one of anxiety? The parent's imitation of the infant's expression, which the infant is constitutionally equipped to perceive (Meltzoff, 1993), is represented, and this representation is mapped onto the infant's own phenomenal experience. The infant's sensation is then organized by his understanding of the reflection of external signs of this experience. The term "intersubjectivity" is appropriate, since the infant's experience comes to be organized around the impact of this experience upon the caregiver. If the caregiver's reaction is exaggerated, the infant's interpretation of his own experience may come to be permanently biased in that direction (people who suffer from anxiety states may habitually interpret a slight acceleration of their heart rate as signifying an impending heart attack). The infant's representation of the caregiver's reaction has important symbolic potential. It can become a meta-representation—a representation of the infant's representation of his experience of anxiety.

We may assume that similar processes operate at higher levels. The child may not have inherent awareness of his own psychological experience, but develops this through perceiving his intentions, desires, and beliefs in the mind of the parent. The caregiver behaves towards the infant in a way that implies that the infant is motivated by wishes, beliefs, or feelings. What the child internalizes at the core of his psychological self structure is not internally emergent self-awareness, nor the caring primary object, but rather the primary object at the moment of reflection. We will return to this issue after considering some qualitative differences in caregiver responsiveness based on attachment theory.

Adult attachment and reflectiveness

We have already referred to the empirical evidence linking attachment classifications of infants to the stability and coherence of the self structure in later childhood. We have also reviewed evidence suggesting that a parent's own attachment classification influences the quality of the evolving relationship between himself or herself and the child. Placing these findings alongside the model of the intersubjective roots of the psychological self considered above, we can suggest several clinically important considerations about the quality of self-development, based on the internal working models of attachment relationships which the parents bring to their interactions with the baby.

The infant who looks for a way of managing his distress identifies in the response of the caregiver a representation of his mental states, which he may internalize and use as part of a higher-order strategy of affect regulation. The secure caregiver soothes the baby by combining "mirroring" of the child's affect with expressions or behaviour that suggest incompatible states. In a recent study (Fonagy, Steele et al., 1995), we confirmed that mothers who soothe their distressed 8-month-olds most effectively following an injection rapidly reflect the child's emotion, but this mirroring is mixed with other affects (smiling, questioning, mocking display, and the like). The discrepancy between the infant's expression of affect and the caregiver's reflection is, we believe, *essential* for the symbolic and therefore containing and soothing quality to be effective and retained. This formulation of sensitivity has the same emphasis on the modulation of the infant's experience through understanding which Bion (1962) incorporated in his notion of containment. The finding that clarity and coherence of the mother's representation of the child mediates between the AAI and the mother's observed behaviour is consistent with the model (Slade, Belsky, Aber, & Phelps, in press). In previous studies, we have reported a relationship between the reflective capacity of the parent, during pregnancy, with regard to his or her own childhood, and the likelihood of forming a secure attachment with the baby (Fonagy et al., 1991).

Insecure attachment, by contrast, may also be seen as an intersubjective process, but this time, rather than the internalization of comforting reflection by the adult, there has been a primitive identification with his or her defensive stance. Winnicott (1967) wrote:

> What does the baby see when he or she looks at the mother's face? . . . ordinarily, the mother is looking at the baby and *what she looks like is related to what she sees there* . . . [but what of] the baby whose mother reflects her own mood or, worse still, the rigidity of her own defences. . . . They look and they do not see themselves . . . what is seen is the mother's face. [p. 27]

Closeness to this mother is then maintained at the cost of substantial compromise to reflective function. The dismissing caregiver defends against aspects of her own psychic reality, perhaps evoked by the infant's helplessness, and adopts an overly coping or simply avoidant stance in the face of the baby's distress. This failure of mirroring is internalized by the infant, who will then attempt similarly to appear to ignore his own emotional experience. At the core of the self-representation is the non-reflecting caregiver. By contrast, the preoccupied parent is likely to represent the infant's internal state with excessive clarity, even caricature. What is lacking here is the distance between the baby's expression and the parent's reflection. The infant needs to find something in the parent's mind which is the same, yet not the same, as that which he is experiencing. If the overlap is too small or too great, the parent's reflection contributes to the baby's arousal rather than modulating it. The infant has no choice other than to repeat this escalation (the resistant pattern) or to avoid it, much as the infants of dismissing parents do. In either case, the key point remains that *the lack of modulated synchrony between parent and baby becomes the content of the baby's experience of himself* (see also Crittenden, 1994).

There is much in the attachment literature which supports the notion that insecure attachment is rooted in the incongruence of internal experience and its representation within the self structure. For example, we know that avoidant infants respond to separation with only minimal displays of distress while experiencing considerable and enduring physiological arousal (Spangler & Grossman, 1993). Similarly, Crittenden (1988) and other researchers have demonstrated that small children who have been abused try to simulate falsely positive feelings. Studies reviewed above (Emde & Buchsbaum, 1990; Lieberman & Pawl, 1990) which showed immature and incoherent self representations as a consequence of insecure attachment are also consistent with this model. At an extreme, the internalization of the parents' defences leads not only to a pervasive failure to represent emotional experience coherently, but also to the construction of an experience of the self around such false internalization (Winnicott, 1960).

The object at the core of the self

The phenomena we have been discussing thus far fall within the normal range of experience. Individuals differ in terms of the quality of self representation. At an extreme clinically we encounter individuals whose self representation is so fragmented as to appear almost non-existent, or so distorted that it seems completely out of touch with real emotional experience. Bleiberg (1984, 1994), for example, has described severely personality-disordered children who experienced a sense of almost total alienation from their core self. We conceive of such children as showing an extreme version of the strategy of insecure infants. Confronted with a frightened or frightening caregiver (Main & Hesse, 1992), they adapt by a wholesale internalization of the caregiver's reaction to them. This leaves at the core of their self structure the representation of the object rather than of the self. Not only is the child then out of touch with his affect, but he also experiences the self representation as foreign to his internal experience, yet very much a part of himself. Internal coherence later becomes impossible to achieve without first externalizing this alien part of the self representation. This is perhaps why young children, classified in infancy as "disorganized" in their attachment, have been shown to behave in an unusually controlling way towards their parents. The object must be consistently controlled in order that it can remain an effective vehicle for the alien part of the self.

The mechanism we are describing is basically one of projective identification, although that construct is perhaps too broad to convey exactly what we intend here. One hallmark of the special category of projective identification we are describing is the desperation felt by the individual to be able to get rid of the unwanted aspects of the self. The alien part must be externalized for the child to feel a sense of being in touch with the real, experiencing self. The closer to the core of the self such an alien object resides, the greater the need for the physical presence of the other, to permit this externalization. For the child who was "disorganized" as an infant, the object who was internalized as part of the self representation is the most likely vehicle for this projective process. Thus, even brief separations may feel like an impossible challenge. Often, in young children, the difficulty is compounded by the continuing need of the child for a mirroring object. They continue to attempt to find themselves in the other, at the same time as externalizing onto the other their alien self-representation. This is very often a self-perpetuating pattern, in which the child struggles to rid himself of parts of himself and actualize them in the parent, at the same time desperately needing the parent to reflect and strengthen the feeble but true core. If the parent, or later attachment figure, is able to accept the projection, and yet retain some capacity for reflective functioning, the course of the child's development may be changed. In our experience, relatively few parents are able to change in this way. Commonly, quite a vicious transactional cycle develops in which the relative strength of the true self weakens and the corresponding need for externalization increases, and the contact between parent and child becomes a struggle which often gets described as a sadomasochistic relationship, though we would see this as misleading in that it suggests perverse erotic gratification as the driving force.

Finding the mentalizing self

We take the view, then, that the acquisition of reflective function is part of an intersubjective process between the infant and his parents (see Gopnik, 1993, for a highly elegant elaboration of such a model). The parent helps the creation of mentalizing models through complex linguistic and quasi-linguistic processes, mainly through behaving towards the child in a way that leads him eventually to see that his own behaviour makes most sense in terms of ideas and feelings determining his actions, and the reactions of others to him, which can then be generalized to other people. The parent approaches the crying infant with a question about his feelings in her mind—for instance, "Do you want a cuddle?" The sensitive caregiver thinks of the child as a person, rather than in physical terms: "Have you been standing alone too long?" "Are you cold?" The parent can bridge internal and external experience sufficiently for the child to absorb patterns and their implications. Ultimately, the child arrives at the conclusion that the caregiver's reaction to him is rational, given the assumption that he is motivated by thoughts and feelings. Unconsciously and pervasively, the caregiver treats the child as a mental agent, which is perceived by the child and used in the development of a core sense of mental selfhood. We assume that this, by and large, is a mundane process, happening routinely throughout early life, not reflected on, and so rarely modified.

Caregivers, however, differ in their ways of carrying out this natural human function. Some may be particularly alert to the earliest indications of intentionality; others, such as parents tending to be withdrawn or depressed need stronger indications before perceiving the child's mental state and modifying their behaviour accordingly. Yet others, such as the eating-disordered mothers evocatively described in the work of Alan Stein (1994), may systematically misperceive the child's states of mind, with resulting deformation of the child's sense of himself. In Stein's sample, bulimic mothers were insensitive to the small child's hunger cues, which, interestingly, in some extreme cases led to either obesity or failure to thrive, underscoring the importance of the mother in helping the child construct a clear symbolic representation of his mental states.

The child's perception and representation of mental states in himself and others thus depends on his observation of the mental world of his caregiver. He is able to perceive mental states to the extent that his caregiver's behaviour implied such states. This he may do when the caregiver is in a shared pretend mode of playing with the child, and many ordinary interactions (such as physical care and comforting, conversations with peers) will also involve such mental contact and exchange. This is what makes mental state concepts such as thinking inherently intersubjective: shared experience is inherent to mental state concepts.

The parent's capacity to observe the moment-to-moment changes in the child's mental state, then, lies at the root of sensitive caregiving, which is viewed by attachment theorists as the cornerstone of secure attachment (e.g. Ainsworth et al., 1978; Grossmann, Grossmann, Spangler, Suess, & Unzner, 1985; Isabella & Belsky, 1991). Secure attachment, in its turn, provides the basis for acquiring an understanding of mind. The secure infant feels safe in making attributions of mental states to account for the behaviour of the parent. By contrast, to some degree the avoidant child shuns the mental state of the other, while the resistant child focuses on his own state of distress to the exclusion of close intersubjective exchanges, or finds it difficult to distinguish between different people's internal states. Infants with disorganized attachment may represent a special category: hypervigilant of the caregiver's behaviour, they use all cues available and may be acutely sensitized to intentional states, and thus may be more ready to construct a mentalized account of the caregiver's behaviour. We suggest that in such children mentalization may be evident, but it does not have the effective role in self organization that characterizes securely attached children.

We believe that what is most important for the development of mentalizing self organization is that exploration of the mental state of the sensitive caregiver enables the child to find in her mind an image of himself as motivated by beliefs, feelings, and intentions— in other words, as mentalizing. There is considerable evidence to support the view that secure attachment enhances the development of inner security, self-worth, and autonomy (e.g. Londerville & Main, 1981). Infants with disorganized attachments, even if they acquire the skill of mentalization, fail to integrate this with their self organization. There may be a number of linked reasons for this: (a) the caregiver is unlikely to be reliably contingent in responding to the infant's self-state and shows systematic biases in her perception and reflection of it; (b) the mental state of the caregiver evokes intense anxiety through either frightening behaviour suggesting malevolence towards the child, or behaviour suggesting fear, which may include fear of the child himself; (c) the child needs to use disproportionate resources to understand the parent's behaviour, at the expense of reflecting on self-states.

These factors combine, perhaps, to make children of some mentally ill parents become keen readers of the caregiver's mind, as the studies of children of mentally ill parents by Zahn-Waxler (Zahn-Waxler, Kochanska, Krupnick, & McKnew, 1990; Zahn-Waxler, Radke-Yarrow, Wagner, & Chapman, 1992) and Lyons-Ruth (1996; Lyons-Ruth, Alpern, & Repacholi, 1993) have clearly demonstrated. However, they may be poor readers of their own mental states, out of touch with their own internal world.

The acquisition of full mentalizing

The experience of the internal world is traditionally referred to in psychoanalytic texts as psychic reality. From Freud's earliest works (Freud, 1900a), it has been recognized that in the young child psychic reality has a concrete quality. An alternative perspective is to see the young child's experience of mental states as characterized by an equivalence between internal and external reality.

In previous papers (Fonagy & Target, 1996; Target & Fonagy, 1996), we have attempted to describe the normal development of reflective function in the child of 2 to 5 years. We suggested that there is a transition from a split mode of experience to integrated mentalization. Primarily from a clinical perspective, we put forward a number of propositions about the development of the psychological part of the self following infancy. These were:

1. Until 3 or 4 years of age, there are two modes of relating internal experiences to the external situation: (a) in a serious frame of mind, the child expects the internal world in himself and others to correspond to external reality, and subjective experience will often be distorted to match information coming from outside ("*psychic equivalence mode*": e.g. Gopnik & Astington, 1988; Perner, Leekam, & Wimmer, 1987); and (b) while involved in pretend play, the child knows that internal experience does not reflect external reality (e.g. Bartsch & Wellman, 1989; Dias & Harris, 1990), but then the internal state is thought to have no relationship to the outside world ("*pretend mode*").

2. Normally, the child of 3 to 4 years integrates these alternative modes to arrive at *mentalization*, or *reflective mode*, in which mental states can be experienced as representations. Inner and outer reality can then be seen as linked, yet they are accepted as differing in important ways and no longer have to be either equated or dissociated from each other. Mentalization comes about through the child's experience of his mental states being reflected on through, for instance, secure play with a parent or older child, which facilitates integration of the pretend and psychic equivalence modes, through a process that may be an elaboration of the complex mirroring of the infant by the early caregiver. In playfulness, the older person gives the child's ideas and feelings (when he is "only pretending") a link with reality, by indicating the existence of an alternative perspective, which exists outside the child's mind. The other person also shows that reality may be distorted by acting upon it in playful ways, and through this playfulness a pretend but real mental experience may be introduced.

3. Intense emotion and conflict can lead to a partial failure of this

integration, so that aspects of the pretend mode of functioning become part of a psychic equivalence manner of experiencing reality. This may be because the atmosphere in some families tends to be incompatible with the caregiver "playing" with the most pressing aspects of the child's thoughts; these are often disturbing and unacceptable to the adult, just as they are to the child. The rigid, controlling behaviour of the pre-school child with a history of disorganized attachment may then arise out of a partial failure on the part of the child to move beyond the mode of psychic equivalence in relation to specific ideas or feelings, so that he experiences them with the intensity that might be expected had they been current, external events.

Reflective function and self development

While mentalization may not be an unequivocally positive experience, Judy Dunn's work (1996) shows us that, at any rate, the understanding of emotion at 3½ years predicts a positive perception of social relations, mature moral sensibility, and the understanding of complex emotions. Stern (1985) pointed out that a sense of ownership of one's actions, whether derived from the experience of forming plans, proprioceptive feedback, or the objective consequences of physical actions on the environment, contributes to the sense of self-agency. In our view, such agency also crucially depends on the quality and reliability of reflective function, as ownership of action is intimately tied to the mental state (belief or desire) that initiated it. It is impossible to conceive of self-agency as fully established by the physical actions of the child, as such a large proportion of these will fail to achieve their intended objective, because of the child's immature physical and cognitive capacities. The recognition of the child's intentional stance by others may then be critical in making the thought "real" for the child. We believe that interaction that safely links perceptions, thoughts, and emotions as causes and consequences of action contributes vitally to a feeling of agency. The earliest foundation is presumably the baby's sense that he causes the caregiver's mirroring behaviour (Gergely & Watson, 1996).

Of course, the core of self-agency must originally lie with the body, where the baby's attempts to exercise control often succeed after early infancy. Higher-level, more complex actions, particularly those that involve others in the child's life, often require the reflective caregiver to make sense of the young child's wishes and translate these for the links between mental states and action to be established. It is to be expected then that children who have experienced neglect or coercive, rigid, frightening, or abusive parenting will frequently feel their sense of self-agency to be feeble and insecure, largely limited to the more firmly established bodily domain.

When parenting is not good enough

Children living with certain deprivations—for example, mentally ill or maltreating parents—are at risk of failing to find their own intentional being within the mind of the caregiver and are thus at risk of poor development of mentalization. There is accumulating evidence that maltreatment impairs the child's reflective capacities and sense of self (Beeghly & Cicchetti, 1994; Cicchetti & Beeghly, 1987; Schneider-Rosen & Cicchetti, 1984, 1991). The pattern of results suggests that maltreatment may cause children to withdraw from the mental world. Physical experiences probably become more important, and this may, paradoxically, drive them physically closer to the ill or abusing parent. Their ability to adapt to, modify, or avoid the parent's behaviour is also constrained by their limited capacity for mentalization.

There are several reasons why traumatic childhood experiences are likely to undermine the development of reflective function.

First, in such families the public world of school and community—where reflective function is common and desirable—is often kept very separate from the world of home, where the unpredictable or incomprehensible behaviour of an adult makes recognition of the mental state of the other dangerous to the developing self. Even where the child benefits from sensitivity and reflectiveness in the world outside home, thereby developing an alternative model of relating and experiencing himself, the models derived from experiences within and outside the family are likely to be kept insulated from each other and limited to their separate contexts.

Second, if understanding the behaviour of his parents requires the child to try to envisage their probable thoughts and feelings, he could then be confronted with attitudes towards himself that are extremely painful to recognize: hatred, fear, indifference. Such experience could destroy the child's belief that one can safely understand others through one's own feelings (Herman, 1992), and the child would be likely to inhibit this capacity in intense attachment relationships, or avoid entering such relationships at all.

A third possibility is that the difficulty is not a result of the traumatic events themselves, but of the family atmosphere surrounding them (which may also occur in the absence of trauma). Alessandri (1991, 1992) found that the difficulties in pretend play of children who had been abused or neglected were mirrored by their mothers' difficulties in taking a playful stance with their child, directing their attention, and engaging in positive interactions. This and other results are consistent with the idea that a lack of a particular social scaffolding may undermine the normal development of reflective function in children whose parents' behaviour may be affected by, for instance, illness, personality disorder, or memories of their own earlier abusive treatment.

Some speculations about pathological development based on the dialectic model

As we have said, a fundamental need of every infant is to find his own mind, or intentional state, in the mind of the object. For the infant, internalization of this image performs the function of "containment", which Winnicott (1967) has written of as "giving back to the baby the baby's own self" (p. 33) . Failure of this function leads to a desperate search for alternative ways of containing thoughts and the intense feelings they engender. The search for alternative ways of mental containment may, we have suggested, give rise to many pathological solutions, including taking the mind of the other, with its distorted, absent, or malign picture of the child, as part of the child's own sense of identity.

With development, and exacerbated by the apparently sadomasochistic patterns described above, this picture can become the germ of a persecutory object which is lodged in the self but is alien and unassimilable. There will be a desperate wish for separation in the hope of establishing an autonomous identity or existence. However, sadly, this identity is centred around a mental state that cannot reflect the changing emotional and cognitive states of the individual, because it is based on an archaic representation of the other, rather than on the thinking and feeling self as seen by the other.

As with children, for adults whose search for mirroring or containment has failed, the striving for separation will produce only a movement towards fusion. The more the person attempts to become himself, the closer he moves towards becoming his object, because the latter is part of the self structure. This may account for the familiar oscillation of borderline patients between the struggle for independence and the terrifying wish for extreme closeness and fantasized union. Developmentally, a crisis may be expected to arise when the external demand for separateness becomes irresistible, in late adolescence and early adulthood. Self-destructive and (in the extreme) suicidal behaviour may then be perceived as the only feasible solution to an insoluble dilemma: the freeing of the self from the other through the destruction of the other within the self.

In some people, for whom separateness is a chronic problem, we have assumed that the experience of self-hood can be achieved only through finding a physical other onto whom the other within the self can be projected. Thus, many will find leaving home very difficult and sustainable only by finding an alternative, comparable figure onto whom the other within the self may be projected. If the other person dies or leaves, a pathological mourning process may be initiated whereby the person feels compelled to maintain a live picture of the other, in order to shore up the integrity of the self.

Another possible outcome of poor development of the psychological self is that the body may be used to contain and enact mental states. In these cases, the child's own body comes to serve the function of meta-representation of feelings, ideas, and wishes. Violence towards the body of the self (e.g. self-cutting) or that of the other (apparently unprovoked aggression, or "mindless violence") may be a way of "controlling" mental states which are invested in bodily states (e.g. the mother seen as part of one's own body) or destroying "ideas" experienced as within the body of the other (Fonagy & Target, 1995).

In both physical violence and self-destructive acts, a number of factors combine. First, in these acts the individual functions in a non-mentalizing mode of psychic equivalence. There is an intolerance of any alternative perspective (it has to be destroyed) and a belief that, by destroying the person representing the idea, the persecuting idea will also be eradicated from his own mind. Second, in both externally and internally directed aggression, there are indications of the persistence of a pretend mode of functioning, in that the individual at one level perceives his acts as inconsequential, except in obliterating the intolerable thoughts. External reality can be ignored: the overdose can be conceived of as getting rid of certain thoughts belonging to another, yet leaving the body unharmed. Third, the absence of mentalizing removes key restraints on action against both the self and the other. Even when someone can intellectually conceive of the impact of their actions on another person, this may be felt as meaningless, empty of emotional conviction (Blair, 1995). Linked to this may be a reason why women more commonly self-harm, while men are more often aggressive towards others. We would suggest that for women, the image of the mother (most often the primary caregiver in early life) more easily resides in one's own body, whereas for men it is easier to externalize this and the thoughts it represents onto others.

In extreme cases, where the child has found no alternative relationship in which his thoughts and feelings are perceived and reflected, his own potential for reflective capacity will not be fulfilled. In cases of abusive, hostile, or simply totally vacuous relationships with the caregiver, the infant may deliberately turn away from the object; the contemplation of the object's mind is overwhelming as it harbours frankly hostile intentions towards the infant's self. This may lead to a widespread avoidance of mental states which further reduces the chance of identifying and establishing intimate links with an understanding object.

As studies of resilient children suggest, even a single secure/understanding relationship may be sufficient for the development of reflective processes and may "save" the child. We do not anticipate that trauma outside the context of a close attachment would pervasively stunt the development of mentalization. It is because reflective function evolves in the context of intense interpersonal relationships that the fear of the mind of another can have such devastating consequences on the emergence of social understanding.

If the traumatized child has had no social support of sufficient strength and intensity for an attachment bond and then reflectiveness to develop, then the experience of later trauma or abuse will probably not be reflected on or resolved. Naturally, the unresolved experience of abuse diminishes the likelihood of meaningful relationships, which, in a self-perpetuating way, makes it harder to reach a satisfactory resolution of the disturbing experience through reflective processes. In fact, a pattern may be established whereby suspicion and distrust generalize, leading to a turning away from the mental state of most important others and an apparent "decoupling" of thinking about people, leaving the person bereft. The "neediness" of people with borderline personality disorders seems to be a step in this direction: no sooner do they become involved with another person than the malfunctioning of their mentalizing capacity leads them into confusion and chaos within the relationship. They may regress to the intersubjective state of earlier mental representation, no longer able to differentiate their own mental representations from those of others, and both of these from external reality. These processes combine, and such people may become terrorized by their own thoughts about the other, experienced (via projection) as *in* the other, particularly their aggressive impulses and fantasies; these become crippling, and most commonly such people reject or arrange to be rejected by their object. Psychoanalysis or psychotherapy can break the vicious cycle by reinforcing reflective capacity.

Psychotherapy and mentalizing

Acceptance of this model does not imply a change in psychotherapeutic practice, or that these ideas are relevant to most forms of later pathology. Many patients with neurotic problems have relatively good reflective capacities, founded (we would suggest) on adequate early attachment relationships and adequate mentalizing capacities in at least one caregiver. In these cases, we see traditional psychoanalytic understanding and the interpretation of current unconscious conflicts as very powerful and able to produce substantial, lasting change. It does, however, call for a reappraisal of the relative importance of aspects of technique in cases showing the kinds of early developmental failure which we have tried to describe. This means that certain more supportive techniques may shift from the status of parameter to mutative components, at least in the early stages of what is likely to be a prolonged analysis.

The focus on reflective function in psychopathology brings with it an implication concerning the role of insight in these cases of severe character and developmental pathology. Insight is an unlikely goal early on, given the profound limitation on listening to and understanding interpretations which these patients show. In some less severe cases, the therapist may be impressed by the patient's apparent receptiveness to interpretations and may become suspicious only in the long term when what seems like the building of insight fails to lead to significant change. Patients such as these acquire insight within what we would see as a pretend mode, where reflection is possible as long as it is kept separate from everyday reality. In other words, the patient plays at being in analysis but is unable to integrate it with genuine feeling or meaning.

What are the analyst's goals when understanding is unattainable, at first, and is in fact perceived as a serious threat? We aim to enhance certain psychic processes. To do this, the analyst needs, of course, to create an environment within which thinking about feelings and ideas can be experienced as safe, perhaps for the first time. There is then the opportunity for the patient to find himself as a thinking and feeling person within the analyst's mind. The analyst presents a picture to the patient that is related to the patient's experience at that moment, but is also sufficiently different for the patient to learn the possibility of alternative perspectives. There is a constant and sometimes overwhelming pressure on the analyst to accept the patient's externalization, and this she must do, in some way, for a refusal to do so brings about the experience of the self as destroyed by the return of the alien other. Yet by becoming this other person, the analyst would have obliterated her capacity to think about the patient. The situation is made more difficult because the simple presentation of the dilemma to the patient, unlike talking to more neurotic patients about the transference, has little effect.

The analyst's task is primarily to remain in touch with the patient's mental state, despite the patient's dramatic enactments: to address and challenge the patient's mental capacities by verbalizing internal states, differentiating feelings, breaking down unmanageable anxiety-provoking experiences into simpler, more manageable entities, helping the development of an "as if" attitude where ideas can begin to be thought about as ideas rather than as reality, yet retaining their links to the internal world, and so on. We think of these interventions as "small interpretations", generally pertaining to aspects of the mental world that are neither unconscious nor overly complex. In neurotic patients, such feelings and thoughts would require no elaboration on the part of the analyst, yet without such background work the analysis of severely disturbed people is, we suggest, bound to fail, ending prematurely or turning into an impasse.

Psychoanalysis inevitably deals with individuals whose past experience has left them vulnerable to current stress and the repetition of adverse early experiences. The treatment of people such as those we have focused on in this chapter involves an elaborative, mentalistic stance. This enhances the development of reflective self-function and may in the long run enhance the psychic resilience of individuals in a generic way, providing them with improved control over their system of representation of relationships. It can equip them with a kind of self-righting capacity whereby through being able to make their representational models more flexible, they can be reviewed and changed. Such gradual and constant adjustments facilitate the development of an internal world in which the behaviour of others may be experienced as understandable, meaningful, predictable, and human. This reduces the need for the splitting of frightening and incoherent mental representations of mental states, and new experiences of other minds can more readily be integrated into the framework of past relationship representations.

The abused or traumatized child, evading or entangled in the mental world, never acquires adequate meta-control over the representational world of internal working models. Unhelpful models of relationship patterns emerge frequently, and the internal world of the child and adult comes to be dominated by negative affect. Caught in a vicious cycle of paranoid anxiety and exaggerated defensive manoeuvres, the person becomes inextricably entangled in an internal world dominated by dangerous, evil, and mindless objects. He has abandoned the very process that could extract him from his predicament—the capacity to reflect on why people do things, what goes on in their minds.

Over a long period, frequent and diverse interpretations about the patient's perception of himself, the analyst, and their analytic relationship may enable him to attempt to create a mental representation—both of himself and of his analyst—as thinking and feeling, together and independently. This can then form the core of a sense of himself, with a capacity to represent ideas and meanings, and create the basis for the bond that ultimately permits new possibilities of separation and intimacy.

Acknowledgements

We would like to acknowledge with affection the long-term, fruitful collaboration between Peter Fonagy and Miriam and Howard Steele in attachment research, and our more recent, very valuable collaborations with György Gergely and Efrain Bleiberg.

CHAPTER TWO

Psychoanalysis and developmental therapy

Anne Hurry

"Where are finished or developing character structures open to influence? We know they are open to many influences, because there are many people who never have therapy and who still undergo quite extraordinary personality changes during their life-time, *according to experience in relationships* . . . sometimes experience through frustration, sometimes through satisfaction, sometimes through a new world opening up to them. And this is largely an unexplored field, but very worthwhile to explore from what we see happen in child analysis."

Anna Freud,[1] quoted in Penman, 1995

P sychic development is a lifelong process, subject to both inner and outer influences, the outcome of a continuous interaction between what is innate or has become inbuilt in us and the relationships and circumstances that we encounter.

---

[1] In this chapter, Anna Freud's comments quoted by Ava Penman are from previously unpublished transcriptions of meetings, chaired by Penman, in which Anna Freud participated during 1970 and 1971.

Today, there is considerable interest in the "innate", in the genetic roots of psychological development and its disturbances, and our growing knowledge here should prove valuable in helping us to offer appropriate treatments. (See Cohen, 1997, for a brief review of organizing or influencing biological factors in various childhood disturbances.) But emphasis on the innate can be used to oversimplify complex psychological phenomena. Biological reductionism, increasingly evident in the current scientific climate, can lead to a kind of therapeutic nihilism: psychotherapy becomes an irrelevancy or restricts its aims, offering only improved management; gene therapy or drug therapies are seen as the answer to psychological difficulties.

Improved management may indeed offer hope for certain conditions but is no panacea, and gene therapy cannot be the answer to problems that are not genetically determined. There is, for instance, no "gene for aggression" (a term used to denote a wide variety of different behaviours). Even could there be such a gene, it would impact differently on different individuals: neither psychotherapy for the hyper-aggressive nor the betterment of social conditions would become irrelevancies, as Rose (1995) has cogently argued. Similarly, there can be no "gene for homosexuality" or "for heterosexuality", and, where the complex manifestations of the various sexualities are accompanied by conflict and pain, they require analysis, whatever their outward form (Hurry, 1994b).

What may prove most remarkable is the extent to which the effects of relationships can modify the effects of genetic tendencies, and the extent to which we ourselves can influence the environment and relationships by which, in turn, we are affected (cf. Lewontin, Rose, & Kamin, 1984; Rose, 1997). It is possible to recognize the role of genes without subscribing to genetic determinism, for, as Rose (1997) puts it, "it is in the nature of living systems to be radically indeterminate, to continually construct their—our—own futures, albeit in circumstances not of our choosing" (p. 7).

Neurological studies have shown that experience affects the development and functioning of the brain throughout life:

> The genome is not sufficient to encode all the details as to which connections ultimately become functionally active. To a startling degree, it is interactions with the environment that

stimulate the more precise wiring of neural connections. . . .
Illustrations of the experience-dependent nature of brain development exist at every level of brain functioning, from the
rapid growth of the brain in early childhood to the subtler
modifications that occur throughout the lifespan. [Pally, 1997,
p. 589].

Brain and neurodevelopment are "use-dependent". The earliest stages of life are particularly crucial, both neurologically and
psychologically. Neurological studies have shown that without
appropriate early stimulation, or appropriate relational experience, there is maldevelopment of the areas of the brain that mediate such functions as humour, empathy, attachment, and affect
regulation (Perry, Pollard, Blakley, Baker, & Vigilante, 1995). And
attachment studies have shown that the nature of an infant's first
relationships, determined by the quality of parental relating available (rather than by inborn temperament), lays down patterns of
relating that, although never conscious, remain a potential influence on all future relationships (Chapter 1).

But we are not doomed perpetually to enact such patterns.
Brain modifications do occur throughout life, and, as Anna Freud
indicated, relationships and events in day-to-day life can provide
an opportunity for change and growth at all stages. Developmental
therapy provides such an opportunity for change through a relationship fine-tuned to the patient's developmental needs. Psycho-
analysis, too, provides a particular kind of relationship, one that
meets the needs of those individuals who have reached the stage
of symbolic or "representational" thinking, but who are held back
from further development by pathogenic influences from the past.
Here, the developmental need is for "insight", for understanding
that can clarify past ties and so allow further development. *The
distinction between developmental and psychoanalytic work is thus a
false one: psychoanalysis is itself a particular type of developmental
therapy.*

The term "psychoanalysis" has been used in a *pars pro toto* way
to cover both classical (insight-oriented) and developmental (inter-
actional/relational) treatment for nearly a hundred years, and this
usage is by now unalterably established. For the sake of clarity, I
shall keep to current usage, so far as possible reserving the term

"developmental therapy" to refer to work aimed directly at furthering development—that is, not via interpretation.

Some terminological confusion will inevitably remain. Anna Freud (1965, 1970) defined the aim of child analysis as restoration to the path of normal, progressive development. This aim is also appropriate in adult analysis, as Jack Novick (1990) has pointed out, describing the "progressive thrust" of adult development as possibly equal to that of childhood. He added: "Psychoanalysis may not only be a means for restoring growth, but an important developmental experience in its own right . . . allowing a second chance for old solutions to be altered and new ones to be created" (p. 432). Such a view respects the forces within the patient that make for change and growth and is consistent with the thinking of the British Independent analysts (see Kohon, 1986).

Our developmental potential can be fulfilled only in a social context, and the first social context is the interactive relationship with the parents, in which infants find—but also, in part, create—the objects that they need. Similarly, in psychoanalytic developmental therapy, patients find or create in the therapist an appropriate "developmental" object. Bollas (1979) wrote of the search for "a particular object relation that is associated with ego transformation and repair" (p. 99). We could see this as a search for health and wholeness—for the experience of well-being, of being in touch with the object and with the self. Winnicott (1960) described a similar active search in the "False Self" organization, in which there was a move towards health: "The False Self has as its main concern a search for conditions which will make it possible for the True Self to come into its own" (p. 143). We could see the decision to begin an analysis—that is, a relationship with an object who will recognize and understand—as indicative of this search and as an outcome of developmental forces.

The search for health and wholeness is more evident in some individuals than in others; in some it may, for defensive reasons, appear entirely absent. The search is not restricted to analysis. Anna Freud spoke of the "extraordinary" changes that people can undergo in everyday life. Burland (1997) has written of "an inherent process for self-healing". Stressing that the self-reparative activities he saw in analysis were used spontaneously throughout life, he added: "Psychoanalysis can be viewed as a technique by which these inherent means of psychological self-repair are mobilized and maximized in a goal directed venture over a circumscribed period of time" (p. 474). Similarly, Ruszczynski (1998) describes the potential for further emotional development and growth not only in the analytic relationship, but in all, since "*All* relationships are a complex and fluid mix of both developmental and defensive interactions" (p. 36).

Classical analysis

For many years, the effective element in analysis was thought to be the making conscious of the unconscious via interpretation. The essential aim was insight and greater ego control. The transference aspect of the relationship to the analyst was of central importance: through it, the patient could revive past relationships and conflicts, and these could then be understood and worked through by means of transference interpretations.

Taken to the extreme, this approach put the patient in a relatively passive position as the recipient of the analyst's understanding. Some analysts, most notably Strachey (1934), held that only transference interpretations were truly mutative—that is, capable of resulting in lasting change. Although Freud himself never subscribed to this view, a technique grew up in which everything that a patient said or did was likely to be interpreted in terms of the transference. Such a technique could result in what Balint (1968) called "a relationship between a highly important, omnipresent object, the analyst, and an unequal subject" (p. 169).

Some classical analysts recognized the importance of what they called the "real" relationship to the analyst (in particular, Greenson, 1967), but many saw the "real" relationship as a potential interference to the analyst's central role as a transference object.

There is no doubt that classical analysis brought great relief to many patients, freeing them from the crippling burden of conflicts stemming from the past and enabling them to find new, more adaptive ways of coping and to build more rewarding relationships. Today, interpretation still retains a central place in the analysis of neurotic patients with relatively well-developed, structured personalities and a capacity for representational (symbolic) thinking.

But not all patients can make use of interpretation. As Balint pointed out, "[Analytic] technique was worked out for patients who experience the analyst's interpretation as interpretation and whose ego is strong enough to enable them to 'take in' the interpretations and perform . . . the process of 'working through'. We know that not every patient is capable of this task" (1968, p. 10). Such patients were (and are) most often individuals still functioning at a dyadic level, where the sense of self was (is) imperfectly or distortedly developed, the structuralization of the personality incomplete, and the capacity for representational thought poorly developed. From the beginnings of psychoanalysis, individual analysts struggled to find ways of working with these patients, but the failure of experiments like Ferenczi's "mutual analysis" (1932) led many to reinforce their opinion that such people were "unanalysable".

Developmental therapy

Although the term "developmental therapy" is relatively new, it is used to describe the kind of work long established at the Anna Freud Centre as a means of helping children with developmental deficits or distortions—within the context of child analysis. Child analysts have always used such techniques as helping a child to be able to play, to name feelings, to control wishes and impulses rather than be driven to enact them, to relate to others, and to think of and see others as thinking and feeling. They have done such work intuitively, and at times, lacking a fully developed theoretical framework in which to view it, they have undervalued and sometimes failed to record it. Anna Freud, however, believed that this "developmental help" called for further study (1978, p. 109).

We have now begun to clarify the nature of developmental disturbances and of our therapeutic responses to them (Fonagy & Target, 1996; Fonagy, Target, Edgcumbe, Moran, & Miller, in preparation; Greenspan, 1997). Developmental work has moved to the forefront of psychoanalytic thinking; it is valued in its own right, it has been made "respectable", and it has even been named. Fonagy and Target (1996) introduced the term "psychodynamic developmental therapy", and a little later Greenspan (1997) wrote of "developmentally based psychotherapy".

Such recognition of their way of working enables child analysts to be more aware of what they are doing, to bring their technique more fully into the compass of their thinking, and so, gradually, to refine and develop their clinical skills. It has also enabled adult analysts to be clearer about the very similar techniques that they employ in work with adults suffering from developmental deficits or difficulties. Previously, such work in adult analysis had been described as "ego support" and seen as a departure from—even a contamination of—"pure" analytic technique, since it involved the use of "parameters". Today, with growing recognition of the developmental element in all analyses, such parameters are becoming recognized as mutative elements (Chapter 1), and the term "developmental therapy" is now also applied to work with adults.

Our understanding of developmental disturbances and of ways of treating them has been greatly enriched by findings from infant observational research, for the interactions that take place within the therapeutic developmental relationship are essentially similar to those that ordinarily take place between the parents and the infant or child. The most relevant recent research findings are highlighted in Chapter 1. To summarize: (a) the outstanding importance of the infant–mother relationship is universally recognized; (b) the infant is seen not as the passive recipient of care and nurturing, but as born with a readiness to attend to people as entities, developing as an active partner in the context of a central relationship, one in which each partner influences the other; (c) the self is built up in relation to the other and to the other's view of the self, and shared experience of positive affect is essential for the development of the sense of a separate and authentic self; (d) the image of the world, too, is built up in relation to the other's image of that world as conveyed to the infant, both affectively and cognitively.

Infant observational studies
and psychoanalytic theory

While research studies must lead us to question some aspects of analytic theory, they confirm or can help us to develop others (cf. Chapter 1: see also Fonagy, Target, Steele, & Gerber, 1995; Shapiro & Emde, 1995).

Attachment theory was initially seen by many analysts as contrary to psychoanalytic thinking. Bowlby's (1958) paper, "The Nature of the Child's Tie to His Mother", was ill received at the British Psychoanalytic Society, and the thinking in his great trilogy, *Attachment and Loss* (1969, 1973, 1980), is only now being integrated into analytic theory. Yet Freud, throughout his writings, stressed the centrality of the early relationship to the mother, describing her importance as "unique, without parallel, established unalterably for a whole lifetime as the first and strongest love-object and as the prototype of all later love-relations" (1940a [1938], p. 188).

Bowlby's thinking confirmed Freud's view of the central importance of the early relationship to the mother, but now within the context of the infant's primary bond with an attachment figure. Although some analysts (notably Fairbairn, 1952) have seen the need for object-relating as primary, Freud and Bowlby do differ here, for Freud saw love relationships as dependent from the beginning upon the need for drive satisfaction: "A child's first erotic object is the mother's breast that nourishes it; love has its origin in attachment to the satisfied need for nourishment. . . . This first object is later completed into the person of the child's mother" (1940a [1938], p. 188).

The concept of the drives as the main motor forces of psychic life (never directly observable) was a hypothesis modelled on the physical sciences of Freud's time and may now have outlived its usefulness. But, irreconcilable as Bowlby's views may be with Freud's stress on the centrality of the drives as primary motivators, acceptance of the child's attachment needs does not mean that we have to deny the existence or importance of sexual or aggressive feelings and wishes.

It is true that the object-relational stance can sometimes reflect a comparative neglect of the role of sexuality (Etchegoyen, 1996; Furman, 1997), although those who work with young or pubertal children cannot but be aware of the impact of changing bodily needs and pleasures on relationships and on the developing self. Today, most analysts would see sexuality as organized within an object-relational context. They focus not on the drive per se, but rather on "when and how its components manifest themselves, how they affect personality development, how they interact with aspects of personality functioning and are, in turn, affected by it, and, not least, the role of the environment in this process" (Furman, 1997). Furman's (1992) observational studies, for instance, have clarified the way in which the toddler's anal preoccupations, interests, and behaviours impact on his development both directly and indirectly—in that they also affect the mother, thus affecting the mother–child relationship, and so, in turn, the manifestation of anal behaviours.

Conversely, both adult and child analysts cannot but be aware that sexual manifestations may arise not only on the basis of autonomous physical stimuli, but also, and importantly, on the basis of the need to defend against painful affect, to achieve a feeling of well-being, or to serve an object-relational aim.

The theory of the aggressive drive has long been the subject of disagreement among psychoanalysts. It has been argued that aggression is so fundamentally different in kind from sexuality, not being rooted in any autonomous physical stimulus, that it makes no sense to use the same term, "drive", to denote two such different phenomena. Clinically, it is in any case more useful to consider the destructive aspects of aggression as a response to pain, fear, and frustration (Parens, 1991).

Where Freud and Bowlby do agree is with regard to the importance of separation. Attachment studies confirm Freud's views on the anxiety induced in the infant by separation from the mother, and they add to our understanding of the ways in which the infant may cope with it. Freud was the first psychoanalytic observer of babies—of his own children and those of relatives and friends (Novick, 1989). From early on, he saw anxiety in children as "originally nothing other than the expression of the fact that they are feeling the loss of the person they love" (Freud, 1905d, p. 224). He held to this view throughout the vicissitudes of his thinking on anxiety. In 1932, for instance, he wrote of the fear of loss of love as a later prolongation of the infant's separation anxiety, adding,

"You will realize how real a situation of danger is indicated by this anxiety. If a mother is absent or has withdrawn her love from her child, it is no longer sure of the satisfaction of its needs and is perhaps exposed to the most distressing feelings of tension . . . here psychological researches trench upon the facts of biology" (1933a, p. 87).

The ethological studies available to Bowlby were not available to Freud, but in the light of the above it seems likely that they would have been of extraordinary interest to him—as would Bowlby's own work. Bowlby saw attachment as serving the biological function of preservation of the species, and the satisfaction of the infant's needs as essential to its survival. Freud had a special interest in the links between psychology and biology. (This is perhaps most evident in his early "A Project for a Scientific Psychology", 1950 [1895], in which he attempts to link neurological and psychological processes, emphasizing the impact of the environment on the organism, and the organism's reaction.)[2]

The infant attachment patterns described in Chapter 1, reflecting as they do the origins of lifelong defensive patterns, inform our understanding of an area first developed by Freud. His most famous child observation was of the "cotton reel boy" (1920g, pp. 14–17). This child would throw away any small object, with an "o–o–o–o" of satisfaction. He had a wooden reel with a string attached and used to throw this away with the same satisfaction, but then retrieve it by means of the string, uttering a joyful "*da*". Freud saw the throwing away as in part an expression of the boy's anger at his mother for leaving, but his main interest was in the coping strategy evident in the game: in throwing away something that he could then retrieve, the boy actively mastered the experience of separation from his mother.[3]

---

[2] To suppose that Freud would not have wished to integrate the findings of attachment studies within psychoanalytic theory is rather like supposing that Galileo would have rejected the discovery of supernovae or black holes (and to reject recent research findings as incompatible with Freud is not unlike rejecting later astronomical findings as incompatible with Galileo).

[3] "Object tossing" in infancy usually begins as an interactive form of play in which the adult retrieves and returns the object that the child has thrown. It is now understood as marking an early stage in the developmental line related to the mastery of separation anxiety (Kleeman, 1967, 1973; Willock, 1990).

Today we would see the boy's behaviour as indicative of serious attachment problems for, Freud noted, at 18 months the child never cried when his mother left him for a few hours, even though "[he] could not possibly have felt his mother's departure as something agreeable or even indifferent". The *only* use he made of any toy was to throw it away. Such restriction would now suggest an overwhelming need to cope with separation, one that seems unlikely to have allowed the development of any interests or zest for life. Indeed, the child was "not at all precocious in his intellectual development", and Freud appears to have taken this as a given. Today, we would question that given, more aware that effective functioning, even when pre-programmed, develops optimally only in the context of an appropriate relationship (Furman, 1992; Hobson, 1995).

The first attachment studies focused on the infant's relationship with the mother, but some recent research has focused on his relationship with the father. Freud's view of the father at the oedipal stage, as love object or rival, is of course well known. Less well known is his recognition of the importance of the earlier relationship to the father. In essence, he saw this (in the case of the boy) as involving a primary identification, the child's "first and most important identification", although it could be reinforced in response to later oedipal conflict (1923b, p. 31).

We are now becoming increasingly aware of the importance of the early relationship to the father. We have known for some time that, from the first weeks, the infant develops a relationship to father that is particular to him (Cath, Gurwitt, & Ross, 1982). More surprising, and important for clinicians, is Steele's recent finding that the security of an infant's attachment to his father (predictable at 18 months from prenatal interviews with father) is not affected by the security or otherwise of his relationship to his mother, or vice versa (Chapter 1: see also Steele et al., 1996). This finding would suggest that infants do not necessarily generalize basic trust, or basic mistrust and fear, and that "transference" of patterns of relating does not inevitably occur in infancy.[4] It follows that a

---

[4] Such is not invariably the case: Field, Healey, Goldstein, Perry, and Bendell (1988) have shown that young infants (3 to 6 months aet) of depressed mothers develop a depressed style of interacting with their mothers which does

secure relationship with even one person, existing possibly for only a short time, may provide the foundation for a mode of relating which can later be utilized when an appropriate object is found. (This has implications for later manifest change, whether in therapy or in the course of life.)

There remains much that we do not know, and perhaps cannot know, of the inner world of the infant. Developmental findings cannot answer all questions. But they can provide a clearer picture of the early years, one no longer obscured by the kind of speculation that was perhaps inevitable when we simply did not know what was possible in infancy. Much of this speculation was based on a view of pathology as rooted in and directly reflecting what had been normal at earlier stages of life. Such extrapolation backwards from the pathological to the developmental was evident in all psychoanalytic schools of thought and could have deleterious effects on clinical work.

Freud's various attempts to describe and date a stage of primary narcissism, for instance, have become meaningless in the light of our knowledge of the infant's readiness for interaction, and they have hindered rather than helped the development of our clinical skills. Similarly, his view of a sense of omnipotence as characteristic of normal infancy and early childhood has become untenable, although this is not yet generally recognized and the unquestioning acceptance of his views here can still have adverse clinical effects: the defensive roots of omnipotence in a sense of helplessness and fear can be insufficiently recognized, blocking the way to the possible development of a realistic sense of competence (Novick & Novick, 1996).

Similarly, Melanie Klein's (1957) view of envy as present from birth is untenable since, as we now know (Chapter 1), neonates are simply not capable of the kind of attribution of motivation to others which she assumes. In extrapolating backwards, Klein blocked fur-

---

generalize to their interactions with non-depressed adults who are strangers to them (i.e. adults with whom they have had no opportunity to build up an alternative model of relating). Unfortunately, Field's paper does not tell us whether these infants related similarly to their fathers—or indeed, whether they had been reared in one- or two-parent families. Clearly, further research is needed here.

ther understanding of the complex affect of envy, and her view
of this affect as a bedrock, a basic given, sometimes led to a way of
working that faced the patient with something akin to original sin
rather than with hope.

Psychoanalysis
as an interactional/developmental process

The interactional frame of reference has added greatly to our understanding of development. Since psychoanalysis is a two-person
endeavour, it is not surprising that this same frame is proving
increasingly useful in our understanding of the therapeutic process. Findings from developmental psychology go far to support
the work of analysts who have stressed the interpersonal basis of
development and of analysis.

From the 1950s on, Balint, Winnicott, and other Independent
analysts in the United Kingdom, as well as Loewald in the United
States, were emphasizing the interactional nature of analysis. They
saw the role of the analyst as analogous to that of the parent.
Deficiencies or distortions in the structuralization and experience
of the self were related to deficiencies or distortions in the early
(dyadic) relationship to the mother. Analysis could provide the
opportunity for a new beginning on the patient's part when the
analyst could provide an appropriate holding or facilitating environment (Winnicott, 1965).

Loewald (1960) described transference interpretation as clearing the way for a relationship to the analyst as a "new object", and
thus to new ways of being and relating.[5] He saw the sense of self
as built up through the internalization of parental images of the

---

[5] Loewald's approach remains fundamental to much recent thinking on
developmental work. Greenspan (1997), for instance, writes: "Structure building . . . does not occur, as is often postulated, out of resolving conflicts; it occurs
from certain features of a relationship that are ongoing in nature. These are the
same relationship features that lead to proper structural growth during development. . . . Conflicts have to be analysed so that individuals will be amenable
and accessible to the type of relationship that will build structures" (p. 374).

child—images conveyed through a multitude of moment-to-moment interactions—and believed that comparable interactions took place within analysis.

Loewald held that processes within "classical" analyses of neurotic patients were essentially the same as those within analyses of patients with obvious ego defects. The difference lay in the level of interaction, rather than the type:

> In . . . borderline cases and psychotics, processes such as I tried to sketch in the child–parent relationship take place in the therapeutic situation on levels relatively close and similar to those of the early child–parent relationship. The further we move away from gross ego-defect cases, the more do these integrative processes take place on higher levels of sublimation and by modes of communication which show much more complex stages of organization. [1960, p. 21]

This view of the importance of developmental interaction within analysis differs from a still current view which would restrict developmental work to the analysis of patients with obvious defect or deficit (Pine, 1994). Such a restricted usage diminishes the importance of the developmental factor in all analyses.

Analysts are increasingly taking the view that one function of "understanding" is to enable patients to make use of the opportunities for growth that analysis provides. Kennedy (1971) described the aim of interpretation (in child analysis) as enabling the child to resolve conflicts impeding his development, rather than as giving insight about the past. Emde (1980c) saw the therapeutic process (in adult analysis) as reopening the pathway to environmental influences, revealing the analyst as a new, potential developmental object. Settlage (1993) stressed the interdependence of analytic and developmental processes, seeing these as functioning simultaneously and complimentarily.

Tähkä (1993) distinguished three strands in the patient's use of the analyst: as *Contemporary object*, as *Past (transference) object*, and as *New (developmental) object*. He related structural change specifically and only to the patient's use of the analyst as a new developmental object. He also saw the transference as providing the opportunity for the analyst to become a new developmental object, in that the analyst acted differently from the original developmental object being sought in the transference. Tähkä stressed that this difference did not involve any deliberate role play: it did provide a "corrective emotional experience", but not in the Alexanderian sense (Alexander & French, 1946). Rather, it was based on the analyst's "empathic and/or complementary recognition of the patient's frustrated and arrested developmental needs and potentials" (p. 231).

The British Independent analysts apart, many writers assume that the patient can make use of the developmental relationship only following interpretation. But it is evident in the work of Balint, Winnicott, and others (see Kohon, 1986) that an analysis may begin with quite lengthy periods in which the analyst does not interpret, but provides a holding environment (i.e., a developmental relationship)—which may eventually enable the patient to make use of interpretation. During such initial periods, the analyst may recognize the patient's affect, but there are patients who feel even such recognition as intrusion and for whom it is therefore necessary to wait. How is it that the patient is able to make use of such a relationship, given his transference expectations of, say, intrusion or attack?

We cannot yet be certain about the answer to this question. But we know that the models of relating built up in infancy can be independent of one another, and that even a single secure/understanding relationship may "save" a child (Chapter 1). While experientially it often seems that analyst and patient together create or discover an alternative way of relating, it may be that this "new" model resonates with and evokes an earlier model built on experiences of self-with-other so minimal or short-lived that it cannot be relied upon and so rarely made use of in current relationships that its existence is not suspected. On the other hand, earlier experience does not have to be the basis of the search for a new way of relating: as the epigenetic course of development unfolds, individuals (or patients) seek and partially create an object and a mode of relating appropriate to their developmental stage, perhaps in part on the basis of earlier models—for example, the oedipal child who confidently woos the parent (or analyst) is the child who has already felt loved—but also on the basis of their developmental agenda. Furthermore, it is possible that a "relational" developmental agenda is operative from the beginning of life, that the infant's readiness to attend to others indicates a (non-conscious) "pre-conception" of the other. Braten (1987) suggests that the infant's brain contains circuits indicating the co-presence of a "virtual other", and that it is through experience that the sense of the actual other is gradually filled in. So it may even be that some "new" therapeutic relationships are indeed new, but built on what Alvarez (1996) calls the "traces of a pre-conception or of a pre-object" which remains undestroyed despite the infant's earlier failure to find or create an appropriate object.

For a patient whose experience has been primarily of pain, neglect, or dissatisfaction, it is a great risk to allow the hope of a more benign relationship, and for defensive reasons he may rely upon an old, malign model. But even in such cases we can see the transference as carrying or accompanied by an unconscious wish for change alongside the defensive need to repeat, as carrying hope that the analyst will act as developmental rather than as transference object. Weiss (1995), summarizing a number of studies linking process and outcome, found that patients worked in accordance with an unconscious plan—a plan to disprove pathogenic beliefs by testing them on the therapist:

> . . . the patient benefits not just from interpretation but, equally important, from his relationship to the analyst. Indeed, the patient may achieve a great deal without benefit of interpretation if the analyst, by his approach, passes the patient's tests . . . the patient benefits from a particular kind of corrective emotional experience, namely, the experience that the patient himself unconsciously is seeking by his testing of the analyst. [p. 26]

Although Weiss's findings are open to criticism (see Caston, 1995), they cast light on some unresolved questions. In asking the analyst to contradict transference expectations, the patient is seeking an appropriate developmental object. This search may be his real agenda, the basis for a genuine, predominantly unconscious therapeutic alliance that can underlie the conscious "working alliance" or even the lack of any overt alliance (Chapter 4).

It is not only in his role as a developmental object that the analyst enables a developmental process to resume, but also in his role as interpreter or "contemporary object". In narcissistically disturbed and borderline cases, the recognition of affect and of the patient's "true self" are priorities if an experientially separate and effective self is to develop (Hurry, 1990). Interpretation does more than clear obstacles holding back development: it may be experienced as a new kind of recognition, and validation of previously warded-off aspects of the self may permit a new integration. "'Feeling understood' is a self-consolidating experience" (Ornstein & Ornstein, 1994, p. 993).

Thus, in practice the theoretical distinction between the analyst's interpretative and developmental roles becomes blurred: the interpreting object is also a developmental object. Anna Freud, speaking of child analysis, commented: "There are many moments . . . where one . . . shows the child that one is different from the parents, merely by understanding, by reacting differently to something the child says or does. That's an element which is very often neglected, which we call the analyst as a new object" (quoted in Penman, 1995). Her comment here is as true of adult analysis: "merely by understanding" the analyst becomes a new object, different from the patient's inner objects.

Today, Winnicott's "There is no such thing as a baby" is paralleled in Ogden's "There is no such thing as an analysand apart from the relationship with the analyst, and no such thing as an analyst apart from the relationship with the analysand" (1994, p. 4). This view represents the culmination of a growing interest in such things as work in the "here-and-now"; affect recognition and attunement; the interaction of transference and countertransference; the importance of role responsiveness (Sandler, 1976), or counter-response, as a step on the path to understanding; and the effects of the analyst's behaviour on the patient, and of the patient on the analyst.

Analysis is repeatedly compared to parenting. In 1979, Hansi Kennedy wrote that "the interaction between child and analyst represents the situation of the infant whose mother can contain, meet and anticipate her child's needs" (p. 25). Many analysts have taken this view, but with an increasing emphasis on the forward-looking aspects of the parental role. Sandbank (1993) described both analyst and parent not only as providing holding of different kinds, but also as aiming to facilitate psychological growth: "A mother holds, protects, comforts, identifies with her children's distress and tries to provide an atmosphere of safety. . . . She also questions, observes with objectivity, encourages progress, envisions the future" (p. 718). We could add that, just as the good-enough mother stretches the infant's range of expectancies, there are times when the good-enough analyst stretches the patient's range.

The analyst–parent comparison has been used mainly in reference to the analyst as a maternal developmental object, and certainly that is where Winnicott's emphasis lay. Relatively little has been written of the use of the analyst as a developmental object analogous to the father. Where such a comparison has been made, it has usually been in cases where the father has been physically or psychologically absent (Fabricius, 1995; Hurry, 1990).

It may be that as analysts we serve in the role of the father more often than we had realized, that patients seek to find or re-find in us both maternal and paternal developmental objects. Herzog (1995), for instance, gives a convincing picture of a 4-year-old's need to find his father in the analytic setting. From the beginning, his patient, Tommy, assessed his analyst in terms of his attributes and capacities, using him in the role of a helping father, one who knew the joys of masculinity. Tommy recounted a "dream" in which, as a little lion, he went hunting with his father. They chased a zebra, but Tommy fell and was afraid that father lion would be angry and would hit him. When the father was not angry, Tommy was relieved:

> Daddy helps me up and says: "Come on, I'll show you how to run and then we'll get another one. I wanted antelope for dinner anyway." I responded: "That's how a little lion learns to hunt, you know, he needs a teacher." "Yeah," said Tommy, "someone who is like him and knows how it feels to run fast and then to jump and strike." "How does it feel?" I asked. "Wonderful, you know that, it's the best thing in the world. I know that you feel that too when you hunt," Tommy said. [p. 269]

Here we can see how Tommy's fear of the transference object—the angry analyst/father—is superseded by his use of the analyst as a benign father, a helper and teacher who is different yet similar, and hence one with whom he can identify. Over time, such relational experiences lead to the internalization of new representations of self-with-other.

Herzog's patient was young, making use of the analyst as father at a stage when this was developmentally appropriate. In child analysis, it is common for such developmental experiences to feed back to, and be reflected in, the child's relationships to his original objects, the real parents at home.[6] But similar experiences in adult analysis, relatively late in life, are also used to develop— and are reflected in—new relationships. Until this has happened, the analysis remains incomplete. Jack Novick (1990) has suggested that it is premature to terminate an analysis if the analyst is still the only person to meet the patient's "primary need" to be listened to and understood—in other words, before the patient has been able to develop a relationship with a "real" object outside the analysis. Similarly, Tähkä (1993) noted the function of analysis as a preparation for new relationships:

> In a successful analysis, [the analyst's] fate as the patient's developmental object may have a course analogous to what the patient's interactions with his original developmental objects should have been: that is, a gradual, relative abandonment of the analyst both as the patient's self ideal and as an ideal love object. The role of the developmental object is not to prepare for himself the developing individual in his care, but for new, age-appropriate objects. [p. 248]

A new development occurring at a chronologically late stage is not experientially "the same" as a development occurring age-appropriately in infancy or early childhood, for it evolves in the context of patterns of interaction with others that have long been laid down. Anna Freud asked, "Can [basic experiences] be undone? . . . and which of them can be undone, which can't and . . . to what age can they be undone? I am pretty convinced that they can't [all be undone]. And I don't know which can be undone, which only leave consequences, which can be influenced later on" (1970, quoted in Penman, 1995). Today, we would not expect basic relational experiences to be "undone". New models of self-with-others built up in

---

[6] However, in the case of children where a parent is lacking, the analyst may serve as a primary developmental object (Chapter 6).

treatment (like Tommy's new model of self-with-father) do not obliterate old models. They are built up alongside the old: the potential for activation of the old remains, particularly under conditions of stress.

For early models of relating are never accessible to consciousness and cannot be remembered autobiographically (Fonagy & Target, 1997). Thus there is "a wider zone of nonconscious mental activity than we have been used to thinking about" (Emde, 1995, p. 416). Although the existence of a procedural unconscious was always implicit in psychoanalysis, it did not become a focus of analytic thinking until Sandler and Joffe's (1969) distinction between the realm of structure (unknowable) and the realm of experience. It is now clear that this distinction is relevant inter- as well as intra-personally: "Much of what is important is implicit, nonconscious, and can only be known interpersonally through actions and interactions" (Emde, 1995, p. 417).

Inaccessible to consciousness, early models of relating are not subject to representational manipulation, and interpretation or "reconstruction" cannot obliterate them. This has implications for the choice of interpretation. From Freud on, reconstruction has been central to psychoanalytic technique, the "cornerstone of psychoanalytic practice, understanding and research" (Greenacre, 1980, p. 39). But while reconstruction can provide meaningful insight into current functioning, it can never exactly reflect early experience, as Sandler and Sandler (1997) have pointed out. Furthermore, when more adaptive and rewarding ways of relating have been achieved in treatment (i.e. new patterns of relating created alongside the old), it is not essential for the patient to "know about" the origins of the old models. Cognitive awareness of these origins does not bring fundamental change, although the patient's knowledge of the rules on which he has relied can be useful in helping him to recognize when he is falling back on old, maladaptive patterns, and so selectively to activate more appropriate and adaptive patterns (Chapter 1).

Reconstruction is perhaps most useful in that it supports the development of an ongoing sense of self, rooted in the past and moving towards the future, experienced as authentic despite the impossibility of "objective" accuracy. Man-kind needs his-story, even though that story is continually revised throughout life, both within and outside analysis. Sandler and Sandler (1984) and Kerry Novick (1990) have pointed to the need to give "historical biographical sense" to the patterns of relating that emerge in treatment. Human beings need to make sense of things. Freud was aware of the need to think in terms of cause and effect, and he even wrote of the "compulsion not to let chance count as chance but to interpret it" (1901b, p. 258). (Indeed, his life's work may be seen as founded in part upon this compulsion; it is one that analysts need to remain aware of, and at times be wary of, for it is natural to assume causal linkages where none may exist: Morton, 1997.)

The oft-repeated comparison between analyst and parent, useful as it is, should also be treated with some caution. Analysts are not parents, however much their work is analogous to parenting. Winnicott wrote:

> Psychoanalysis as we learn it [i.e., classical analysis] is not at all like child care . . . But in the part of our work as analysts that I am referring to, there is nothing we do that is unrelated to child care or to infant care. In this part of our work we can in fact learn what to do from being parents, from having been children, from watching mothers with very young babies or babies unborn. [1963, p. 252]

Anna Freud commented along similar lines:

> The borderline between therapy and upbringing. . . . has never been fully characterised by anybody . . . much happens in therapy which also happens in upbringing and certain things happen in upbringing that also happen in therapy. [quoted in Penman, 1995]

The borderline remains unclear. What is certain is that while analysts do meet some developmental/relational needs, they do not satisfy instinctual needs.[7] What is to be hoped is that the analyst recognize and relate to the patient as he is, on the basis of the patient's needs, not primarily on the basis of the analyst's own narcissistic needs, externalizations, or projections (Tähkä, 1993). It is important that while the analyst's overall attitude may be be-

---

[7] Of course, in the case of children, analysts cannot satisfy basic needs for ongoing bodily care, nourishment, protection, and so on. Where such fundamentals are lacking, environmental provisions are necessary.

nign, she does not necessarily accept all aspects of her patient. She may have to refuse to relate in the way that the patient sets up, before the patient can begin to relate in another way.

Analysts are certainly not ideal parents. A parent behaving as we do would be experienced as very rejecting: regularly after fifty minutes, we turn our patients out, and we leave for weeks at a time. Hamilton (1987) suggests that the analyst differs from the mother who creates a secure attachment, in that the patient's feelings of security are constantly disrupted "by the same figure who offers help, sympathy and understanding" (p. 72). This disruption may occur through separation or, as Hamilton points out, as a result of the analytic work itself, since analysis of unconscious phantasy and defence inevitably undermines the sense of safety. Therapeutically, this may be all to the good. Underlying models of insecure attachment are inevitably brought to the fore, allowing for their recognition within the analytic relationship—that is aspects of the transference emerge and coalesce around "real" aspects of the setting, and in response to the analytic work itself, and are thus less likely to be bypassed. At the same time, the developmental relationship can be grounded within realistic limits: the patient has to confront the reality of separateness and separation. Furthermore, as Stewart (1989) points out, the setting makes it inevitable that we "fail" our patients in an appropriate way, giving them the opportunity to experience Winnicott's necessary and "legitimate" hatred. (Of course, it is also true that the disruptions, threats, and failures of the analytic setting may be too great for some vulnerable patients, and in such cases some environmental provision may be necessary.)

We are not parents, but in our developmental role we are perhaps more evidently "ourselves" than in our interpretative role. In developmental interactions, we are (and need to be) at our most spontaneous. Of course, we are also "ourselves" when we interpret, but interpretation can to some extent be described in a way that is common to all, however individually it may be slanted. Developmental work is rooted in the individual personalities of patient and analyst, and in their interaction.

It is only recently that we have begun to study the effects of the individual analyst's personality upon the analytic process. Kantrowitz's work points to the outstanding importance of the fit between patient and analyst, or "patient–analyst match". Her long-term follow-up study (Kantrowitz, 1995) calls into question much that we thought we knew regarding analysability, process (including such things as the resolution of the transference), and the stability of analytic gains. The *only* factor that she found relevant to outcome was patient–analyst match. Given the spontaneity needed in developmental work, this match is probably most important with regard to the developmental aspects of analysis.

It is not only the patient who develops during the course of an analysis. As Kantrowitz (1997) has commented, "Once analysis is viewed as a process influenced by and impacting on both participants, it would seem expectable that the analyst, as well as the patient, would be affected by participating in it" (p. 128).

The practice of analysis has long been seen as therapeutic for the analyst, but in classical thinking this effect was attributed to the benefits of ever-greater insight, since the work involved continual stimulation of conflict for the analyst and hence the need for further analysis or self-analysis (Glover, 1937). Now while it is certainly essential for the analyst to be aware of her own contribution to the analytic situation, we would not today see insight, outside the context of an ongoing relationship, as therapeutic in itself. (Indeed, in a survey of practising analysts, Kantrowitz, 1997, found that while almost all showed some change and growth in knowledge over the course of a treatment, those who consulted with a valued colleague showed "profound" change.)

The change within the analyst is now beginning to be seen in a developmental framework. Kantrowitz (1997) has suggested that processes of change within the analyst may be essentially similar to those within the patient:

> If the patient's psychological change comes about, at least in part, because what goes on between patient and analyst is different from what the patient had previously experienced—i.e., frightening or disappointing expectations about the other and/or oneself are not repeated, or if repeated are reworked, reunderstood, and then relived with a different outcome—then something parallel is likely to occur for the analyst. The patient may become an old/new object for the analyst in parallel with the analyst's being an old/new object for the patient. [p. 145]

This may indeed be so at times. For instance, it is known that many gifted psychoanalysts have had depressed mothers, and it may be that in the practice of analysis they reaffirm a pattern of relating in which they can enliven the withdrawn object, are not helpless in the face of pathology. But it is to be hoped that they are aware of any continuing need to restore the object, rather than driven to act out this need. It is, after all, the patient who pays the analyst, as Tähkä (1993) points out.

Kantrowitz's view of change within the analyst is slanted towards the correction of pathology, albeit through a developmental relationship. Tähkä (1993), however, sees analytic work as providing a stage-appropriate developmental relationship, one analogous to the parent–child relationship and accompanied by appropriate "generative pleasure" or "generative pain":

> To make full use of his function as a new developmental object for the patient, it is important that the analyst not only tolerates it, but is able to maintain a lasting interest in the patient and a stable motivation for a "generative" interaction with him. . . . A crucial sign for the presence of such a motivation is the analyst's felt concern for his patient. . . . However, it is important that this concern is of a "generative" kind, and not significantly based on neurotic guilt or countertransferential rescue fantasies. The most dependable sign of an adequate "generative" attitude towards the patient is the analyst's felt freedom to experience fully the whole gamut of parental feelings and pleasures that accompany his role as a new developmental object for his patient. [pp. 241–242]

Here we have something new. Tähkä is fully aware of the potential for pathology in the analyst, and of his possible countertransference use of the patient—for instance, to relieve guilt or overcome helplessness. Elsewhere, he points to the risk of the analyst's seeking to gratify his own infantile needs via the patient, especially in developmental work (pp. 249–250), and the risk of his using the patient as a source of narcissistic gratification (pp. 255–256). All these risks have been discussed in the literature, and all demand ongoing monitoring of the countertransference. What is new is Tähkä's recognition of the analyst's legitimate experience of parental-like feelings, pleasures, and pains.

To fulfil their developmental potential, human individuals need appropriate developmental objects throughout life. One cannot be a parent without a child, or an analyst without a patient. We have discussed the oft-repeated analogy between the developmental roles of parent and analyst. Much less interest has been shown in the developmental role of the patient for the analyst . But Tähkä notes that the interaction between analyst/parent and patient/child is affectively a "real" interaction, although one in which the patient's needs come first; where shared, empathic pleasure becomes the patient's own. Tähkä adds: "This letting the object keep the pleasure for himself is followed by a secondary pleasure in the subject for the loved person's feeling good and for the knowledge of having contributed to that oneself" (p. 244). For the analyst to feel pleased at the outcome of his work is no less appropriate than for parents to feel pleased as they see their child develop.

In short, as a developmental object for the analyst, the patient ideally is not one through whom the analyst contradicts old transference expectations, but one appropriate to the analyst's developmental stage of parenthood (or grandparenthood), a current developmental object realistically perceived in terms of needs that will change over the course of the analysis, just as the child's needs change.

I do not wish to imply that the developmental aspect of our work is always rewarding or pleasurable. Far from it. Parents may see their child's development go awry, and analysts may see their patients' development blocked or twisted despite their best efforts. Patients who use hatred and aggression as a defence against loving feelings and vulnerability (Furman, 1985; Hurry, 1994a; Isaacs, 1934), or who define themselves in terms of aggression (Fonagy, Moran, & Target, 1993), often set out to destroy any attempt to understand and may seem determined to create a malign treatment relationship. Their underlying question as to the possibility of another kind of relating may appear totally inaccessible. With these patients, the developmental aspect of our work is crucial. Yet they necessarily evoke Winnicott's (1947) "objective or justified hate", and to remain in touch with our capacity for "objective love" may tax all our personal resources (Chapter 4). While in the end such a challenge can greatly further our own development, and is rewarding in its own way, getting there can be tough going.

For some time, it has been fashionable to speak of psychoanalysis as an "impossible profession", and perhaps to see our work in this way has provided us with some (masochistic) narcissistic rewards. It is true that psychoanalytic work can be very difficult, and it can fail. But, overall, it is very rewarding:

> . . . there tend to be effective inner prohibitions in analysts' minds against admitting that they are enjoying their work, as an extremely interesting and rewarding way of making a living; something that they have chosen deliberately, and that they would not change for any other work in the world. It is a work that provides its practitioners with never-ending possibilities for creative insights, as well as with a rare versatility of professionally legitimate and useful gratification. Instead of an impossible profession, it could be characterized as a privileged work of the few. [Tähkä, 1993, pp. 253–254]

Developmental therapy
in work with children

Until recently, our thinking on the developmental aspects of adult analysis was relatively uninfluenced by child analysis, although child analysts have always combined the developmental and interpretative approaches in their work. Useful links are now being made (Daldin, 1994; Fonagy, Moran, Edgcumbe, Kennedy, & Target, 1993; Furman, 1994b; J. Novick, 1990; Yanof, 1996). Yanof in particular has noted how the discontinuity between child and adult work blocked mutual learning. Why should this have been so?

Edgcumbe (1995), describing Anna Freud's ambivalence about what she called "developmental help", suggests that we may have inherited this ambivalence, that we may still look down on developmental work as not "proper analysis". This is so. But it is more than that. Child analysis grew up in the context of adult work, at a time when the established model of analysis emphasized the making conscious of the unconscious via interpretation of the patient's free associations. But children do not free associate: they talk, they act (i.e. they do things), and above all they play, although some are not able to play. Often they require the analyst to take a role in their play, to carry those externalized aspects of the child's self which cannot be integrated within it, or to enact the role of feared or longed-for inner objects.

In giving form and voice to aspects of the child's self, or to his inner objects, the analyst "naturally and inevitably draws on and reveals aspects of her own psyche" (Birch, 1997, p. 65). The analyst's personality is thus more actively revealed in such play than it ever can be in adult analysis. In enacting a role, she follows the child's guidelines, spoken or unspoken. "You be a cross teacher", the child may say, or, "You be a mummy crocodile who never bites her baby". Or, as the keeper at Heaven's Gate, the child may simply hold out his hand to the "sinner", demanding a record card. In being that necessary cross teacher, that non-attacking mother, or that sinner, the analyst is also herself—that is, she cannot "act" from the surface, but must draw upon aspects of herself that resonate with similar elements in the child, but with which she is herself comfortable. Only then can the child begin to feel them as acceptable or bearable within himself.

Such real participation in the child's play imposes technical demands that are unique to child analysis; for, even while playing, the analyst must retain (or consistently re-find) the capacity to reflect, to be aware of the nature of the interaction between herself and the child, and to judge if and when interpretation may be appropriate. All this is very different from classical adult analysis, to the extent that some adult analysts have seen child analysis as "not proper analysis".

Child analysts, too, have tended to devalue the work they find themselves doing. Despite our increasing knowledge of the developmental importance of play, few child analysts are immune from feeling that they "ought to" keep on interpreting. Ablon (1993, 1994), warning against this, has shown how the analyst's need to impose his own structures via interpretation can interfere with the child's need to structuralize and master. And Arietta Slade (1994) writes:

> Even experienced therapists feel a pressure to interpret and make sense of play for their patients; somehow, such exchanges seem like *real* therapy, whereas playing per se does not. I still find myself feeling uneasy and guilty when a child

and I have been "simply playing" for a long time, and I often begin wondering how I can bring us back to what we're *really* supposed to be working on. Winnicott was right: it is sometimes safer to be clever than to play. [p. 104]

Today, interpretation of the child's play is increasingly seen as inappropriate and even harmful at times, for it may interfere with the child's discovery and exploration of the self, or undermine his age-appropriate ways of mastering conflict (e.g. Abrams, 1993; Mayes & Cohen, 1993; Neubauer, 1994). The pendulum has swung far from its original classical position, where play was seen mainly as providing the opportunity for interpretation of disguised unconscious conflict. It still does provide such an opportunity (see p. 63), but it is now seen as intrinsic to growth, as the child's mode of discovery, a metaphor that expresses his realization of the potential within himself and within his relationships to others—a metaphor more meaningful to him than the adult metaphor of the analytic interpretation.

Winnicott (1971) was the first to recognize the full importance of play and the risks of interpretation; he saw play as fundamental to the analytic process with both adults and children. Juliet Hopkins, who was supervised by Winnicott, notes how, while he did interpret play when appropriate, "he was more interested in the way that children themselves use play to reflect and facilitate the development of the self. He decried 'running commentary' analyses, which, by verbalizing everything, steal the child's experience of his own creativity. . . . Winnicott recognized that, through playing, therapy of a deep-going kind may be done without interpretative work" (Hopkins, 1996, p. 24).

Describing her work with a 3-year-old, Hopkins brings to life the role of interaction and play in the development of the sense of self and other, prior to the stage when interpretation can be meaningful. Her patient, "Paddy", had no speech and was not toilet-trained. He had never shown signs of attachment and often wandered off and got lost. He showed no awareness of danger and no response to pain; he never played, but roamed about eating dirt and rubbish. At first, Paddy wandered around the consulting-room, clambered over the furniture, threw toys, and made a lot of noise. Hopkins found herself responding intuitively, verbalizing what Paddy was doing and feeling. Winnicott supported this approach:

> Winnicott spoke of the importance for children of naming their emotions, intentions and body parts. Naming, he said, makes shared and therefore socially acceptable what previously was only private fantasy. Putting children's experiences into words gives them greater self-awareness and hence greater control; it allows fantasy to be checked with reality, it increases the capacity to remember and it reduces guilt. . . .
>
> Fortunately, Paddy warmly welcomed my attempts to feed back in words what he was feeling and doing. He began to look eagerly at my face to see my interest in him reflected there. . . . Paddy appreciated that my face and words mirrored his experience and so confirmed his existence. He began to talk, to point to himself when he wanted something and to call himself "Paddy". He seemed touchingly overjoyed to discover that he possessed his own thoughts and feelings. He had arrived at feeling "I am".
>
> For Paddy, the discovery of "I am" was accompanied by the parallel exploration of "we are". Paddy took great pleasure in having or doing the same as me. He was thrilled to discover that we both had blue sweaters, both had buttons and both could draw circles. He liked to imitate me and be imitated. We "clapped handies", blew raspberries and made animal noises. Thus we established mother–baby games which normally originate in the first year. These games express a mutual identification in which the infant distinguishes between the "me" and the "not me" while retaining through play the potential for assuming either the mother or the baby role. . . . Paddy had not yet begun to experience me as a separate person whom he missed between sessions or whom he could imagine to have a separate personal life of my own.
>
> Winnicott had observed that the development of play depends upon trust. Paddy's first venture into play with me must have been based on his growing confidence that I would continue to prove reliably friendly and emotionally available, able to respond to his spontaneous gestures.
>
> I remember asking Winnicott how I could enable Paddy to move on to the next stage of development—surely interpretation was needed now? But no, it seemed that one form of

playing could lead spontaneously to another. Playing could be both a reflection of the therapeutic process and a means of bringing it about. Paddy began to pretend. His first pretend play, like that of many babies, took the form of pretending to feed me and inviting me to pretend to feed him. . . .

Winnicott knew that this new capacity for togetherness was essential for providing the context in which Paddy could risk discrimination and tolerating differences. Paddy started to become interested in observing and exploring my body and focused on differences in our clothing and anatomy instead of on our similarities. All the toys had previously been held in common, but now he selected "his" cars and bricks and allotted me the others. . . . The difference between "me" and "not me" was becoming increasingly delineated.

During this period Paddy gradually developed a powerful attachment to me. He greeted me with enthusiasm and felt very rejected when it was time to go. Disillusionment was painful. He was forced to confront my separateness and to face his anger about it. Hide and seek became his favourite game. This enabled him to play out his anxieties about separation and loss of contact and about retaliation and attack. He would jump out of his hiding place to frighten me and liked to kick me on occasion. These games of hide and seek enabled me to verbalize his hopefulness that he would not be forgotten when out of sight and that I would want to find him when he disappeared. I was becoming for him both a mental image which he could recall in my absence and a separate person in the external world who came and went. [pp. 22–24]

The work described here is almost exclusively developmental in nature. Hopkins interacted and played with Paddy intuitively, in a way clearly analogous to the mother's play with her infant and toddler. She came close to interpretation in her verbalization of Paddy's hopefulness about her wish to find rather than forget him. To have focused on his fear of loss would have failed to validate his newly discovered hope. I am sure that Hopkins' "in-touchness" and evident delight in playing with Paddy were also important.

The progress of this treatment is very clear. Interpretation was out of the question at first, for Paddy's lack of development was evident in all areas. He had never been able to establish any kind of secure attachment, and, lacking that essential, he had, as it were, got stuck. The gradual building-up of a secure mode of relating, expressed and confirmed in the hide-and-seek game, enabled the development of a much greater degree of structuralization. Paddy became capable of symbolic play and gave evidence of unconscious conflict. Only then did interpretation become appropriate.

The game of hide-and-seek is an important one in child analysis (and often in adult analysis too, but in disguised form). It is a hopeful sign when it first appears, pointing to the child's dawning awareness that the other can and may wish to have him in mind, even when absent. It is most hopeful when the child can allow the analyst to hide, as well as hiding himself—for there are children who use the game in a primarily defensive mode, always being the ones to hide. They dare not risk the dreadful experience of failing to find the needed object, so they have to make the analyst the deserted and abandoned one. When this manoeuvre is used omnipotently, or accompanied by sadistic pleasure, it can be difficult to relinquish. The analyst may have to refuse to play rather than gratify the omnipotence or sadism, although some children are able slowly to recognize that the feelings that they are driven to externalize *are* bearable, since the analyst can bear them, and they may then be able to accept and integrate them.

Hide-and-seek is a later development of the "peek-a-boo" game, for, as Willock (1990) has noted, "The essence of peek-a-boo is the controlled interruption of visual contact with another person, primarily a love object, followed by the pleasurable re-establishment of contact" (p. 322).[8] Some children use peek-a-boo as well as hide-and-seek in their search for the object that can be reliably found and re-found and will, in turn, reliably find and re-find. Often these are children whose primary objects have been able to

---

[8] Willock, building on Kleeman's work (1967, 1973), proposes a developmental line related to the mastery of separation anxiety and the integration of autonomy, evident in "a sequence of play proceeding from active peek-a-boo to object tossing, being chased, hiding, early hide-and-seek, the bye-bye gesture, verbal bye-bye and other uses of language." He adds: "The steps in this series of games connote increasing levels of confidence that despite separation, the primary object is still there and reunion will occur. Each new step on this developmental line thus expresses and contributes to the growth of basic trust" (Willock, 1990, p. 322).

play with them and to take delight in mutual rediscovery. (Willock, 1990, notes that a capacity to play on the mother's part, as well as adequate maternal care, is necessary for the emergence of active peek-a-boo, i.e. peek-a-boo initiated by the infant [p. 322].)

Some children also need to discover or confirm that the object will recognize and respond to them in sound and can take delight in a spontaneous mutual exchange in this modality too, one echoing the early pre-verbal dialogue between the mother and her infant[9] (Chapter 3).

Interactions such as peek-a-boo, early forms of hide-and-seek, or the mother–baby dance in sound are falsified by interpretation (Stern, 1985, p. 163). When analyst and child are occupied almost exclusively in such early relational experiences, this is very clear, and most—but not all—current child analysts would participate without distancing via interpretation.

Nevertheless, it remains true that play, particularly repetitive or stereotyped play, can also be indicative of conflict that the child is unable to resolve without interpretation. Yanof (1996), exploring the question as to how far analytic work with children needs to be brought to their conscious awareness, concludes that analysis proceeds on the dimensions of both insight and relationship; much depends upon the child's capacity for self-reflection and level of development.

Most children who come for treatment differ from Paddy in that they are only partially "stuck". The sense of self, and of self-with-other, have developed to some extent, but patchily. In some

---

[9] Trevarthen and Marwick (1986) have found that this early mother–baby dialogue, or "motherese", has rhythms in common in all languages, and is usually high pitched. Alvarez (1996) notes Trevarthen's suggestion that the baby's sensitivity to certain rhythms and pitches is innately laid down in the brain, and she adds: "When one sees these children light up and pay attention the moment the voice of a colleague or parents changes to 'motherese', one feels Trevarthen must be right" (p. 533). Alvarez suggests that clinicians working with autistic children may find it useful to attempt to communicate with them in similar rhythms. I believe she is right, and, moreover, that such communication is useful in the analysis of many less fundamentally disturbed children. Some, like "Tom" (Chapter 3), make direct and spontaneous use of "motherese"; others may do so in more disguised form, e.g. by asking the analyst to sing to them (Chapter 4).

areas there may be normal, or even exceptional, developmental progress. Such children are usually those who have received both "good-enough" and "playful-enough" maternal care, but care that has been interrupted or inconsistent because of psychological difficulties or external circumstance. These children present with a combination of developmental difficulty and conflict; here, the question as to how to sort out this mixture was first posed by Anna Freud.

The first two child-analytic training institutions in this country were founded by the great pioneers of child analysis, Melanie Klein and Anna Freud—and both were inevitably much influenced by their classical background. For both, interpretation was the sign of a "proper" analysis, although Klein emphasized interpretation of a child's deepest anxieties, and Anna Freud, interpretation of defence.

Yet Anna Freud was above all a developmentalist, well aware of the child's developmental needs, and working always in the context of his developmental level. Her ambivalence towards the developmental aspects of analysis may have been partially rooted in her loyalty to her father's work. Certainly, she was always aware that developmental deficit called for help via relationships. Back in 1949, she wrote of pathologically aggressive children that "the appropriate therapy has to be directed to the neglected, defective side, i.e., the emotional libidinal development" (p. 42). But at first she did not see such help as coming within the purview of analysis. The aim of analysis remained the widening of consciousness and increased ego control. Non-interpretative interventions were seen as "education", different from and even "diametrically opposed" to analysis. By 1965, while she still viewed "the truly analytic measures" as the only effective treatment for the infantile neuroses, she saw an admixture of such measures and of the "subsidiary therapeutic elements" as beneficial in many non-neurotic cases. Among the subsidiary measures, she included such things as suggestion, reassurance, verbalization and clarification of internal and external danger, verbalization of affects, and even the stimulation of fantasy.

She recognized the dual role of the child analyst as transference object and "new" object—the latter close to today's "developmental object"—and pointed to a possible tension between the two roles:

> If [the child analyst] accepts the status of the new object, differ-
> ent from the parents, he undoubtedly interferes with the
> transference reactions. If he ignores or rejects this side of the
> relationship, he disappoints the child patient in expectations
> which the latter feels to be legitimate. . . . To learn how to sort
> out the mixture and to move carefully between the two roles
> . . . are essential elements of every child analyst's training.
> [1965, pp. 38–39]

Here Anna Freud recognized a dilemma that can exist in both adult and child work. She often considered this issue. She was aware of children's legitimate developmental need to be understood, and clinically I think she was not so far from Winnicott's "Needs should be met, wishes should be analysed" (quoted in Tonnesmann, 1980). But intellectually her agenda was different: she seems always to have regarded anything other than "true" analysis for neurotic children as regrettable: they had, she said, a tendency to "misuse" the transference relationship for "a corrective emotional experience".

But in the case of developmentally stunted children (those with "grave libido defects"), she came to believe that a therapeutic change could be set in motion by "the intimacy of the analyst–patient relationship": "On the basis of this new and different emotional experience, the child may move forward to more appropriate levels of libido development, a therapeutic change set in motion within the outward setting of child analysis, but on the basis of 'corrective emotional experience'" (1965, p. 231). Here, her use of the term "corrective emotional experience" has no pejorative overtones. Thus, by 1965, defects in relating had become a focus of "developmental help" within analysis.

Anna Freud was very clear that for developmentally disturbed children, such help took precedence over the revival of the past within the transference—indeed, that the latter might well be contraindicated:

> If you try to help [a child with gravely stunted development]
> by making the past alive once more, you don't help her, be-

cause partly the past is alive anyway, much too alive, and partly there is no power inside her strong enough to deal with the past. [quoted in Penman, 1995]

She went on to explore the interaction between the infantile neuroses and the developmental deficiencies, seeing these as inextricably bound together. She often considered how developmental lack or damage might be helped in treatment, and, as Edgcumbe (1995) pointed out, she set us an agenda: "*to the extent to which developmental harm can be undone belatedly, child analysis may accept it as its next duty to devise methods for this task*" (A. Freud, 1978, p. 109).

Child analysts at the Anna Freud Centre have taken up this task with enthusiasm. In a series of papers, Fonagy and his colleagues put forward a model of mental functioning which gives us a new way of understanding some kinds of developmental disturbance and the ways in which they can be helped. This model has illuminated the nature of developmental therapy with adults as well as with children and is implicit throughout much of this book. In brief, Fonagy and Moran (1991), and Fonagy et al. (Fonagy, Moran, Edgcumbe, et al., 1993; Fonagy, Target, et al., 1995) proposed a distinction between a "representational" and a "mental process" model of the curative factors in analysis. Within the former, interpretation aims at making new links between representational structures. But in patients with developmental disturbances, whole classes of psychological functioning may be inhibited or undeveloped, and these patients are likely to be unable to make use of interpretation.

Their inhibited functioning (except in cases of constitutional defect) is seen as defensive in nature, but as possibly of very early origin: "Before defence mechanisms proper are reliably established, the child is able to prevent unpleasurable mental experiences by inhibiting the evolving mental process itself, which is a more generalised, primitive defence" (Fonagy, Moran, Edgcumbe, et al., 1993, p. 42). Environmental deficit or danger often initiates such inhibition, since "where the early environment is broadly unfacilitative, the use of most mental functions will be met by disappointment and unpleasure" (p. 32). Such processes as feeling, wishing, thinking, and imagining may all be affected. An abused child, for example, may forego all thought about the mental state of others rather than face the terror of his mother's murderous wishes.

We should add that a seeming inhibition of mental processes may be the result not only of the use of primitive defence, but also of a failure to develop due to the lack of an appropriate relationship—that is, the outcome of deficit rather than of conflict. As Alvarez (1996) has pointed out, an apparently withdrawn autistic child may be an "undrawn" child, rather than a defended child.

The analyst's task is to engage inhibited or undeveloped processes within the analytic encounter, and there are many individual ways of doing this. Fonagy et al. (Fonagy, Moran, Edgcumbe, et al., 1993; Fonagy, Target, et al., 1995) suggest that central to these is a focus on the thoughts and feelings of both patient and analyst. They hold that the notion of inhibited mental processes points up the therapeutic value of a mentalizing or reflective capacity and offers a conceptual bridge between child and adult work.

The child analyst engages inhibited or undeveloped processes through his relationship with the child, and this will vary from analyst to analyst. Within the context of the relationship, the analyst may make use of consciously selected "educational" measures—as, for instance, in providing the too-easily aroused child with a means of self-regulation, showing a frightened child a way of controlling peremptory urges, talking with a child about the way that others may respond to the way he relates, or even in providing information that makes sense of the child's experience of his family and of his world (Hurry & Sandler, 1971). But often such measures are employed spontaneously, just as they are in the course of the parent–child relationship.

The use of any educational or supportive measure inevitably changes the child's relationship to himself and to his analyst. It can, for instance, enable a child to feel safe enough to make use of interpretation. Anne-Marie Sandler (1996) describes such an intervention:

> Carlo, aged six-and-a half, initially enacted his feelings of helplessness by identifying with a train engine, which he saw as the most powerful vehicle in existence, immune to all danger. The engine was never to be allowed to run dry, so Carlo

drank large quantities of water throughout the hour and uri-
nated freely in the session. To prove that the engine remained
powerful he climbed onto the window sill while whistling
shrilly like an engine. He pulled down the curtains and said
he was going to jump through the window. . . . The therapist
introduced the idea that really powerful engines have brakes
and that strength meant being able to use these brakes to stop
and start whenever the engine wanted to. Gradually Carlo's
game changed to one in which he would turn his brakes on
and off and stop at stations to let people in or out. This provided welcome intervals during which the therapist could
start giving explanations and interpretations. The engine game
was elaborated by the introduction of a mechanic who wanted
to understand how the train worked so that he could prevent
breakdowns and damage. [pp. 279–280]

For Carlo, the sense of "having brakes" was an important and new
experience. One of his greatest terrors sprang from his inability to
be or to feel in control of inner impulses, and his greater feeling of
safety seems to have stemmed mainly from his new sense of being
in control—but it also sprang in part from his changing view of the
therapist as someone who wanted him to be safe and who could
help him to keep himself safe. In other cases, it is often the changing relationship to the therapist as the provider of safety which is
primary. Ann Alvarez (1992), writing of work with abused children, describes how,

One child was able to talk about the abuse for the first time,
and really remember it, as well as his fear and finally even his
outrage, only after some months of therapy when he realized
his therapist protected him and enabled him to "get past"
some dangerous boys in the corridor leading to the school
therapy room. [p. 159]

Alvarez's outstanding work with autistic and atypical children
suggests that a particular kind of treatment relationship may enable some developments not simply to resume, but virtually to
begin. She points out that the analyst may function as a "reclaiming
object" (we would call this a developmental object)—the mother
who is "enlivening, alerting, claiming and reclaiming" (1992, p.
197). Where a child has encountered the most fundamental relational deprivation, Alvarez believes that his ability to use an

enlivening therapeutic relationship may be founded not on any earlier model of relating, but on his inherent "preconception" of a living human object (1996, p. 527).

Alvarez did not consciously choose to become a reclaiming or enlivening object but found herself being one, speaking "with a great sense of urgency". Perhaps she could do this because she did not have to deny her own need to relate. Tähkä (1993) has stressed the relevance of the analyst's object-seeking need; it is a factor in all analyses—although to be effective rather than intrusive it must not be overwhelming. It may have a bearing on the patient–analyst match: clearly not all analysts could have allowed themselves to feel the urgency felt by Alvarez, an urgency so needed by her particular patient. Other patients may need more naturally re-served analysts, at least for periods, although we do of course find ourselves responding differently to different patients, and differently to the same patient at different times.

In 1995, a series of meetings at the Anna Freud Centre was devoted to discussing interventions that the reporting analyst felt were not "truly analytic", but that had proved effective in helping the patient to move on. Presenters were often uncertain as to the rightness of what they had done and had questioned what they were doing even as they did it. Such questioning is proper: inter-ventions that depend primarily upon a spontaneous interaction do demand subsequent scrutiny: the risk of countertransference act-ing-out is obvious. On the other hand, too much scrutiny, or doubt about propriety, can be the death of spontaneity.

In most of the reported interventions, the analyst had reacted spontaneously in a way opposite to that sought within the transfer-ence, usually in a situation of therapeutic impasse. Julia Fabricius suggested at the meeting that such interventions indicated a "coun-ter role responsiveness". They were often followed by a quite dra-matic shift in the child's way of relating to himself and to the analyst. Such a shift was evident in Ann Harrison's case, "Martha" (Chapter 5). After a holiday break, Martha spent weeks sorting bricks, discarding the irregular "messy" ones, and building towers, utterly impervious to any interpretation. The analyst, feeling "a bit stuck and hopeless", said that she wanted to make something with the other bricks—and she went ahead and made a house using the discarded "messy" bricks, despite the child's protests.

It is not pleasant to be obliterated, and perhaps when the analyst felt "stuck and hopeless" it was not merely that she felt no analytic progress was being made, but also that she missed any experience of mutuality and genuinely did want to build something herself. Yet she was still in touch with her patient. She could not but bring something of herself in choosing to build a house, but the house also had relevance to Martha. In short, only this analyst could have made this intervention, and only in interaction with this particular child.

The intervention was clearly pivotal—after it, Martha was able to experience and communicate feelings and object needs. In presenting herself as having a mind and wishes of her own, the analyst had cut across the child's defences in a way that made it evident that it was safe to be separate and different. It seems that, despite her overt protests, Martha had unconsciously wanted her analyst to act in this way, to serve as a developmental object who could allow her to be separate and who would contradict her omnipotence.

Such interventions may well be under-reported, given child analysts' persisting feeling that they do not constitute "proper analysis". Nevertheless, in published clinical accounts, one can sometimes see how the analyst's direct contradiction of transference expectations, often in word and action, is crucial in enabling a child to move on.

Dr Herzog's patient, "Tommy", the boy who was to use him as a benign identificatory figure, had earlier insisted on wearing a Superman costume. Through his identification with this all-powerful individual, Tommy fended off his fears of smallness and vulnerability. He also had a car, "Night Rider . . . an automobile with many problems", which he used as a vehicle for the expression of his fears. Herzog (1995) writes:

> Tommy soon reported that the car's underneath pipe was not growing sufficiently and that surgery would be necessary. I, with noteworthy insistence, opposed this development, even going so far as to refuse direct orders that a surgeon be summoned for surgical intervention. Tommy was both startled and enraged by my unexpected obstinacy. He butted his head into my midriff and then withdrew into coquettishness. This enactment, which illuminated castration anxiety, aggression

and theory of father–son interaction ... was followed by Tommy's shedding his Superman outfit. [p. 266]

Here, the analyst's refusal to adopt the expected transference role of the castrating father, and one who saw Tommy as inadequate, in need of repair, enabled Tommy to feel secure enough to relinquish his magical identification with Superman. We cannot be sure what would have happened if Herzog had agreed to the operation; it is possible that further elaboration of Tommy's fantasy would have followed. Similarly, it is possible that, had Herzog attempted to interpret the role of the car as a vehicle for Tommy's externalizations, Tommy might have begun to explore and integrate his feelings of littleness and vulnerability. But it is equally possible that Tommy needed the experience of a father who would protect rather than castrate him before he could begin to face the extent of his fear, for unconsciously he sought just such a developmental object in his analyst.

It is important that no particular one of the many possible ways of responding to Tommy's request for an operation is *the* "right" way. There is no "right" intervention at any point in an analysis. Or, rather, there is a "right" intervention for a particular analyst with a particular child, one that will enable that particular analytic duo to continue on their unique therapeutic road—but this may well be the "wrong" intervention for another analyst. What is crucial is that the analyst be aware of the effects of his intervention. As Chused (1992) points out:

> Every aspect of useful analytic technique has its problems. Benevolence towards children, while useful in engaging them in the process, can limit their freedom to express negative feelings. Similarly, an emphasis on verbalization and historical reconstruction in child analysis may push a child to prematurely communicate with words rather than action, leading to submission or resistance, and a limitation of what is explored. ... Benevolence and verbalization have their place. The danger lies in their being employed without scrutiny. [p. 183]

It is also important that the analyst be prepared to move between the developmental/relational stance and the interpretative, as Anna Freud described. Where a child is too frightened to perceive his analyst as non-threatening whatever he does, interpretation may be effective. But where interpretation seems only to confirm a child's fear, the overt provision of safety may in the end prove more effective. Both developmental relating and understanding are necessary; each can potentiate and reinforce the effects of the other. This is as true in adult as in child work, although perhaps less obvious.[10]

As Anne-Marie Sandler (1996) has pointed out, "there is no hard and fast dividing line, in the analysis of children or of adults, between pure interpretation and developmental help" (p. 281). An analyst who uses only interpretative interventions nevertheless provides an ongoing developmental relationship (will he, nill he), not only in that he consistently provides recognition of the patient's self, but also in that interpretations carry the implication that the patient's view is open to possible question. Chused (1992) notes that "Complex nonverbal messages are frequently transmitted along with verbal interventions. When we 'neutrally' question a perception or experience, we are conveying that there are alternate ways of perceiving and experiencing life" (p. 171). Thus transference interpretations inevitably carry the unspoken implication that the analyst may not be as the patient perceives him, and the patient's awareness of this contributes to his being able to use the "analytic" element in the intervention.

He may also be helped to use an interpretation when its formulation takes into account his developmental need for a particular kind of relationship, or, as Weiss (1995) has described, when it is in

---

[10] For instance, the adult patient who condemns himself for what he is, does, and thinks usually perceives his analyst as unaccepting and condemning. Here, interpretation is inevitably felt as further condemnation: "You are wrong (again) to see me in this way." It may be months before the patient can hear the interpretation as it is meant. In the interval, the analyst's genuine acceptance of the patient will have been conveyed in a multitude of subtle ways, often nonverbal, including tone of voice and rhythm of speech, i.e. the analyst, wittingly or unwittingly, has provided a developmental relationship. Here, too, the analyst must be prepared to move between the developmental/relational stance and the interpretative. To continue to provide acceptance without clarification of the patient's externalization of critical inner objects would rob him of the opportunity to be aware of the way that he relates to others, and to opt for more growth-promoting ways of relating.

line with his unconscious plan to disprove pathogenic beliefs by testing them on the therapist:

> Our research supports the hypothesis that the patient . . . is more insightful immediately after the therapist passes a test or offers him an interpretation helpful in disproving the beliefs, and that he benefits over the long term from interpretations that he may use to carry out his plan. [p. 7]

We have seen how a child responds when the analyst, in refusing to adopt the transference role assigned to him, passes the relational test that the child has set. Such a refusal offers evidence that the analyst can respond in terms of the child's needs, and hope that he will do so again. An interpretation can offer a similar hope: the extent to which it does so depends in part upon its taking into account the child's developmental object-need.

Thus the abused child (or adult) who invites the analyst to take part in a sexualized interaction—that is, to repeat the abuse—will not at first benefit from interpretation of his need to repeat, but from interpretation of his need to know that the analyst will not re-enact the abuse: "You want to make sure that that's not going to happen here, with me, whatever you say or do." Similarly, the consciously terrified child may hear interpretation of his fear as a confirmation of danger, but when the interpretation is phrased in terms of the child's underlying wish for protection—"You want me to keep you safe"—protection begins to become more of a possibility in the child's mind. Later, when a sense of safety has become more established, he may be able to explore the roots of his fears. Or, the child who believes himself to be his analyst's least-preferred patient will often be able to use an interpretation that recognizes his underlying longings—"You want to be my best, cleverest boy"—before he can bear to explore the ways in which he feels so unacceptable. When his being "the best" is perceived as thinkable in the analyst's mind, it can become thinkable in the child's. In short, effective interpretation often begins by offering hope in the context of the developmental relationship between patient and analyst. Here, again, "developmental" and "analytic" work are inextricably interwoven within the therapeutic process.

PART II

Clinical work with children

CHAPTER THREE

"Tom":
undoing an early
developmental hitch

Anne Hurry

A t 10 years of age, Tom was a miserably unhappy, anxious child. He would run away from home or threaten suicide, saying that his parents did not love him. He walked in his sleep and had nightmares. He was failing at school, hated the teachers, and felt that they hated him. He hated and fought with his older brothers.

Tom was from an intact and fundamentally loving family, but early illness, hospitalizations, and medical procedures had traumatized him and had caused his parents great concern. Painful physical illnesses, including middle-ear infections, continued up to an operation at the age of 3 years. Tom woke, screaming, during the operation. Throughout latency he remained vulnerable to infections, and he often had headaches or tummy aches. These reinforced parental concern for his health.

Tom's early illnesses served to initiate a masochistic mode of relating. Physical pain, and later also psychic pain, became a way of reaching and controlling the object. Yet this was only part of the picture. The capacity for positive object-relating which emerged in treatment suggests that, in early pain-free times, mother was able to relate happily with him.

The pain that Tom underwent from early babyhood, and the shock of the medical assaults, must have given rise to aggression that could not yet be directed towards a separate object. This may have created an *Anlage* for Tom's later somatization and turning of aggression against the self. By 3, when Tom had his operation, he would have been able to focus aggression upon the object. We know that in such situations the mother who cannot protect is experienced as the attacker. In treatment, Tom certainly expected attack from me. Yet protective figures were there from the start, although they could not be trusted.

Tom's analysis began in 1995, when he was 11 years old. At first he did not feel safe enough to play. When he was able to, he used his play to indicate his underlying questions about me—about my willingness to accept or reject him, protect or endanger him. The intensity of his fears (or his conviction as to his pathogenic beliefs) gave this play a driven quality, and I found myself acting as a developmental object, contradicting his view of me and enabling him to feel safe enough to use interpretation.

There came a point when Tom was ready to use play primarily to catch up on lacunae in development, rather than primarily in the service of undoing past learning, and I interacted with him in the way that I felt he needed. Much of our interaction had to be *entirely* spontaneous. There was no question of my consciously choosing when or how to respond, as one may choose the timing and phrasing of an interpretation. I could reflect, but only afterwards. I was often unsure as to what was happening and questioned whether I should be being more "analytic".

Throughout Tom's analysis, I served as both developmental and transference object. Developmental work ran parallel to the work of understanding, each process potentiating and facilitating the other, as Settlage (1993) described. Tom was at first unable to make use of "interpretation", but the relationship with me often enabled him to use it, while interpretation often enabled him to perceive and make use of that relationship. This interplay can be seen in the following overview of Tom's analysis. The "Comments" on each stage of the analysis focus on technique, with particular reference to the effects of developmental work on the unfolding of the transference, and vice versa.

Beginning treatment

At first, Tom was too frightened to speak, or even to investigate his box. He would draw, but if I watched, my attention seemed an unbearable weight. Attempts to take up his fear seemed only to confirm it.

I found a way of reaching him through writing stories. In order that reading about himself (even in displacement) would not be too humiliating for Tom, I was careful to include positive aspects. The first story began, "Once upon a time, there was a boy who liked lots of things. He liked animals, especially rabbits and dogs, and sometimes he liked watching TV". It went on to describe the boy's dislike of French, big brothers, and scary ladies. Tom read this solemnly, with no comment.

The third story ended, "So the lady made a lot of guesses about what the boy might be feeling, and wrote them down. Will Tom help her? Will he tick the things that are right, or cross out the guesses that are wrong?" For the first time, I had used Tom's name in the story, and I was wondering whether this would alarm him. But he did correct it, leaving in "Did he think she would be very cross?" and ticking that he wished to know all about his box and the lady but thought that she might think it "rude" to want to know.

This written exchange brought enough safety for Tom to inspect his box and politely play games like Ludo. But he remained guarded, mistrusting my willingness to help. He drew scenes of danger: people would be skiing down mountains with chasms ahead, but the rescue helicopters would fly away. Tom rejected interpretations in terms of the relationship with me, as though these were meaningless.

It was weeks before he could respond when I took up his conflict about talking and tell me how *he* saw his problems. At school, the teachers did not like him and the French master picked on him. At home, his brothers were to blame for his unhappiness. They would taunt him until he attacked, then tell on him. He agreed that then he hated them and wanted to die. He especially wanted to die when his parents told him off, feeling that they didn't love him at all. I brought in his fear that if I knew about these hating feelings,

I might not like him. When Tom agreed, I went on to puzzle about his wanting to die when angry with his brothers: perhaps he wanted to kill them? Tom agreed.

Another difficulty had to do with the things his brothers called him, like "Runt". I noted his vulnerability to their taunting. Could it be that he believed what they said? "Yes", said Tom, "When they say it such a lot it's impossible not to believe."

Then there were his nightmares. He didn't remember them, but there was something about people killing him. Here I introduced the idea of the unconscious, telling him about pushing thoughts to the very back of one's mind, and how they could go on bothering one. I noted his view of me as "killing" him if I took a piece in Ludo. People could appear very dangerous and killing. But the question was why: could he have turned around a wish of his own—did he want to kill Mum and Dad when they were angry? Tom could confirm that. From then on, his use of projection in sessions lessened and he felt safe enough to "kill" me in Ludo by cheerfully winning. His nightmares stopped.

In the following weeks, Tom seemed to be further testing my reaction to his aggression, telling me how pleased he was when he attacked his brothers. But his guilt remained. The trouble was, he said, there was *nothing* good in their relationship: he hated them. This made him so bad he deserved to die.

Tom's conflicts were experienced primarily in relation to his real objects, although in the transference I remained potentially dangerous. He drew a man in a boat nearing a dangerous water-fall. I drew a helicopter—but he added guns, making it an attacking machine. He did have some hope that I might be willing, if not able, to keep him safe. He built card houses, wanting me to preserve them between sessions. But he avoided the risk of disappointment by deciding that it was fun to knock them down.

He also avoided any discussion of the possibility that he might miss coming over the summer break. In fact, he enjoyed this holiday and sent me a postcard. He came back pleased to see me, chatting away about the holiday. This reaction confirmed my view that I was still primarily a real contemporary object.

COMMENTS

Tom's initial fear and frozen reaction to interpretation led me to feel that I had got to find a way of making a relationship with him. This feeling, in its turn, influenced the development of the analysis and the balance between "relating" and "understanding".

At first, the way was through writing. My asking Tom to help by correcting the stories put him in a position of partial control, thus mitigating his fear. It gave evidence of my willingness to see him as good, as capable, and as an active partner in our work. It also indicated my willingness to reach out to him. These factors enabled him to make use of the "understanding" in what I had written, and we could move on to spoken communication.

In the initial phase, I did not "interpret" as such, but recognized conscious feelings and thoughts that were troubling Tom: his aggression and death wishes, his fears of unacceptability, his guilt and wish to die. By verbalizing such things without condemnation, I was creating the possibility in Tom's mind that he might be recognized, understood, and accepted as he was, thus laying the groundwork for Tom's eventually being able to accept himself.

I also introduced him to the possibility of thinking about himself (and others) in questioning his reactions and beginning to wonder about possible links. I introduced the idea of the unconscious and even of defence mechanisms, such as repression and projection—though not in those terms! I also pointed to the value of recognizing feelings in telling Tom how the repressed could go on bothering one, or the projected make one afraid. This carried the implication that I did not wish him to be afraid or bothered—for every intervention we make is heard not only for its content, but also for its sign value with regard to our own attitudes.

Masochism and omnipotence

On returning to school, Tom was miserable. He was beginning the two-year curriculum for public school entry exams at 13 and was genuinely worried. But he also used this worry to manipulate his parents: he talked of suicide, and he couldn't get to sleep, so mum came and slept in his room. There were weeks of quite florid masochism. At the school gate, Tom would refuse to get out of the car, grumbling miserably away to his mother.

And he certainly grumbled to me! He would begin sessions by saying that he had had "the worst day ever". Sometimes he could face the uncomfortable reality that everybody had to go to school. More often he was angry about the "unfairness" of life and demonstrated this in many ways: if I had some luck in Ludo, he would moan, "It's not fair". When I made a joke of this, moaning away like him, he was clear: "It's not fair if I'm not winning."

Sometimes he could respond to interpretation of the anger in his masochism by letting himself have a nice time. He told me, for instance, how life was especially bad because he had a headache "all the time". I said his anger at being made to go to school might be expressed in headaches, adding that headaches could get to feel worse if people found them useful, like for getting out of school: it would be sad if he got stuck with them. "I know", said Tom, "I'm not going to let them get on top of me". He built a magnificent seven-storey card house, finishing with a minute of the session left. "I know—", he said, "we'll spend it admiring my house."

Gradually, mum became firmer, and Tom began to struggle not to moan before school. Usually he lost the struggle, and two further elements in his masochism became clear: not only was it used to manipulate the object, it also represented both an attack and a testing of the object's real concern.

Feelings of being unprotected, uncared about, and endangered were exacerbated by a minor car accident. Tom was pleased to have this "really bad news" to tell. He drew another dangerous skiing scene with a useless helicopter. When I took up his uncertainty about whether anyone would care if he were hurt or killed, Tom said quite calmly that he didn't think this applied to me, but it did apply to mum and dad. I said it was no wonder that he threatened to kill himself, to see whether they would get worried, and he gave me a quick grin.

His parents had hoped to transfer Tom to a less academic school. He nagged them unmercifully about this, although he knew that there were no vacancies until the following year. When I picked up his disappointment and anger towards his parents and me for not finding a new school, he denied that he wanted to make me feel bad with his unhappiness, but agreed there was a bit of a wish to make mum feel bad.

Unable to control his school situation, he became increasingly controlling of me. In playing squiggles, he told me exactly what to draw (hardly "playing"!). Outside treatment, he bitterly resented any controls. His presentation of "poor me" obscured the fact that troubles at school were often the result of his doing exactly as he pleased. Thus, he told of a horrible teacher who gave him lines and didn't like him. When I puzzled about the fact that yet another teacher had turned against him, adding that there had to be a reason, Tom admitted that he had moved the teacher's chair so that one leg was over the hole in the floor, and the chair had tipped. It was so funny! I agreed it probably was, but noted that the teacher would inevitably be cross. I added that though he hated people telling him what to do, grown-ups often could. Tom was indignant. No one should contradict his wishes: if they did it was unfair!

COMMENTS

As Tom's habitual masochistic mode of relating came into the transference, it became appropriate to interpret with regard to his parents *and* myself. I made no attempt to draw his conflicts exclusively into the transference, or to interpret the continuance of his major focus upon the parents as defensive. Thus, I accepted Tom's assertion that his uncertainty as to whether anyone would care if he were hurt or killed applied to his parents, but not to me. Similarly, I believed that he wanted to make his mum feel guilty, but not me. The *potential* for such feelings and wishes was clearly present in the transference. Insistence on drawing that potential into awareness would, I believe, have skewed the development of the transference and would have had serious effects within the treatment relationship, contradicting Tom's growing experience of me as recognizing his ongoing feelings and thoughts, an experience that was both a developmental and a treatment priority.

Tom was able to think about painful matters partly because he genuinely was unhappy, but also because I drew attention to and questioned his masochism and omnipotence, both explicitly and implicitly. Thus, when I took up the extent of his hatred of being told what to do, I pointed out that adults often were in a position to control him. Or I used joking enactments, as when I moaned away like him—"It's not fair!"

This kind of confronting and clarifying had implications within the treatment relationship. It conveyed the message that omnipotent masochism was hardly an ideal mode of relating, but this was conveyed in the context of my concern for Tom's well-being and happiness, again both implicit and explicit, as when I told Tom it would be sad if he got stuck with headaches. Moreover, I was always prepared to respond positively to non-masochistic ways of relating, as when I sat for a full minute admiring his card house.

"Tom-Pin"

At this point (Week 25), there was a change: Tom's conflicts came more fully into the transference, and there was a consistent theme: his testing *my* concern for and willingness to find and protect him.

First he used a pin to explore the question as to whether I wanted him in the world. In the pin "game", we had the beginnings of play, but driven and repetitive play. Tom would throw the pin into the bin, hide it, or lose it in his box. I made it my job to find it. For weeks, Tom was urgently busy attacking Tom-Pin, wrapping it in Sellotape and leaving it to suffocate, or beating it remorselessly. It was my job to save it. Eventually, Tom-Pin was given to me for safe-keeping at the end of sessions: "It's your job to look after him."

Until Tom had had sufficient contradiction of the transference through the pin game, it was not possible to explore the self-condemnation behind his feeling that he should be thrown away. But eventually he could begin to face his guilt, telling me that Tom-Pin was being mistreated "Because he is bad". His anger towards me felt especially bad and had to be displaced or turned against himself. But in the week before Christmas, when I wondered why Tom-Pin should be attacked when it was I who was leaving, Tom's knife slipped and hit my leg. He announced that I should be sentenced to life imprisonment in a cell with a carnivorous ferret. At home, he said he hated me for going when he needed me.

COMMENTS

The shift into the transference of Tom's longing for acceptance and safety, his fear of rejection, hatred, and abandonment, was facilitated by mother's growing ability not to collude with his masochism, and by the growing importance of the relationship with me: Tom now had real hopes of acceptance, however faint, so his fears of rejection and loss were inevitably greater. From this point on, I interpreted mainly within the transference and could take up current difficulties with the parents as displacements from the relationship with me, again in the context of evident concern. I did search for the lost pin, and I did protect it.

Suicidal and self-attacking enactments

Given the assurance that I would protect the pin, Tom's enactments shifted back to his own body. He would twirl the scissors near his face, or turn his gun upon himself. When I took up his protecting me by attacking himself, the gun swung towards me. But as Christmas approached, the attack turned towards himself, and in the last session he announced that Tom-Pin was dead. When I took up his belief that I *really* hated him and wanted him dead, he got under the desk and "shot" himself.

Tom returned from the break less distant from his feelings of deprivation and loss. His feet were starving, he said. When I wondered whether I had been starving him all holiday, he responded "Maybe". Rage and fear were brought to the sessions through talk of horror movies. Here Tom was in part testing how acceptable his violent, frightening fantasy world might be to me. He told of a lady who could not go home for a whole week after seeing *Silence of the Lambs*.

School exams were approaching, and sessions became filled with competitive football, with Tom determined to win. If I got a goal, he would roll on the floor enacting rage and misery, or bang his head on the desk (again, hardly mutual play). I interposed a cushion, saying that I would do this until he got the message about not hurting himself. When I took up how stupid and awful not winning felt, linking with the time when he was little and his brothers really could do everything better, he stopped the head-banging.

In the week before exams, Tom missed a session because of a muddle over times. At home he regressed to his old ways, and in sessions his self-hurting escalated as he tested my safety rule. Instead of banging his head on the desk, he lay on the floor and banged it. As I tried to protect him, our interaction began to take on the quality of an excited tussle, so I took a stand. I said I couldn't now protect him from this head-banging, for he had got too big and strong, and I needed him to help me protect him. But he was *really* not allowed to hurt himself, and if he couldn't stop, we would finish the session until he could manage himself. Tom was utterly wounded. All activity ceased; he lay on his tummy under the desk, making himself very alone, genuinely hurt, but also trying to make me feel awful.

Self-attacks were never again unmanageable. With less enactment, Tom could re-acknowledge his feeling of being bad. Not doing well also meant being bad: when he got only 30 percent in maths, Tom turned the gun upon himself.

He sought refuge from feeling "little and stupid", partly in omnipotent sadistic fantasy, but also by reversing roles in a rather new way. He had a silver ball which he could spin on the desk so that it returned to him. He offered me a go and, when I failed, spent a session patiently teaching me. This was not a passive-into-active triumph: although he enjoyed being the one who knew, he was not putting me down. He encouraged me, and finally I succeeded. I congratulated Tom on his teaching ability, and he was pleased.

Comments

As Tom's enactments shifted from the pin to his own body, I was again prepared to protect him, but when our interaction became sexualized, I had to set limits. In refusing to interact in a sexualized way, I also inevitably refused Tom's continuing wish for direct protection, and this was genuinely hurtful to him. I did not consciously plan what I said, and it was only later that I realized I had combined my rejection of Tom's regressed aspects with a recognition of his more grown-up potential: "He had got too big and strong." I had also asked him for help, again indicating my view of him as capable. I had hinted at the possibility of his identifying with my protective function: "I needed him to help me to protect him."

In this context, my stand against self-hurting provided enough safety to enable Tom to use interpretations of his need to defend against his anger towards me. We could begin to explore the roots of his self-hatred and guilt, and, for the first time, we began to make links with the past, to see the roots of Tom's equation of "stupid" and "bad" in the early and ongoing relationship with his brothers.

This interpretative work opened the path to more benign ways of relating. I did not analyse these, but reinforced them. It would have been possible to interpret Tom's teaching me how to spin the silver ball in many ways. Instead, we had a real interaction, one that reinforced his view of my image of him as capable and giving, and one that he was aware we both enjoyed.

Blind seeking and non-verbal communication

Tom now became occupied with two new activities. The first was precipitated by the imminent Easter break: Tom shut his eyes and searched for me. But after that I usually had to search blindly for him. I would speak of how it felt to be lost, alone in the dark, and unable to find someone. The second activity began most sessions: Tom would make wordless noises, or tap on the table. I would respond by echoing, with a slight variation. If I was not affectively involved in this communication, if I distanced myself by wondering about it, Tom would react with anxiety and omnipotent defence, becoming the almighty Whiplash.

At times he could use noises in an automatized way, and I was concerned that this not become a resistance. This was a misplaced concern. I once really hurt his feelings by wondering if his not using ordinary talking was a way of avoiding something. Tom switched to playing peek-a-boo, as though he had lost me. But he re-found me through the peek-a-boo game (so now we were playing!).

During the Easter break, Tom got lost in a large city. After the break, he made "a really enormous fuss" to his mother about going back to school. He didn't know why it felt so much worse. He thought it might be linked with the break, but his affect was missing until I noted that he had *really* got lost, after we had looked at the lost feeling so much here. It seemed that he felt I was just letting him get lost, had gone off not caring about him. It also seemed that he was taking out his disappointment and anger with me on mum. I wondered about his feeling that I would not like him if he brought his anger here more fully. Tom didn't think so, but then he asked if I minded if he brought his hamster.

My acceptance of his hamster provided no real reassurance, and he reversed our roles, showing me what it was like to be shut out. He showed what a cheat my offer of a relationship felt, starting to communicate by making noises, but hiding behind his box when I responded. He told me, "Go away, I'm never coming back!" or "Go away, nobody likes you". When I linked this with holiday feelings, I was made to miss him even more. He would be dead, and I could not even go to his funeral. Told to telephone about the funeral, I could reach only voices that said, "I will pass you to the next caller". Sometimes he was dead from natural causes, sometimes from suicide. When I took this suicide as a revengeful abandonment of me who had abandoned him, he swung his gun around to shoot me.

For several weeks, we continued to explore these themes. Gradually the hope evident in the blind-finding game, so smashed by the holiday, reappeared as he began to allow me to find him. He made an igloo for himself and withdrew into it to sleep but invited me to come and wave to him through the window.

This time, when feelings of abandonment were increased by several bank holiday gaps, he had much less need to turn his anger on himself. He could shoot at me, although he also wanted to preserve me. He would kill me off and then restore me to life. He used the blind-finding game not to make contact, but to triumph over me, leaving me lost and helpless. His anger took a more sadistic tinge. He would bring me back to life to have the *pleasure* of re-killing me. He would go into conference with his puppet Badger Bill, to discuss how I should be done away with or tortured. With his aggression more available, there were relatively few self-hurt-ing or suicidal enactments, and those that did occur appeared largely in the context of attacking or abandoning me.

But suicidal wishes gained a new intensity when Tom received poor exam results. He did not tell me how poor, but he would bang his head with the tray, rejecting both interpretation and protection. He seemed unreachable until I said that I didn't know why he was so unhappy, but perhaps if we were not able to talk about it I had better write. Tom gave me a pen, and I wrote directly about him and myself. Tom ticked that he was very unhappy, and that he wanted to kill the teachers. He thought that the unhappiness was to do with the exams, and that he did feel stupid and bad. As for being extra cross with me, he thought "Maybe".

He then was able to tell me that he had got only 25 percent in maths and felt despairing. His other results, too, were not as good as last time, and he knew that this was because he had not done enough work. So we clarified that the problem lay primarily in work. Although this did not obviate his feeling of stupidity, I think that it was important in suggesting an avenue through which he could effect change. Certainly he had more hope. He sat doodling a helicopter, no longer a useless or attacking machine. But his final doodle indicated the persisting alternative to success: he drew a shield with the motto "Victory or death".

He remained preoccupied with death, but we were able to explore how when he felt stupid he felt not loved, and when he felt not loved he felt that mum wouldn't care if he died, and then he felt he wouldn't care if she died. This was painful for Tom: as I spoke he lay on the couch with his head in the cushion, looking up briefly to say "a bit" or "only sometimes". However, I could recognize with him how much worse this felt than hating his brothers, whom he did not love as he loved mum.

COMMENTS

The seeking game contained Tom's hope that I would want to look for him, while his feelings of being abandoned in the dark were externalized onto me. I *was* prepared to look for him, and as I did I would speak of how lost and abandoned I felt. I think Tom needed evidence that I would seek him, and evidence that I could bear these lost feelings, before he could feel them as bearable enough to hear my linking the game with his feeling that I abandoned him.

So painful was my leaving that conflicts had to be displaced away from the transference, and Tom acted out in the holidays, getting lost in reality. I could interpret this displacement, also taking up Tom's fear of my being unable to accept his anger—which led eventually to his beginning to face his death wishes towards me and, later, his mother.

Interspersed with this work was our lively non-verbal communication—a kind of mother–baby dance in sound. I think Tom was finding that he could recapture an early good experience, one that he had felt was lost. Some of the reasons for his need to do this would become clear later. At this point, I knew only that the regression felt natural and benign—part of Tom's active search for health and wholeness. I therefore did not attempt to interpret it, but provided the needed response and space for growth.

From Tom's reaction when I distanced myself from our communication, I learned to allow him the kind of relating that he needed, to allow him the experience of attunement. In Tom's analysis, attunement acted as an emotional transaction in its own right, therapeutic in and of itself (Chapter 1: see also Rayner, 1992). Such experiences can be conveyed only very partially in words. Daniel Stern's thinking points to those times when interpretation is contraindicated: "To the extent that events in the domain of verbal relatedness are held to be what has really happened, experiences in . . . other domains suffer an alienation" (1985, p. 163).

Tom did not permit such an alienation. His agenda was very clear when he reacted to my attempt to interpret his non-verbal comments as a possible resistance: he re-established our non-verbal link through peek-a-boo—that is, he re-found me as a developmental object. This ability to elicit an "adapted response" from me indicated a relational competence very different from his old way of relating via omnipotent masochism (cf. Novick & Novick, 1996) and probably indicates an earlier capacity for "micro-repair" in the beginnings of the relationship with his mother (Chapter 1). Its re-emergence in his analysis made possible an experience through which he could repair lacunae in his experience of competence, one of a number of such experiences on which we could build.

"Heaven's Gate" and the "Intrepid Voyager"

We began playing "Heaven's Gate", a game through which Tom could explore and work through the various roots of his guilt. We played almost daily for weeks. As gatekeeper, Tom would keep me waiting for entry to heaven, while he sat with his computer, putting my record card through the machine. Invariably I would be sent to hell because I was "a very bad person". Thus Tom avoided the pain of superego condemnation through externalizing unacceptable aspects of himself and identifying with the cruel and condemning superego.

When I gave him the dates for the second summer break, Tom vividly conveyed his feeling of being abandoned to external and internal dangers through a game of shipwreck, in which he sailed the dangerous shark-filled seas. He was the "intrepid voyager", who could shoot all the sharks. But everything that he relied on let him down: his raft broke, and there was no food on the island. When I linked all this with his feelings about my abandoning him, he could struggle back on to the rocks, until he got to the people island. But the islanders didn't want him and sent him away.

It was less painful to expose me to danger and rejection. Tom would tell me that it was perfectly safe to put my hand in the water—and only then would I hear about the piranhas. A shark carried me off to the Mississippi, where the coastguards came to my rescue but demanded money. As I had none, they left me to sink. When I took up Tom's fear that I saw him only for the money, he lay on the couch screaming into two cushions. But he denied any pain, telling me that he only wanted to test his voice, or singing repeatedly, "I feel good".

More genuine hope did surface before the holiday. In the last week, he allowed himself to rediscover me through peek-a-boo, and he returned to Heaven's Gate. The gatekeeper, Johnny Wishbone, was a psychic who could read your hand and tell your future. Mine was to be shot and then revived. Then I was allowed to keep the gate and had to read Tom's hand. Putting in the holiday dates, I told of Tom's coming journey across the water, of how he might encounter various dangers, but would in the end return. Tom enjoyed this. He asked about his success line, and I said the success line and the hard-work line were close together. It was up to him how close he could get them, for they needed to come right together for success in exams. I told him that I was saying this because I didn't want him to be so unhappy again next exams. Tom asked solemnly how I thought the lines were doing, and I said I thought they were getting closer.

As gatekeeper, I let in all who came to Heaven's Gate. When Tom took back the role, he too let everyone in—perhaps indicating the beginning internalization of a more benign superego. Certainly, Tom had more hope of being acceptable to me, faults and all, so that fears of abandonment were much less overwhelming.

He had the confidence to express his wishes before the break, wearing a T-shirt with the motto, "Fido, and don't you forget it". And he could openly reproach me on my return for going "for a whole month". He was still preoccupied with loss, but in the blind-finding game it was our mutual re-discovery that was important. Now Tom took the role of seeker; he would stand very still when he found me, with a smile coming even before he opened his eyes. As I began to pick up his pleasure in feeling more secure about finding, he conveyed this even more vividly. Now when he found me, he would pretend he hadn't noticed. Then he would come back, saying, "Did you think I couldn't recognize you?"[1] Finally, he was able to express simple delight: "Oh, it's you!"

The continuing modification of the superego was very evident. Tom became more discriminating as well as more benign. No longer was I sent straight to heaven or hell; I would be sent to a halfway house while the judges weighed up the balance of good and evil. And with the modification of Tom's self-condemnation, suicidal enactments and threats lessened greatly, taking only a token form. Tom would begin Monday sessions by lying on the

---

[1] Joan Raphael Leff (personal communication) has suggested that the ability to tease in this way can signal a resolution of ambivalence, an awareness that loving can predominate over hating.

couch pretending to be dead. Finally, I spoke of his parents' possible contribution to this stance. Remembering how ill he had been when he was little, I added that sometimes when people were worried about a baby's life they were very pleased when the baby got better, but couldn't help going on worrying. I wondered if he thought his parents worried. Tom didn't know. But he changed from playing dead, to playing that he couldn't use his legs and had to move around on his arms only. He struggled to move up the couch towards me, but this was difficult on the soft surface. I commented that it would be easier if he had a rope, and he stretched back his arms for me to help pull him along, which I did.

There were no further suicidal enactments. From now on he was free to enjoy life.

COMMENTS

Our work in the "Heaven's Gate" game remained largely in displacement. I did not interpret Tom's identification with the superego, his externalization of his felt badness, or his need to play the game while it remained alive and continued to develop. On the whole, I interpreted only when the play got stuck, becoming rather mechanically repetitive, a "game" rather than "play". At such times, I would note how Tom seemed driven to the game although his heart was not in it, taking up external or internal precipitants, such as a school rejection, or guilt over particularly murderous feelings.

With the continuing working through in externalization of Tom's guilt, and given his experience of me as the benign gatekeeper, Tom changed without my taking up his need to externalize. Alongside his bitter anger at my felt rejections came his growing hopes of a relationship that could be trusted. His delight on finding me in the blind-searching game far outweighed his fears of loss. The reflection and sharing of his pleasure in finding was as important as had been the reflection of past pain.

Tom was nearly ready to go ahead and to enjoy life. But he remained preoccupied with death. What finally freed him was the recognition of his underlying awareness of his parents' concern for him—which we could explore later in terms of his response to that concern.

Perhaps most importantly, Tom was freed from the need to regress to masochism by the slow discovery and eventual belief that his struggle to reach and relate to the object in a positive way could be met by an object who would not only be there for him, but who would also reach out to him.

It could be argued that I should have interpreted as Tom struggled to move up the couch towards me. A more "classical" analyst might have taken up his wish for help, or his defensive stance, or his denial of independent competence, and so forth. As with Tom's teaching me to spin the silver ball, there were many possible interpretations.

My choice of intervention here was based in part on my countertransference, and in part on my long-term knowledge of Tom and the background of our work together. His suicidal wishes had been very fully analysed, and now his playing dead did not seem quite real—his heart was not in it. I was not at all worried for him; rather, I found myself wondering about the role of his current relationships in perpetuating his stance. So I commented on his parents' possible continuing worry for him. Tom "didn't know" about this, but changed from being dead to struggling to move up the couch towards me, using just his arms. As he did so, I was aware of an impulse to give him a hand. But we were much further on together, and I was not sure a hand was what he needed (an unneeded hand can be an infantilizing hand). So I made a statement that indicated the possibility of help, in the form of a metaphor that Tom could utilize in his own way: "It would be easier if you had a rope." Tom could have ignored this, rejected it, played that he had a rope, he could even have used the "rope" for self-destruction. But instead he stretched out his hands for me to help, and I did.

It seems to me that interpretation at this point would have been wrong: I think Tom needed this final bit of evidence that I could reach out to him. Certainly, the essence of this and other interactions does appear to have been internalized. In the following year, Tom was free to experiment with moving around in lots of different ways, still in my presence but now no longer needing my help.

Growing up, but touching base; enjoying life, discovering the world and his own capabilities

For the first two years, Tom's analysis had followed a clear path: his need to discover the possibility of secure mutual relating and the analysis of his narcissistic vulnerability, self-condemnation, and conflicts over aggression had occupied us virtually to the exclusion of all else. But now, with the onset of pre-puberty, drive-powered wishes and fears came tumbling out pell-mell. Issues of control were important, but I did not interpret these, knowing that Tom would find his own standards and controls—as he did. On the whole, I simply accepted the oral and anal derivative material that figured so frequently and interpreted only when Tom was getting into difficulties over guilt or sadism. (Tom's masturbation guilt was analysed through the Heaven's Gate game.)

During this period of instinctual buffeting, Tom was growing up. Analysis remained important to him, but life outside became increasingly attractive. He still found it difficult if I left him, but he was able to leave me for such events as his thirteenth birthday.

To explore the world, one needs a secure base (Bowlby, 1988). Tom still needed to touch base from time to time. Sometimes he seemed like a young child playing happily in the presence of his mother. He would make discoveries about the immediate world. One day, as he lay on the floor rolling around a bit, he discovered a mark like a 7 on the underside of a chair. This intrigued him. He discovered other similar shapes in the angles of the furniture and said, with wonder, "There are sevens everywhere!" He seemed too to be rediscovering his old capabilities, while simultaneously finding new capacities. He experimented with moving around in different ways on the floor, propelling himself just with his legs, or pulling himself along by his elbows. But he also took pride in being able to leap across the room faster and faster.

In touching base, he continued from time to time to communicate with me non-verbally. We began one session with shared noises. Tom had a cold. He pressed his fingers to the hinge of his jaws, telling me that this shifted the mucus in his ears. I recognized what a nuisance this was for him, as it must have been when he was little and couldn't hear because of ear infections. What Tom remembered was the desperate frustration of a later time when he had stammered and couldn't make anyone understand him. He used to stomp off angrily into another room.

I think this was an important forerunner of his later running away and suicidal wishes. Indeed, the memory that Tom brought next further clarified his earlier despair and view of the object as not understanding or caring. He remembered his operation, and biting the nurse, and being wheeled to the operating-room. That was all *he* remembered, but *mum* remembered being with him and then she couldn't be with him any more and she could hear him calling "Mum, mum!" and then the noise stopped, because they must have slapped the mask over his face. I noted how horrible it must have been for mum not to have been able to stay with him, and how horrible for him feeling that she was leaving him to all this. (Later, before termination, we were to explore his need to defend against awareness of his mother's pain.[2])

In the following week, it became clear that learning French had been so difficult because it revived the old horrors of mutual non-understanding. Tom was lying on the couch making gentle kitten-like noises, which I would reflect and extend. Gradually the noises became more like words, although unformed ones, and then suddenly we were talking French. At the end of the session, he said good-bye in French, "*à bientôt*".

There was no need to interpret the link with Tom's language learning difficulties, or with his hatred of the French teacher. These difficulties went, and Tom even got interested in learning a bit of German. He seemed to have made the use he wanted of communicating through noises. Thereafter, it rarely occurred and then only in token fashion: Tom would briefly make non-verbal sounds as though to check that I was still prepared to relate with him in that way.

Over this last year of intensive treatment, he showed very positive changes, increasingly able to enjoy life, to relate to others, to try to understand them as well as himself, and to invest in his

---

[2] Dr Steven Shulruff has suggested that the blind-finding game contained Tom's testing of my capacity to bear the pain of separation, in contradistinction to his mother. His suggestion further illumines the meaning of that game.

school work. He seemed almost to be having a love affair with the world, but a teenage love affair, trying to understand its nature—and the nature of the universe. But he still needed the security of knowing that I was there for him, and when he was threatened with the possible loss of a session (because of a change in the school timetable), he chose to have an extra late lesson instead.

He began the following week by asking: "Would you like to see some pure excellence?" This was his history book, and I was to admire every page. He had all A's, and I congratulated him. At this stage, his ability to be proud of himself was still dependent on the object's willingness to be proud of him. He was to bring many other excellent pieces of work, his need for overt admiration gradually lessening. He became more interested in the content of what he was showing me than in getting my admiration. Erna Furman (1992) has clarified the importance of the mother's "standing by to admire" to the child's achievement of a separate self. Tom was now able to be proud of himself, and he usually no longer needed me to be proud of him.

During the year, Tom coped valiantly with a series of tests and exams. He planned his own revision, carried it through, and gained entry to the school of his choice. He himself was surprised at how much he had changed. I think that the change in his ability to work was due in part to his internalizing my view of him as effective, and in part to the gradual lessening of his omnipotence: it was no longer "unfair" if he was not automatically top, and success was now something you had to work for.

As Tom continued to explore life, heavy metal music and sadistic comics were replaced by jazz and biography. His play began to lose its urgent quality. At times, I felt rather bored, and I thought that he did. But he came religiously to sessions. Then he was faced with another choice: between coming to a session or attending a class in design technology. He was able to give up this session when I took up his fear about what other patients might be getting, linking with his feelings about his brothers.

Of course, underlying fears persisted, but Tom could cope differently with them. In the "Intrepid Voyager" game, he could land beside me with confidence, saying, "You are the people island". Confidence brought freedom. Tom's view of himself was expressed in the motto on his T-shirt: "Young, Single and Free." He seemed freer at home as well as in sessions and could often appreciate his brothers. He no longer expected to be supplied with everything he wanted but did jobs to earn things.

Just before the third summer break, he left his junior school. I was impressed with the extent to which he was in touch with his affects. He had to pack up all his books, and he felt "not sad, but sort of wrenched away". It had been "so automatic" going for so long. He looked back over the classes and companions he had known, and he looked forward to public school and to getting taller. He hoped that his voice would deepen gradually rather than break in an embarrassing way. He looked forward to fishing and shooting on his holiday, and he enthusiastically described the social life of meerkats—they had their own families, unlike the murderous hamsters he had focused on before.

His old automatic superego condemnation was now replaced by a philosophical questioning. In identification with a modern jazz performer, he was reading Nietzsche's *Beyond Good and Evil*. He was not grandiose, knowing that this was difficult and that you often had to go back over a sentence to see what it really meant. He shared part of a chapter with me, and, when I found it difficult, he explained: "It's about the point of life really." He brought his final school-report. The headteacher had written: "It is hard to express my pleasure in the extent of change in Tom." This change was evident in all areas of Tom's work and in his social adaptation.

COMMENTS

My developmental role continued as Tom grew: increasingly my function was to be there to be left (Furman, 1982, 1992). In being there, I had to meet, recognize, and validate Tom at many levels, from that of basic attunement to that of present teenager and future explorative, thoughtful, eager, and effective young man. I hope that such recognition will mean that Tom can retain the ability to utilize personal constellations stemming from many levels of development, and that he will retain his sense of wonder.

During this year, I interpreted less than before, largely because interpretation would have interfered with Tom's prepubertal development. Sometimes I was tempted to interpret more, but I had a strong sense that this would be inappropriate and would block the opportunity for Tom to find his own way. Nevertheless, I remained Tom's analyst throughout, a contemporary object who could help him to sort out interferences from the past. It was in this year that we did crucial work on the impact of early trauma and deafness. Here Tom's primary use of me was realistic, the transference a pale reflection of what it had been.

Transference work was to figure importantly again in the termination phase, immediately following the period described here. Termination took a further year, as Tom progressively opted to cut down on sessions. I felt it important that he be able to leave me, and we did considerable work on his fears of hurting me. Thus, in the final phase I was again both developmental and transference object.

Clearly, much remained unanalysed at the end. For example, we never worked through Tom's oedipal conflicts. These had been expressed in displacement—for instance, in stories of how Spiderman swooped down to rescue his beloved Auntie May at the altar. I felt that to undo such displacements would work against Tom's developmental progress, pulling him back to his original objects when he needed to be distancing. (Moreover, he clearly had oedipal hope: if Spiderman had been doomed to failure, I might have felt differently.)

Finally, I should note that I found it rewarding to work with Tom, enjoyed playing with him, and was never worried that he might kill himself. I think this was an important therapeutic/developmental factor, in that here I was different from Tom's parents who had inevitably been so worried about him. Happily both parents did have the capacity to enjoy being with Tom, a capacity that could come into its own as he became able to relate positively to them.

CHAPTER FOUR

"Paul":
the struggle to restore
a development gone awry

Anne Hurry

F or most of his analysis, "Paul" maintained he did not want to come, and he tried to manipulate the ending of treatment. Towards me he was sadistic, degrading, mocking, and insulting, often consciously hoping to render the situation unbearable for me, and to force me to finish with him. All earlier attempted interventions at a number of different institutions had broken down or come to nothing. By the time he was 11 years old, Paul's difficulties were such that analysis seemed his only chance, even given his expressed unwillingness to come. At this point his Irish parents were prepared to insist on his having help. They were alarmed by his extreme hatred of his younger sister and by his crippling phobic symptoms and contamination fears. Family life had been taken over by their attempts to cope with Paul's difficulties.

There were many other problems. Paul had nightmares of vampires and rats, and he would not eat meat or food that had to be chewed. He was extremely messy, spilling and smearing his food. He was clinging and demanding and often "abusive, offensive, and insulting". Not surprisingly, he had no friends.

In his diagnostic interviews at the Anna Freud Centre, Paul denied that he had any problems and repeatedly said that he did not want to come, that his only problem was his sister, Ruth. But the diagnostician observed severe anxieties stemming from the oral, anal, and phallic levels of development. Paul's object relationships were highly disturbed. His ego functioning was unevenly developed, and there was evidence of persistent concrete thinking and difficulties in symbolization. Defences were primitive and maladaptive, externalization, projection, and displacement being outstanding. The diagnostician concluded: "Paul's is a grave disorder ... a developmental disturbance of a very severe kind. Intensive treatment ought to be tried, but may not be successful ... a future psychosis cannot be ruled out."

As his analyst, I was gradually to discover that Paul's hostility was partially rooted in his need to preserve his defensive stance. He sought to live in an anal world, in fantasy the solitary ruler of a dead, destroyed universe filled with rotting bodies. He could not accept any vulnerability or loss, and he sought omnipotently to control his objects. This stance provided some safety in the face of both oral and phallic terrors, as Shengold (1988) has so vividly described. Analysis therefore represented an enormous threat, and Paul sought constantly to render me the helpless one, to destroy or control me.

In the transference, I frequently represented his hated sister, Ruth, or the hated mother who had borne her. It was important that I recognize the extent of this hatred: "Do you know how much I hate you?" He attacked Ruth and me in barely displaced ways, stabbing at the box on which he had drawn our faces, threatening me with a knife, and describing manifold tortures. Such attacks would alternate with symbolic attacks upon himself or suicidal threats. Often these had a manipulative quality, but at one point there was a real risk.

Both within and outside treatment, Paul maintained his fragile self-esteem by externalizing the many unacceptable aspects of himself and, identifying with the attacking and shaming superego, condemning these in me and in others. Such attacks were also sexualized, powered by sadism. Paul not only felt better when he could make me the bad, despicable, helpless, and shitty object, he also thoroughly enjoyed making me suffer.

Above all, Paul had to maintain his hatred lest he become aware of his own needs or of any loving feelings—to do so would have meant becoming aware of his terror of being unlovable and of intolerable guilt and shame. Desperately he invited my hatred, both to buttress his own and to achieve a "real" relationship of the only kind he knew.

Thus, with grim determination, Paul tried to create in me an anti-developmental object, one who would hate and reject him and who in so doing would confirm his identification with hating, with evil, with unacceptability, and with dangerous power. His longing for a developmental object who would not accept this view of him, who would not hate or reject him, but who could enable him to come into touch with loving feelings was desperately warded off. Yet it was not totally inaccessible: from quite early on, it was expressed in disguised form, and at various points in treatment Paul clearly experienced loving feelings towards me. Although too vulnerable to express these in words, he could express them in actions, as in giving me his photograph. But with each such move came renewed terrors, or confirmation of his transference fears, and he was driven to re-establish himself as only hating and hated. It was not until after treatment had ended that he could begin to integrate the work that we had done.

It is striking that despite Paul's conscious rejection of analysis— his "anti-alliance"— only once did his analysis feel "stuck". One theme developed from another in an appropriate and logical progression. While these themes were rarely (if ever) explored verbally in fine detail, there were times when Paul could use even a minimal amount of "analytic" work: his underlying developmental needs powered an unconscious but effective therapeutic alliance.

Starting treatment

From the beginning, I recognized that Paul had cause for righteous anger, in that he was *made* to come, though at first he would mock my attempts to say this. Initially, he brought his hatred of Ruth and his castration anxiety, but this was in the context of his longing for an exclusive relationship and his determination *not* to relate to the potentially unsatisfying, dangerous, deceiving, and rejecting object.

Paul began by telling me that there was nothing wrong with him and that one meeting would be quite enough. But he was intensely curious about others I might see, and whether they too had boxes with equipment. He first made a paper fortune-telling device and, in telling my fortune, forecast an important aspect of the transference: "You will become ugly."

He was fascinated by the toy gun, firing it at himself. When I said that he could not *really* hurt himself, he appeared delighted with my having given him the opportunity to break a rule. He leapt from his chair, fell to the floor, and rolled in simulated agony. He quickly decided that I was to blame: perhaps he had fallen over my foot.

At packing-up time, Paul again enquired about other patients. Jealousy was to be an important theme, and his hatred of his sister his *leitmotiv*. To him, there was only one way that I could help: by getting rid of Ruth. She should be made to suffer, killed like cattle. When I commented that if she were butchered she'd be like meat, he roared with laughter, tore up paper, ate it, and made paper fangs for himself which he inspected in the mirror.

Daily he insisted that he did not want to come, while simultaneously finding it hard to go. But the first weekend proved that he could not settle in, and he returned determined to have nothing to do with me and to provoke his parents into finishing. He cut off a lock of hair, hoping that mum would say he couldn't come if I let him do things like that. He considered suicide as a way of getting mum to stop sending him.

An alternative was to totally control and enslave me. When I did not obey his orders, he hurled insults at me and threatened me with the knife. Told he was not allowed to hurt me, he put the knife to his lip: if he cut himself, mum would say she would not let him come. But he ended this session by asking: "Do you like seeing me? I mean, would you if you weren't paid?"

I would make it clear that while words were acceptable, physical damage was not. When necessary, I would remove the knife, telling Paul that I would return it when he felt he could manage. In general this was effective, but he had to test me with a physical confrontation. He wanted to ring the NSPCC and tell them how cruelly he was treated, how hungry and starved he was in the treatment prison. He was determined to use the entry-phone, which I did not allow, and he went for me. I held him, telling him that I would do so until he was able to control himself. After token attempts to kick, he did take charge of himself. However, he had never been *really* out of control, or *fully* determined to hurt me, for he could in reality have kicked me, as he was to comment with some surprise. He now openly expressed a wish to kill both Ruth and me.

I was concerned about having begun treatment only four weeks before a holiday break. In the week before Easter, I introduced two technical changes. Firstly, since Paul's provocative threats to break things carried the risk that treatment become simply a gratifying tussle for him, I introduced a sanction: if he deliberately broke something, I would suggest to his parents that he use his pocket money to pay for it. Paul accepted this limit, and I only once had to bring it into play.

Secondly, I provided him with biscuits and a mug for water. I did consider whether I was trying to present myself as only a "good object". But I felt that Paul's view of me as starving or endangering him would not be overcome by two biscuits, and I did think that he needed some suitable concrete mode of conveying his conflicts around eating, a mode that would contain a *potential* for good, unlike the one he had chosen, which was to eat quantities of paper, asking, "Is it bad for you?" His attitude to his biscuits became a reliable indicator of his attitude towards me: his suspicions and fear quickly emerged, as he said that the water smelled or he writhed in pain because the biscuits were "poisoned".

As Easter approached, he repeatedly announced how delighted he was. But he also planned to run away: his parents would be glad to get rid of him and I would say, "Good—he won't be coming any more." I noted his view that I was so glad to get rid of him that I would give him poisonous biscuits, adding that this must be an awful feeling. Paul asked: "Do you see anyone as bad as me? I mean a child or an adult, anyone?"

Over the holidays, all his defences were reinstituted, and on his return he tried to get me to finish by damaging things in the waiting-room. Alternatively, he decided to spend all his session reading. I instituted a ten-minute reading rule, and he accepted this, though asking why he couldn't read all the time. I said it was because I would feel I was cheating him: if he read throughout sessions, I could not help. "You *are* cheating me", he said, "by making me come." I agreed: I was cheating the bit of him that wanted not to be bossed and wanted to make his own decision. When he nodded vigorously, I explained my dilemma, in that I believed that he was at risk—just as if he was in a burning house and denying it, I would still try to get him out (cf. Sprince, 1971).

Paul responded by asking: "Do you interpret dreams?" Clearly, he had heard the concern for him evident in my explanation, and his response indicated a real underlying potential for positive relating. (He was, of course, aware that analysts were interested in dreams.) It also indicated some underlying hope of being understood.

He said he had told mum his dream: there was a lion in his room, and he took a thorn out of the lion's foot and the lion became friendly. In the morning the lion did a pooh in his room—the lion did faeces—and mother thought the cat had done it. When he said it was a lion, she was frightened, but he explained to her that the lion was friendly.

The content of this dream refers to a relationship in which Paul helps the lion by removing the source of his pain, thus clearing the way for the lion to "become friendly". Paul takes the active role. His hopes that I may be able to help him in a similar way, too fragile to be allowed more direct expression, are expressed in reverse form. His fears, too, are clearly indicated: he (the lion) may prove unacceptable because he is perceived as dangerous, and because he is too dirty and messy.

Although these themes were far from fully accessible at the time, Paul's communication did help me to retain hope. The dream could be seen as forecasting the course of the analysis, although it was not until a year after finishing treatment that Paul could allow himself to "become friendly". This change did not, of course, come about because I had removed the source of Paul's pain, but rather because I could help him to bear that pain by recognizing it and by providing a model of relating other than the sadistic and destructive model on which he currently relied.

What we were able to talk about at this early stage was Paul's own "cross part" that he felt bad about and wanted to control, his "killy" feelings: he got very mad at Ruth and mum and felt like bashing them. Sometimes he did bash mum. Once she bashed him, and he bashed her back, and she was frightened! But another time he bashed her first, so she was very angry. I noted how scary it could be, not only to have mum so angry, but also to have her frightened. I linked this with his need to fight with me and his hope that I would be neither frightened nor very angry.

Paul was in touch and interested when I took up the poohs in the dream as indicating another side of him: the side that wanted to make a mess. When I commented on how little children could feel quite proud of poohs, the very first thing they made, he laughed and happily told me a poem about them. (There was no sign of the fear of my reaction evident when he had changed his wording from "pooh" to "faeces".)

This brief working together in no way signalled a conscious working alliance. Paul continued deeply to resent coming and dog-gedly blocked or distorted any understanding.

Summer I: Castration fears

Paul had signalled his castration fear and the risk of a defensive female identification in the first week. He had made a Plasticine man, but could not finish because it needed "something between the legs". He tried to make a woman instead, but this was too difficult, because he would have to make "two other things".

Soon after Easter, he told how a footballer wanted a divorce because his wife was interested only in his wiggly knob. In addition, Ruth wanted to be a boy, and she cried if she had to wear a dress. It was always the female who was the castrator. Paul became convinced of the reality of his fears of me when he lost the top of his pen. He was so sure I had it that he tried to catch me out by pretending to go to the lavatory but quickly coming back to check on me.

He warded off his fear with raging attacks on me or Ruth. When I first took up his underlying fear about girls, he shouted "Ruth's pooh, she's pooh, she's shit gone wrong" and stabbed at his box, his face contorted with hate.

Later, I raised the possibility that little sisters might be jealous of big brothers. Paul thought it daft to be jealous of a boy. It was better not to have a willy: when you were born the nurses came and did this dreadful thing to you. Besides, you got erections. As he spoke, Paul cut his Plasticine into tiny pieces. He then stuck it together, saying it was exactly like before. He fixed pieces of Plasticine onto the knife blade and went to stab the box again, but hesitated lest this made the Plasticine fall off. When I began to take up his fears, he said, "Let's not talk about this".

Later he told me that Ruth wanted plastic surgery to turn her into a boy, adding that she and mum ate meat: "They are lions!"

Though he switched away from this threatening topic, he did so by creating a warm moment with me. He performed "Singing in the Rain", and I joined in. Even this minimal amount of work seemed to have been relieving, for that week he said that Ruth did not know about the women who went "Snip, snip" to boys, and that if he had the choice he would rather be a boy. He began a non-attacking phallic game, attempting to land his aeroplane in the mouth of a vase, but as usual he left this session telling me I was "dead shit".

Safer anality

He was more comfortable with shit. He would fiddle with his Plasticine, muttering "Mess it up . . . shit!" He ordered me around, telling me to pick up things he threw on the floor, or he would "make shit". Sessions would end with Plasticine left on the couch for the next person to "lie in shit", or with spilt water and paper aeroplanes all around the room. One day, Paul surveyed this scene with a satisfied smile: "I have made a complete and utter mess of everything." There was no sadism in this statement, simply anal pleasure, and at times he would show a continuing capacity for such pleasure, happily moulding his Plasticine into sausages, while settling in under the blanket on the couch, assuring me he hated it here.

When the threat of castration loomed, or the end of the session approached, his happy anality would become attacking. He threatened me, "I'll fart", warning me that his farts smelled worse than other people's.

At times, his products were used as a mode of making contact as well as a way of attacking or testing my attitude, and I would recognize both aspects. For instance, towards the Christmas break, Paul again began eating paper. He took spit-laden paper gobs and put them in my sandal. I noted both the attacking element, and the gift giving. Paul said that he wanted me to keep the blobs there for ever, until I was buried. When told that I'd remember him anyway, with or without the blobs, he lay on the couch, saying, "I don't know why, but I just want to stay here and go to sleep".

In the week before Christmas, Paul pressed Plasticine tightly into an old toiletpaper tube, and half offered it to me. I took up his wishes and fears about my accepting what he felt might be his dirty bits, making a link with early times when perhaps he had got muddled about mum's reaction to his *poohs*, and mum's reaction to *him*. Paul said I did have funny ideas, but half lay on the table, asking me to sing to him, while he broke little bits off his Plasticine and plopped them on the carpet.

Testing me to the limits

On our return from this break, Paul seemed to be struggling to hang on to his hostility, constantly interrupting potentially happy activities to rage at me. But he wanted to know whether I was pleased to see him, or glad that he was alive: snuggling on the couch, he told me about swallowing some money when he was small. He then pretended to swallow a coin. When I held it and took up his testing my wish to keep him safe, Paul assured me that he could die if he did swallow it. When he was little, dad had rushed him to hospital. He thought dad had wanted him to live, but he wasn't sure about mum. I noted the sad feeling that maybe mum would be glad to get rid of him, adding that that did not make him into a person who should be got rid of, but it was no wonder that he wanted to know what I felt. After testing this out quite vigorously, making real attempts to get the coin back, he settled down to sleep.

But an external factor precipitated a florid renewal of hostility. There was a change in my timetable, and the patient who now followed Paul tended to ring the bell early so that Paul was acutely aware of him. It was clear that he felt the dawning closeness with me had been smashed. It was less painful to focus on his hatred of

Ruth, and he frequently wished her dead, or never born, whilst stabbing his box and chanting, "Kill, kill!" He denied any jealousy here, but regularly attempted to prolong his sessions, excluding the next patient.

Hostility to me avoided the pain of not being my only patient. Regularly he began sessions by calling me obscene names and holding up two fingers. He tried to provoke me with token attacks on the furniture; he pretended to cough over me and did spit at me. He reiterated repeatedly how much he hated me. When I took up his use of language as being a kind of making a mess with words, like shitting or peeing with them, Paul lit up: "I like that! I'd like to pee all over the room and all over you."

As his attacks continued, as he unremittingly mocked and spattered me with dirt-words, I found him thoroughly unpleasant. There came a point where, close to despair, I questioned to myself whether it was omnipotence, rather than any real therapeutic hope, that kept me going, and I thought seriously about whether I should bring this treatment to an end.

To my surprise, Paul began our next session by asking, "Would you like me to make you a dustbin?" He made me a cardboard wastepaper basket, and I thanked him, saying this was generous. Paul responded, "Generous—that's me!" This was a genuine and meaningful gift. He now wanted gifts and supplies from me. He wanted my admiration too, showing me his schoolwork, or trying to play chess well. Now, when I spoke of mixed feelings, he was very quiet.

It is clear that the change in Paul's attitude was a consequence of his awareness that he had tested me to the limits. I had to question how far the change was placatory, rather than reparative and indicative of his hopes. But I was sure that in sessions it did not have the feel of conforming.

The fear of sexualized loving with its attendant terrors

In a non-hating atmosphere, Paul became prey to fears of sexual interaction (his sexual wishes all projected onto me). Loving feelings had to be warded off because they were so potentially sexualized.

He sneered at me, "I suppose you think I love you", and told of lessons about sex. There was a fish that laid its eggs in the water, and the sperm was put in the water and the fishermen ate it: "Yuck!" It was much worse to eat sperm than eggs, and worst of all to eat people—and I must be a cannibal. He demonstrated pretend cuts, first on his leg, and then directly through his trousers, as though cutting off his penis. I said that quite a lot of boys had fears they could lose their penises, remembering that he had expressed the view that I had let him get cut once already. Paul agreed: of course I had. When I commented on my cannibalism, he announced: "You are made of relics, bits of other people." He wondered what had happened to his foreskin after circumcision, but he did not respond when I took up his fear that it might have been eaten, just as he feared his penis might be.

He told a story about a boy and a schoolmistress who had sex. The teacher raped the boy, was put in prison, and raped the guard. When I said that it seemed that talking about these things might even feel as though I was after him, Paul roared with laughter, but he was able to listen when I showed him the pattern in our talking.

He regressed to eating paper: the second Easter holidays were upon us. In the last session before the holiday, he flipped one of our two dice onto the floor, then flipped the other to join it, saying that he had sent them both to hell: it was better to have a companion.

Summer II:
Mother, death wishes, suicide, and violence

He returned with an evident hope of having someone to be with, in whose presence he could play. He brought a picture-set he had had when small and played happily with it, or enjoyed games with me. He was still unable to cope with ambivalent feelings: the being-together-times were interspersed with attack and insult. We would be playing happily, and he would mutter, "You stupid fool", or "You ugly bitch", not knowing why these words had emerged.

But we had built up enough of a relationship for him to be able to bring some of his fundamental fears: namely, fear of his mother's hatred and death wishes, and fear of his own violence. These fears would give rise to serious suicidal wishes, and together we would look at other ways in which he might cope with his violent feelings.

His fear of his mother's killing wishes came more directly when his tadpoles got sick and died. Paul was convinced that mum had given them the wrong food, just as I poisoned his biscuits. With the mother-doll he enacted the story of "Supermum". He stuffed Plasticine under her skirt, making her pregnant. She became malevolent and all-powerful, killing the baby and the father. The people, the animals, and the angel tried to stop her, but all were killed. God decided he would get rid of Supermum himself. Paul made a Plasticine God, like "a big sausage". But Supermum killed God too.

I commented on how frightening Supermum was and how powerful mums could seem. I added that mum had told me that she did sometimes lose her temper. Paul responded, "She is always losing her temper". By the next session he had "forgotten" Supermum, but in the following weeks I did hear more of the reality of his home situation.

Soon I became Supermum, all-powerful and threatening. Paul would greet me sneeringly, "You're pregnant"—pregnant not with a baby but with "a pig–toad–frog-and-yourself cross". I had "screwed more times than an electric drill". Alternatively, I had never screwed. "You did a shit that smelled so foul the lav wouldn't take it and it jumped out of the pan and up your . . . ." I talked with him about his view of me as so powerful, and his persisting anal view of birth, including his own. Most meaningful to him was the question as to whether his birth was wanted at all. Again, he queried whether I wanted him to stay alive, deciding "You probably do . . . but only because you could be sued . . . and you might feel a bit guilty too". When I linked this with his uncertainty about his parents' feelings, he responded, "Elementary. . . . How can I know? Maybe they want me around, but maybe they only don't want to get the NSPCC put onto them." Instancing several examples, he explained why he felt bound to doubt his parents' feelings; and even when mum controlled her anger towards him, he could see that she was angry.

He continued to greet me with vituperative comments about my baby, or about Ruth. He alternated between thoughts of suicide and murder, and fantasized sadistic attacks on Ruth. He agreed that he wished to make Ruth suffer just as he felt that she had made him suffer, and he immediately asked, "When are the summer holidays? . . . I took some Paracetamol the other day."

I felt that this indicated a real risk in the context of his flooding and rapidly displaceable aggression. However, it was not himself but Ruth that he attacked. After an argument that mum had wanted Ruth to win, he kicked Ruth "as hard as I could with all my hatred". Mum said that he might have to go to Court. What would happen about that? And what would happen if he really damaged Ruth? He was openly frightened both of the consequences and of feeling so out of control of his hatred. I tried to provide him with some hope of control, linking the attack on Ruth with his feelings here, but adding that while it was ok for him to *feel* as angry as he really was, he was not allowed to attack Ruth. I believed that he could control his violence. He had told me that he had thumped a cushion. I thought that this was a good idea: if he felt his rage was intolerable, he could bang something else. And I said directly that I did not want him to take the violence out on himself: the other day he had been telling me about taking Paracetamol. "I did think of that", said Paul.

The issue of how to control his violence became central. Sometimes Paul despaired: "I can't not kick her back—I hate her so much." But he also practised taking his anger out on the couch. There were also signs of a conscious hope of being different: in a charity swim, he collected £26, saying happily, "So I might save someone's life?"

Risking love, but choosing hate and destruction

Paul could now allow more warmth towards both mother and me. He was able to touch her, even rubbing her hands to warm them up. They had moments of closeness. He could show some concern for her and would try to do things for her, such as fixing her bicycle. At times, both appeared to want to create an idealized mother-and-baby–hood. Paul put his head on her breast, chanting "Mummy, mummy", and she found herself spooning food into his mouth while he sat "like a baby bird" beside her.

After a brief absence, Paul was pleased to return to sessions, and he brought a handsome photograph of himself, saying shyly, "If you like you can have it". He sought my good supplies, and he demonstrated his phallic skills. "I don't know why, but I just want to play with my yo–yo."

But positive feelings made the restrictions of the analytic situation hard. He wondered about my seeing him outside sessions, and he tried to borrow money. He complained bitterly about my "funny rules"—above all, my not telling him about myself. When I discussed this with him, he brought the fear that if he knew about me he might *really* hurt me, like the boy at school whose mother had died—death just kept coming up in conversations with him. The second summer holidays were looming, and his conviction as to my underlying hostility surged up. But there was also a real—if split-off—hope. He sang "Loving you no matter what you do" and sat limply back in his chair, holding a plastic drink-bottle to his mouth, letting the water just flow in.

He returned after the holidays determined to engineer termination, all good experiences between us obliterated, and only hating me. On seeing me, he would stagger back, enacting horror: "You're so ugly I cry to look at you." Although he sang "Help me if you can I'm feeling down", it seemed that the break had confirmed the risk of those positive feelings he had been able to own. Paul avoided any attempts to understand this change. At home, he began a campaign of bullying and nagging his mother to let him stop treatment.

This stance, which predominated for some six months, continued to ward off narcissistic pain and actively invited the rejection that Paul feared. (Once, when I took up his attempts to get me to dislike him and get it over with, he asked urgently: "Do you like me? Do you?") And hatred continued to protect him from the dangerous sexuality felt to be involved in any kind of loving.

Hatred also carried his longing for a *real* relationship. Now, far from fearing to hurt me, he set out to hurt. "Your mother's dead, isn't she? She died in pain." Or, "Your husband's dead, isn't he? There are flowers on your husband's grave, but somebody else put them there." As he taunted me, he would lean forward, peering into my face, hoping for tears. He became very quiet when I took up his view that really hurting felt like the only way to get past my funny rules and reach me.

Guilt was steadfastly avoided, though often indicated. Everything became my fault, and I became the torturer. Paul insisted on having a horrible time in sessions. If he forgot and had a nice time, as on one day when he drew his room for me, he would recall himself and issue a stream of vitriolic hate. For the first time, our work seemed really stuck.

I gave much thought as to how best to cope with this malign situation, how not to seem to be participating in such sadomasochistic interaction. Finally, I decided to knit, explaining that I was there to listen and talk with him, and was indeed happy to do so, but that I was not joining in the shit-words game and would be knitting while he talked in that way. While Paul used this as cause for further accusation ("You're neglecting me!"), it did gradually produce some change—a lessening of overt sadism, a turn towards more distanced games, and the use of me to help with his homework. But possibly most importantly, it enabled me to bear the onslaught with equanimity and genuinely to wait for him (cf. Gabbard, 1989).

Nevertheless, his campaign to finish continued, and mum found it hard to withstand his reproaches and bullying. One evening, she rang me, saying Paul was threatening to kill himself. I made it clear that he was not at risk, and that in this instance the threats were primarily manipulative. But Paul arrived triumphantly next day: *father* had agreed that he could finish after a year. He made a list of the remaining sessions, crossing one off each day. He either luxuriated in hatred or tried never to speak to me again.

I'm not bad—you're bad. I'm not good—I'm bad

Having achieved the potential destruction of our relationship, he had to ward off guilt more urgently. He told how a murderer wanted to be gassed. He himself believed in capital punishment— except for "shrink killing". His fear of being and wish to be all evil were evident in his story of the Jedi.

I had commented that it was indeed possible that he would use the whole year to prove how much he hated me, and to strengthen his wish not to come by having a horrible time here. However, we could try figuring out why he hated me so much—what had happened to his other feelings. Paul assured me that he only hated me; it was like the *Return of the Jedi*, where the hero has to fight his father. The father keeps saying that he himself is all evil, though the son believes that there is good in father and refuses the Jedi's order to kill father. Then the Jedi tries to make the son all evil, telling him that he is being filled with hatred. So the father throws the Jedi into the reactor, and there is a great explosion. Thus he proves his son right about there being good in him, and saves his son from being taken over by hatred.

Sadly, although so much had gone on since "the lion became friendly", there was to be no overt understanding from this story: Paul continued to try to enact it with me, retreating into torture fantasies.

He now repeatedly called me a Nazi, or Hitler's mother. He took a volume of Freud from the bookcase, wanting to write "Salman Rushdie" in it. Freud annoyed him, just as Rushdie annoyed others, and Rushdie's books were burned just as Freud's should be. When I commented that this was what the Nazis had actually done, Paul was intrigued and enquired closely about Freud. But he was to use this to make me to blame for all his felt evil. For instance, when I would not let him dump his heavy bag on my foot, telling him that I was not helping him to carry out his hurting wishes, he responded, "You think I'm sadistic", and set out to prove that he was. It felt better to exalt in being all evil than to feel partly good, and he denied that he had ever been good or generous. He asked for his waste-paper basket back and, when I refused, remembering how he had offered to make it for me, said, "I must have been mad when I said that." He forgot that he had ever given me his photo.

Summer III: Finishing but keeping a link

On returning from the Easter break, he said that after he finished treatment he would come back and kill me. Then an event occurred that provided concrete evidence that he was not "all evil". While he later attempted to deny or pervert this episode, he was unable to blot it out. By accident, Paul really hurt me. He was bouncing his rubber eraser on his tennis racquet. He was controlled and had agreed to keep it safe. But the eraser bounced on a corner, flew off at an angle, and hit me in the eye. Paul was horrified. "I'm sorry, I'm sorry! I wasn't aiming at your face! Have I hurt you?" I said he had, but I had managed to shut my eye first.

Paul's primary feeling was of concern and guilt, but soon his attitude changed. "That was funny!", he gloated. I said that he hadn't felt that: rather, he was frightened and shocked. He continued to gloat: "You say I am a Nazi: you bring out all my sadism!" I said that I hadn't said he was a Nazi, though I thought he partly functioned in the same way, and that he'd be sad if he turned into a Nazi. In fact, we could understand some more from what he was doing now. Nazis glorified their cruelty so as to feel good about it—they were not born Nazis. This gave Paul pause. He asked a series of questions, like "Do you believe in animal experiments?", seeming to be questioning the reality of the externalizing transference.

It became more difficult to maintain his view of me as only evil. Occasionally he forgot to cross off the remaining days, or to say goodbye by calling me "bitch". Occasionally, he shared with me something that pained or angered him, or he enjoyed himself in sessions. He invented "a fun game" and let himself decide to play his guitar because it was fun. From time to time, he could tolerate my taking his sadism as an act. I could mention the possibility he stay after the end of the year without its being felt as a challenge. Once, when he was counting the days until the end, blaming me and the sessions for his not being able to have golf coaching, I said that next year he would be able to have all these things, but added that he wasn't to misunderstand: he was, of course, welcome to stay longer if he wanted to. Paul said, "I've never thought of that— well, just for a fraction of a second!"

Paul did end his treatment, after nearly three years. In the final weeks, his longing to stay was very evident, although still denied. For instance, he gave me a carefully detailed picture of the route from the station to my house, commenting that if he ran away a nearby empty house would be a good place to live, because it would be nearer me. Then, realizing what he had said, he exclaimed his disgust.

He often seemed conscious of mixed feelings and could agree that he maintained his hostile stance from "pride". We were able to do some more "analytic" work: for instance, on the link between his current loneliness and the time when his younger brother was born. Moreover, he remembered his hostility to Ruth as having begun when Ruth was jealous of this brother, so that we could begin to see the extent of his guilt over his own jealousy.

He did in the end maintain a link with me. He could grieve over not seeing my knitting finished and asked me to send him a photo of it. I said that I would not do that, because it seemed a kind of pretend that he did not want a link with me, but I would write to tell him when the knitting was finished, and he could come and see it if he wanted to. Paul said, "I see what you mean", and that he would like me to write.

In our last session, the question of limits was all-important. Paul reverted to all his old threats to break my things, asking, "What can you do?" But he stopped all threats when I commented on his wish to know that the limits were still there. Finally, he picked up the mug I had given him, asking if he could break it. I said it was his, and for some moments he held it suspended, looking at it; then he said, "I don't want to break it. . . . I don't want to destroy it", and he put it down.

Follow-up

When Paul ended his analysis, I feared that his guilt might drive him to establish me as such a bad object that he could never return, but in the end he was able to integrate some of our work after he had finished. Mother, who remained in contact with me for about six months, reported that within two months he was "a changed boy", enjoying talking with her and the rest of the family, beginning to make friends. After four months he told her that his reaction to his phobic objects might lie within himself, rather than in the objects themselves, and his phobias and contamination fears gradually waned.

A year after termination, I wrote to Paul as I had promised, letting him know that I had finished my knitting. He first responded with a "horrible" letter but soon rang and asked to come to see me, saying that he had realized that he no longer had to be horrible to me. It seemed that he was genuinely happier in his day-to-day life. Ruth was still "a fearful nuisance", but he could cope with her.

There was evidence of more age-appropriate conflicts with his family, but his underlying fears of being unwanted and his longings to come first were still very evident.

He tested my trustworthiness with an important question. He had once stolen a ruler: had I known? Told that I had not, he responded: "Good, so you weren't fooling me." But he remained wary of my possibly rejecting him, telling me that he was never coming to see me again. Consciously, he was clearly afraid of being trapped back into treatment. I recognized this fear with him, and by the end of the interview he said that he thought he would come again, but "not for a long time".

He still found it hard to have to share but was prepared to try, asking if he could use a whole notebook to draw in, or whether I might need it for other patients. And he found it hard not to have the relationship for which he longed: the last thing he told me was how much he had always longed to go through the door that leads from the consulting suite to my home.

Discussion

As early as 1934, Susan Isaacs detailed the uses of hatred to defend against loving feelings, sadness, helplessness, and guilt. In working with a child who so used hatred, I found that I had not only to accept both aspects of his ambivalence, but also to be prepared actively to provide a new and more positive mode of relating. Anna Freud (1949), linking pathological aggressiveness in children with a lack of fusion, wrote that "the appropriate therapy has to be directed to the neglected, defective side, i.e., the emotional libidinal development". But where any loving feeling or need is perceived as too dangerous, there is a risk of therapeutic stalemate. Erna Furman (1985) has described how such children strenuously resist any reminder of loving feelings and justify their aggression by "not loving and not remembering".

Paul's repeated attempts to get me to finish with him can be seen as a way of testing my preparedness to hold on to him, like the running away typical of hyper-aggressive, conduct-disordered children. Willock (1990) has described such children as having a core of extreme narcissistic vulnerability masked by their aggression and primitive defences. His moving description captures the essence of Paul's dilemma:

> The child's underlying belief is that no-one really cares about him, that . . . he is unable to engage the loving concern of caregivers . . . [and that] there is something grossly repugnant and unlovable about him that makes others turn away in disgust . . . he therefore feels driven to devise strategies to force caretakers to become involved. . . . Frustrated and enraged that he has had unsatisfactory and sometimes abusive rather than the more optimal, developmentally supportive relationships with his parents, the child's longing for such crucial human interactions continues, at least unconsciously. Needless to say these yearnings are intensely conflictual. Frightened of such wishes, the aggressive child tends to repudiate them aggressively. [p. 327]

The therapeutic challenge with such children is to withstand the extreme countertransference reactions they inevitably provoke, and to maintain one's commitment to them. Interpretation alone is at first useless. It can be effective only in the context of hope—and hope is dependent on the child's allowing himself to be aware that the analyst is not rejecting him. Any such awareness is so frightening that it must repeatedly be obliterated, and the certainty of rejection re-established. To agree to terminate treatment would be to join with the child in the destruction of hope, reinforcing his pathology.

It is evident that above all I had to be an object who would not reject Paul—that is, a benign developmental object. It was only in the context of this new relationship that he could begin to use more interpretative work. But in no way did I behave towards Paul with any unusual warmth or kindness. Given his transference expectations of falsity and his radar-like capacity to pick up disguised affects in others, such an attitude would have been experienced as completely false.

From the beginning, I had to meet Paul's developmental need for controls and limits, I had to insist that we keep him, myself, and the room safe. I had to contradict his assertion that I should accept whatever he did. Most child analysts today accept that limit-setting is appropriate in the treatment of aggressive and sadistic children (e.g. Alvarez, 1985: Daldin, 1992; Edgcumbe, 1971; Furman, 1994a; Lanyado, 1990; Sandler, Kennedy & Tyson, 1980). Where parental controls have been lacking or inconsistent, interpretation alone is ineffective and fails to meet a developmental need. Acceptance of Paul's attacks and cruelty would have been felt as a masochistic submission, fuelling his omnipotence and sadism. Furthermore, to have provided no limits would have reinforced his fears as to his own dangerousness and felt evil, as well as fears as to his ability to control his aggression. (In this regard, he needed more than limits—he needed specifically tailored developmental help to enable him to move from physical to verbal expression and to find ways in which he could control himself: cf. Edgcumbe, 1971.)

Honesty is important here. An analyst who appears not to recognize the difference between good and bad cannot be an appropriate developmental object, and at times it is appropriate to express condemnation or anger with regard to a particular piece of behaviour. I did express real anger towards Paul, even though rarely. For instance, he once waited outside until I had begun work with the patient who followed him. He then walked through the garden and up to the window, where he performed a mocking and cavorting dance. I left the session, went outside, and said in very angry tones, "Stop that at once, and don't you ever do it again!" Paul looked frightened and quickly left. In fact, he was relieved not to be allowed to destroy the next patient, although he tried to use the incident to make me feel guilty. (The following session began with a reproachful, "You shouted at me!" I said: "In more than a year I've shouted at you twice—I think we'll both survive.")

It was a big step when Paul could tell me, "Teenagers need limits, you know". Analysts, too, need limits. Those I employed were often necessary for my sake as well as Paul's, for I had to work within the limits of my own physical and psychic tolerance (cf. Lanyado, 1990). Such tolerance will vary from analyst to analyst. I often did not know at the time why it felt right to accept a particular piece of behaviour, but I did gradually find that some concrete representation of the interaction between us, accompanied by words, could be effective when words alone were not. You will remember the spit-gobs, the coin, the eraser: Paul's need to be met at this level of concrete representation reflected his continuing difficulty in symbolization in some areas, and it also pointed up his experience of the gap between parental feelings and parental words and actions.

Many writers have noted the risk of the analyst's being drawn into a sadistic interaction, (e.g. Alvarez, 1985: Burgner & Kennedy, 1980; Daldin, 1992). With Paul, the problem was less how not to participate, more how not to be *perceived* as participating: I had openly to state my dislike of his way of relating and to refuse to share it. Furthermore, since he often experienced neutrality as rejection or sadism, and interpretation as unbearably humiliating and attacking, I had at times to find ways of sidestepping his mode of relating and invite him to relate in another way before he could even hear me. It was sometimes just possible to call out the potential for benign relating in him. For instance, if he tried to madden me by creaking his chair, I might respond by turning this into music, adding a tune or tapping a rhythm, and we could have a "good" time together.

But more usually, when Paul seemed completely mired in hatred, spending session after session in verbal messing and cruelty, it took thought to find a way of helping him to see that I was not joining in a sadomasochistic interaction with him. It could be said that, through such interventions as telling Paul that I would knit until he could relate in another way, I "taught" Paul that sadism was not acceptable. (Analysts "teach" their patients more often than we have recognized: the very decision to interpret some mode of behaviour can imply that it is open to question.)

Willock (1990) has described how a child may embrace a devalued, negative identity "in order to ward off the more painful feeling of emptiness associated with his feeling of being fundamentally unloved" (p. 327). The more patients like Paul long for a developmental object who will see them as potentially good, the more they cling to an image of themselves as "bad". This view provides a way of mattering to others when any other way seems hopeless. And the transformation of their horror at the "evil" self-image into the conviction that they have chosen it by-passes guilt and becomes a means of narcissistic aggrandizement. In the transference, these patients seek to transform the analyst into an object who will confirm this "evil" view of themselves (and analysts who believe that they have no conscience unwittingly reinforce this manoeuvre).

In sometimes daring to admit the positive or loving aspects of his self representation, Paul could also admit them in me. He could have some hope of my gratitude for his present, my admiration of his photo, my enjoyment of his guitar concert, my pleasure while singing in the rain, my involvement in his invented game. I met this hope in showing just these responses, and he was able to feel them as genuine, not "fooling".

But during his analysis such good experiences were repeatedly obliterated. I have mentioned the challenge posed within the countertransference by children like Paul, and there was at times a risk of my rejecting Paul, of therapeutic despair and withdrawal. Alvarez (1985) has vividly described the impact that constant destruction of any "good" moment or live interchange can have, adding that "The therapist . . . may have to struggle hard within herself . . . to survive and transform the endlessly repetitive countertransference experience of defeat and hurt". She recommends an attitude of "fortified neutrality" to provide sufficient distance for thinking. I found that I could achieve the appropriate distance only if fully aware of the extent of Paul's sadism and wish for malign relating, for, in such a context of hatred, it was natural to invest in hope after any good experience with Paul. I had to learn to expect destruction—and yet not be over-fortified, but remain open to the possibility of warmth and creativity.

Children like Paul, honed by experiences of emotional disguise on the part of others, are fine-tuned to awareness of any underlying negative response. I think that Paul often knew how he had made me feel, and that it was important that I myself recognized that at times I found him "horrible" and "inhuman". Without such awareness on my part—if I had "fooled" myself—I think he would have despaired of achieving recognition not only of his destructive aspects, but also of his loving and reparative aspects, in his case a graver lack. In addition, he would have despaired of finding genuine positive aspects in me. I am not implying here that verbalization of the countertransference is necessary. Indeed, I believe that such verbal revelations are usually inappropriate (and very different from the occasional expression of anger or sharing of pleasure discussed above). But affective interchange does not depend on words. The episode of the waste-paper basket provides good evidence that Paul was aware of what I felt and confirms Winnicott's (1947) observation that the patient who seeks objective or "justified" hate must be able to find it, or he will not be able to find "objective love".

It was remarkable that in our final sessions Paul could so clearly indicate something of his underlying vulnerability and yearning, even though he had to disparage and deny that yearning until the very last session. It was remarkable that he could also indicate a real move from his identification with his destructive aspects—"I don't want to destroy it." In the end, Paul did internalize and integrate a good deal of our work. (His later comments to his mother about his phobic objects echoed things that I had said that, at the time, he had apparently ignored or sneered at.) The changes he showed after termination, and the fact that he could maintain a relationship with me, and even return to see me, rather than use termination as a justification for feelings of rejection and hatred, give grounds for realistic hope for his future.

Aknowledgement

The thinking in this paper has developed from that in an earlier paper (Hurry, 1994). I am indebted to Dr Robert Furman for his illuminating discussion of that paper (Furman, 1994a).

CHAPTER FIVE

"Martha": establishing analytic treatment with a 4-year-old girl

Anne Harrison

I n this chapter, I describe the early months of treatment of a little girl in five-times weekly analysis. I focus on the particular quality of the difficulties that she brought and consider what it was that we had to struggle with together for interpretative work to begin.

"Martha" was 4 years old when she was referred for assessment. Although intelligent and musically gifted, she was disabled by fears and phobias, a need for rigid control, and, above all, an inability to form relationships outside her immediate family. At home, she demanded to be bottle-fed, to be carried, to use nappies, and generally to be treated as a baby. The referral was initiated by her nursery school, who were alarmed that now, in her last year before school, she continued to avoid any real engagement with staff and seemed entirely to blank out the presence of the other children. Her parents were doubtful about the referral at first, feeling that, although she was odd and difficult, this was perhaps an unavoidable aspect of what made her special.

Martha is the elder of two children and has a sister, Maria, eighteen months younger. Her parents moved to this country from South America as students and were married in their later 30s. The marriage was not a particularly happy one, but the parents were clear that Martha was very much wanted and loved. The account that they gave of relations within the family was striking, having as its central premise an understanding that the child disliked her mother and loved her father.

The pregnancy itself had been trouble-free, but the birth difficult and mother had been unwell for some days after. She tried to breast-feed but gave up after a few weeks because Martha could not latch on. Almost from the very start, it seems, father had interposed himself in the relationship and had taken over as much of the baby's care and feeding as he could. Mother remembers consciously feeling excluded by the time Martha was a few months old.

Relations with Maria were more straightforward for both parents, and more satisfying for mother. Nevertheless, it was clear that Martha was now established in a position of dominance in the family. She had reacted to Maria's birth with a period of intense nightmares, and within a few months she had begun physically attacking and tormenting her, as she continued to do. Neither parent felt able effectively to intervene and to take a stand against Martha's persecution of her younger sister.

At the same time, Martha's relationship with mother established itself as stormy and battling, and this too was to continue, with Martha shouting her defiance and rejection and, on occasion reducing her mother to tears. There was one kind of experience, however, that mother and daughter were able to share: when mother sang, Martha would sit close to her and seem to be absorbed. With father, the relationship allegedly remained exclusive and benign at all times. They read together and, with time, have begun to play on the computer. Both parents spoke with ready pride of Martha's intellectual precocity. At the same time, however, her demands to be treated as a baby had become more direct and insistent; father had been pleased to gratify them, readily feeding her with a bottle and carrying her in his arms.

Both parents seemed to be in two minds as to how to view the situation. On the one hand, there clearly was great concern for Martha and a wish to do the best for her well-being. On the other, father appeared to feel that Martha's hostility to her sister and stark rejection of one parent in favour of the other was no more than the natural, Freudian order of things, and mother in her be-wilderment seemed to accept this. Similarly, even while the parents described the difficulties that Martha's aggressive, regressive, and controlling behaviour caused at home, and the growing range of her fears of dogs and other animals, they stressed what an unusual and loveable child she was. It seemed as though Martha's specialness could come only at some emotional cost both to herself and to her family. Both parents were dismissive of the nursery school's concern about Martha's failure to form relationships, particularly with other children; nevertheless, when told of our very real concern about the fragility and imbalance of her psychic development, they accepted our recommendation for analytic treatment.

I saw Martha for the assessment and found her indeed unusual and arresting in her way. She was small for her age, with a pretty, serious little face and an odd composure in her manner. She seemed without self-consciousness or even self-awareness, and she came with me readily in order to explore the box of playthings that she had been told I had. This she did, naming various articles in turn, and using several of them in a deliberate and controlled way: for example, she separated the Lego bricks into piles according to colour and made marks with each of the felt-tip pens in turn on a sheet of paper. On the second day, she was eager to repeat what she had done the day before. When she spoke, her words were hard to follow (although she spoke clearly after the first month), but she spoke only to ask me for something. There was no exchange between us, and anything I said she ignored, as if she had not heard me. I was left with the sense of a child who felt terribly precarious beneath a thin veneer of confidence, at risk of being overwhelmed if she allowed herself to experience me—or any-one—as separate from herself.

We began analysis about a month after the assessment, al-though for Martha it was as if there had been no real gap. She remembered all the things that we had done and was happy to return to them. Over a period of three or four weeks, our repertoire of activities increased and particular ones were elaborated and established as favourites. Most important of these was a game she called "big ball and little ball", where one of us, usually Martha, made endless, tiny balls of Plasticine and rolled them across the table for the other to catch and incorporate into one large ball.

Another was for her to sort the Lego not only according to colour, but also by size, so that only bricks that were identical were allowed to be put together, while any odd-shaped bricks were discarded. With my help Martha then built towers, which she classified according to how tall they were, but she ignored anything that I might have to say about this: for example, that the little balls might want to be safe inside the big ball, or that one tower might want to be bigger than another.

More hopeful was Martha's fondness for four plastic pigs that she had found in the toy box; she returned to look at these every day and identified them as Mummy, Daddy, Martha, and Maria. With time, she began a tentative kind of play with Martha-pig, while I put words to what it was the pig might be wanting or feeling: "She's hungry, she wants to play, she likes to splash in water." Martha did not respond directly to these comments, but seemed to use them as cues for what the pig might do. Gradually, the pig acquired a character as someone who loved to splash, stamp, be difficult, and generally make a mess, and she was named "Messy Pig".

We had begun analysis about six weeks before the summer break, and sessions continued in this rather ritualized way until then. We resumed in the autumn, with no real acknowledgement from Martha that there had been a gap. Our activities became more rigid and controlled, and we played even more big ball and little ball and Lego towers. There was one innovation: out of the family of pipe-cleaner dolls Martha selected two figures, a big sister and a little sister, whom she called "Big Girl and Little Girl". Often at the start of sessions she got these out and looked at them wistfully, moving them towards one another until they touched and then drawing them apart. She listened, but did not comment, while I talked of Big Girl and Little Girl being like her and me and of how we, too, could be together only for a little time, but then, sadly, had to go away and leave each other.

For weeks after starting back, we were taken up with the business of Lego towers. First the irregular bricks—which Martha now called "the messy bits"—were discarded. Then, inevitably, came the construction of a row of uniform towers.

In a crucial session in our fourth week back, I took a different stance. As usual, the Lego was tipped out, the red bricks put in a pile, and the five odd bricks discarded with the ritual words, "I don't want that one—it's messy". Again I was told that I could have the white bricks, and again Martha set about sorting out the red bricks according to size and shade of red. One by one, each pile was built into a tower, with help from me at predictable points to hold the towers steady.

When the towers were made and the time came to compare one with the other, Martha ignored anything I said that did not belong with the "big, bigger, biggest" classification of the towers—for example, how the big tower might feel very important or the little tower might want to catch up. She also ignored my wonderings about what else we might be able to make with the bricks. We were now well into the session, and, as before, I was starting to feel a bit stuck and hopeless.

This time, however, I said: "Now, you've made your red towers, but today I want to make something too, with the other bricks. I want to make a house." Martha ignored me at first, but then began to watch in rather a worried way as I started to use bricks of different colours together. She said "No" several times. When I included some of the messy bricks in the structure, she said, "Not to touch—those are the messy ones". Now, instead of enquiring in various ways what made the messy bricks messy, I said: "I don't think they are messy, they are just different from all the other bricks; each one is different and I think maybe it feels all by itself." Martha stared at me and then reached out and fingered one of the messy bricks. I said: "I think that maybe the messy bricks are a little bit lonely and would even like to join up with the other bricks to make a house." Martha stared some more and then, as I said that it was time for us to tidy away, began to add the remaining messy bricks to one of her towers, murmuring, "It's all right, it's all right". I said: "Yes, I think it is all right." As we put the bricks back in the box, Martha took out a plastic stethoscope, put it on, touched my arm with it, then put it away. I said: "You know, I think you would like you and me to be close and really get to know each other, but it's so sad, because every day, when we do get close, we have to say bye–bye to one another." Martha did not reply, and we set off downstairs together.

She came quickly when I collected her for the next session. On the way upstairs, she told me that she wanted to play with Big Girl and Little Girl. But when we got to the room, she initiated a game of peek-a-boo, something we had played once or twice before the summer, but not since. I said that Martha had not seen me since yesterday and that now she felt glad to know that I had come back. Sometimes, I continued, we didn't see each other for a much longer time, like at the summer, and then I thought that she really did feel afraid that she might not ever see me again.

Martha did not reply, but got out Messy Pig and made her stamp on the table and stamp and splash in a dish of water. I remarked on pig's activities and wondered what she was feeling: was she cross or excited, or was she having a good time? Martha ignored this and got out Big Girl and Little Girl. Holding one in each hand, she brought them together several times, as if they were rushing towards one another, while I spoke words for each of them, exclaiming that it had been such a long time since they had been together and how pleased they were to see each other. Then I spoke for Little Girl and said how worried she had been that Big Girl was not going to come and find her. Martha giggled at first and then began to look upset: "No more", she told me, "no more". I said that it felt very sad for her to hear about Little Girl's worries about Big Girl not coming back, because she I thought, too, some-times felt a bit like that.

Martha stared at me; she said nothing but looked calmer. She was clearly torn between her wish for us to go on playing and her fear of strong, distressing feelings. She then said that she wanted us to play on the bed [the couch]. I said that that was a good idea, because then Big Girl, Little Girl, and Pig could all be together and no one would fall and hurt herself (as Martha often did). She looked doubtful about including the pig, but brought her over and fairly soon invented a game in which each of the girls rode on Messy Pig's back, while she exclaimed repeatedly, "They're having a good time!"

Towards the end of our time, Martha came and stood beside me. "What's your mummy's name?", she asked. I thought for a moment and said: "When you and I are close and have a good time—like Big Girl and Little Girl—it makes you think of your mummy and how you love it when you feel close to her." Martha looked at me for a moment or two, saying nothing, then turned away.

For a child like Martha, feelings of any kind bring a terrible threat of being overwhelmed and made helpless. She protects herself from this, not only by the rigidity of the control she imposes, but also by denying and blanking out on the experience of difference and separation and even the awareness that her object is different from her. In this way, she tries to keep at bay the force of her desperate, messy feelings but pays the price by reinforcing her awful sense of isolation and omnipotence.

What analysis must offer a child—or adult—with this kind of incapacity is something prior to an understanding of her feelings. First of all, there has to be a means to experience them and a space in which it can feel safe to do that. The analyst is a new object for a child, and, through an experience of her that is reliable and unthreatening, the child can come to risk knowing of her as someone separate. My resolve to do something different with the bricks was, of course, a stepping out of the strict role of comment and interpretation and was born, in part, out of my own frustration. What it offered Martha at the time, however, was a chance to see not only that mixing the bricks and including the messy ones was safe, but that an experience of me as separate and outside her control was something bearable after all.

When we talk to a child in an analytic session and offer games and activities, we are, in a way, teaching new skills—but not as an end in themselves: this is not behaviour modification. Language and play offer the child a means to represent and symbolize the feelings that immobilize her; they begin to form the material of affective thinking and communication. It is out of this that the analytic dialogue can grow and, with it, understanding, relief, and real—rather than omnipotent—control. In the second session described, Martha was able to have something of the freedom of being able to experience her feelings, by means of the externalization onto Little Girl and, of course, the stamping, messy pig. She was able, too, to hear me interpret the anxiety that this caused her and to be reassured by that. The experience of contact between us and of being understood by me naturally intensified for Martha a wish for us to be close to one another. But when her wish to be close to me inevitably brought with it all her longings to be close to and know her mother, she located this wish in my mind, not her own— to protect herself, of course, but also to wonder and to ask about.

With patients for whom the experience of their own feelings can seem so dangerous, the analyst and her thoughts may serve to model the capacity to think and feel which the child herself is lacking.

After these two sessions, things became more lively. Martha and I often played with Big Girl and Little Girl, greeting each other and being together. Messy Pig was active too, stamping and splashing and making a mess; she often crashed into Big Girl and Little Girl and sometimes attacked them. On several occasions Little Girl attacked Big Girl, and Martha looked relieved when I acted the part of Big Girl, not being angry but "knowing" about Little Girl being cross and upset with her for having to wait so long to play together. (In time, of course, the Big Girl and Little Girl material would have to be taken up in relation to Martha and both her mother and her younger sister, but at this early stage, when my most immediate concern was to open up the possibility of thinking and of being understood in Martha's mind, it was essential for it to be interpreted primarily within the relationship to me.)

Martha was more dubious about my sympathy for Messy Pig, who, I said, felt so messy and horrid that she was sure that nobody liked her. Soon we had a new activity: painting. Martha got out the paints that I had put in her cupboard, and she said that she wanted to use them. For more than a week, sessions were given over entirely to making a mess. Martha mixed only black and smeared and covered the paper and her hands indiscriminately. She agreed that she, too, was making a mess, just like Messy Pig. The task of clearing up—herself, the paint trays, and the table— seemed as satisfying for Martha as the painting itself. For a time, she insisted on taking the soggy sheet of paper home, and every day, as I left her in the waiting-room, I heard one or other parent exclaiming on the beauty of the painting and struggling to identify what it represented.

After a bit, with my help, Martha began to mix other colours, too, but then she would flood them with black or brown, "making it all mucky", or "making dirty, mucky black". She rolled the words about in her mouth with real savour. Inevitably, too, she began to splash me with paint, usually when we were clearing up. She was a bit nonplussed when I said that I didn't want to be splashed, or took the brush away from her if she continued, seeming surprised that I neither indulged her nor lost my temper. She agreed that when she splashed me she was being a bit like Messy Pig. One day when she began to splash, I suggested that we got Messy Pig out and that she could do the splashing. Martha accepted this idea immediately and Pig was brought to splash and mess in the paint water, while Martha exclaimed that Pig was "a really Messy Pig!" Next day was Friday, and Martha told me on the stairs that she wanted to make mustard colour today and that there would be no splashing. I said that a big bit of her really didn't want to splash me, but that it was hard for her not to, especially when I said that it was nearly time for us to stop and that maybe we could use Pig to do the splashing, like we had done yesterday.

We settled in to mixing colours and exclaimed together on the mustard that we made. Martha then put black in all the colours, made them mucky, and said that they were "lovely", "beautiful", "fantastic". I said: "No, I don't think that one looks lovely now, I think it looks all mucky." Martha gave me a hard look and flicked a bit of paint water onto my hand. I said: "Oh dear, you're splashing again and I don't want to be splashed; what are we going to do?" She flicked another bit water at me and I reached across and held onto her brush saying, "I think that I'll have to hold on to this now if I don't want to be splashed." Martha said "But I want it!", and I responded "I know you do, but I don't want to be splashed— maybe we need Pig to help us."

Martha ignored this and began to paint her hand with black paint, glancing up at me as she did so. I watched and then remarked that she was making her hand all black, whereas she'd only put a little black splash on mine. I said: "When you splash me, you feel afraid that I am terribly cross with you and that I think you are very bad." Martha stopped painting her hand and put down the brush. I said: "But we're lucky, because we've got the sink and lots of water, so we can wash our hands." Martha agreed, and we both washed our hands.

Later, when we were clearing up, she began to splash again. I reached out to take the brush, and Martha said immediately, "Get Pig!" She rushed over to her box, got Pig out, and brought her to the sink. Pig was put in the mucky paint water because she was messy and cross and stamping. I wondered if Pig felt cross and upset because today was Friday, and we were not going to have a play tomorrow because it was Saturday, nor on the next day, because it was Sunday. Martha listened to this but did not say anything. Pig had a wash and was dried, and Martha said that she was "better".

However, when I said that we really did have to stop now and put things away, Martha threw Pig at me and burst out, "I don't like you!" She stood looking shocked and apprehensive. I sat down beside her and said: "Sometimes you do feel cross with me and really don't like me, especially when I say no and that it is time for us to stop." I said that it was very hard for her, because she so loved us to play together and to be friends, and she felt afraid that all her cross, upset feelings would spoil it and make me not like her. Martha searched my face intently and seemed to relax. She asked me to help her to take off her apron.

For a week or two now she had been choosing little bits of paper "to take away". Earlier in the week she had seemed to agree when I said that she wanted something to take away, so that she wouldn't feel sad when we said goodbye. She now chose two scraps of paper, and when I said "Like you and me", she said "Yes", identifying the large scrap as me and the smaller one as herself. She made the smaller scrap give the larger a good thump, put them both together on the table, and set about putting things away in her cupboard.

When this was done, she asked me to close the door "like yesterday". Several times before she had wanted to shut the cupboard door tight, but had made no response when I said that she might want to keep me safe in the cupboard, so that I would be there when she came back. This time, however, when I shut the door, she said, "Anne stay here—all day", adding, "I want to play tomorrow". I said that I knew that she did, and that she felt very sad when she knew that we wouldn't have a play then. Martha took up her bits of paper and said, "It's a butterfly and a wasp—a little butterfly and a big wasp", and we set off downstairs.

The burden for a child like Martha, for whom the psychic elaboration of feeling states has been inhibited, is twofold: lacking a capacity to structure and differentiate her inner experience, she is alone and helpless with a great agglomerate of feeling which threatens constantly to overwhelm her; at the same time, and because of this, she is trapped in a state of primitive, magical thinking, in which she feels herself to be terribly powerful and terribly bad.

Martha's situation at home has not provided the help she needs to begin to master the force of her early wishes and resentments. Caught up, perhaps, in her parents' minds with their own needs and identifications, she is both idealized and exploited in the tensions between them. With no reliable boundary or limits set for her, she is at the mercy of all the rage, envy, and frustration that she feels towards her mother and of her own terrifying fantasies of vengeance and punishment. There has been nothing to protect her—or her little sister—from her jealous fury towards her, or to help her to moderate it with feelings of love and empathy. Finally, the sheer confusion for Martha of feeling herself both encouraged towards precocious intellectual development and, at the same time, actively invited to regress to infancy must have left her frozen and despairing that she could ever gain coherence in her inner life.

The analytic setting must allow the child to feel secure enough to begin to think. In stopping Martha from splashing me, I put limits on the enactment and the immediate discharge of her aggression and offered her a displacement for it through the activities of Messy Pig, which we could then think about together. I showed her, too, that I had needs and wishes for myself and that, crucially, I could look after these and so look after her.

Left with no structure to mediate the violence of her impulses, Martha is caught in the toils of her own omnipotent fantasies where she projects this violence and dreads its coming back at her in dogs that bite and wasps that sting. It also finds a place in her own primitive conscience, and Martha punishes herself in bitter self-condemnation. At this time, Martha often fell and sometimes bruised herself, and in the sessions that came after this we began to see Messy Pig being dashed to the floor and to talk about her hurting herself because she felt so naughty.

In helping a child to see the difference between fantasy and what is real, the analyst brings the child relief. This is the very stuff of analysis and interpretative work. But the child must have confidence that the analyst can tell the difference between one kind of thing and another, and it is sometimes from the analyst that she learns to make distinctions. Furthermore, in discovering the possibility of a genuine control over herself and her messiness and of a genuine capacity to make things better—for instance, in washing her hands, cleaning the paint trays, and wiping the table—Martha no longer had to fall back on grandiosity and denial.

Similarly, an ability to give names to her feelings and to discriminate among them allows the child to feel less overwhelmed and emotionally messy. No longer constricted by anxiety, her mind becomes able to make connections and gains strength and structure, as she internalizes her experience of being understood by her analyst. As the threat of unthinking rage and helplessness receded from Martha in the session that I have described, she was beginning to allow herself to know how small and vulnerable she really felt and to feel that it might be possible to let me know of her sadness and of her longing to have me with her.

CHAPTER SIX

"Donald":
the treatment of a 5-year-old boy
with experience of early loss

Viviane Green

"Donald's" early development unfolded in a chaotic environment. His young parents had not planned for a baby. They battled acrimoniously, separating in his first year. Thereafter he had no permanent home. Mother was an alcoholic, and father would take over when he felt that Donald was at risk, or Donald would stay with his aunt and uncle.

It was father who approached the Anna Freud Centre's Well Baby Clinic for help in managing the baby's outbursts of kicking and screaming. He kept regular appointments. Mother came twice; she sought to convey her love and interest in her child, but she went to great lengths to conceal the extent of her alcoholism. Both parents tried to stabilize their son's rather chaotic routine, but father felt overwhelmed by his parental responsibilities and had difficulty in setting limits.

When Donald was almost 4 years old, he began to attend the Centre's nursery school. An appealing and intelligent child, he enjoyed a wide range of activities. He was proud of his physical abilities, and he had a playful imagination. But he found it difficult to contain his aggression and would bite other children without provocation. He became attached to the staff but was defiant and provocative towards them. His anxiety and unhappiness were evident in his agitation and severe nail-biting.

Soon after his fourth birthday, his mother died in an accident while away visiting her family in Liverpool. Ironically, Donald's life became more stable. He lived with his father and regularly visited his aunt and uncle. But his difficulties intensified both in the nursery and at home, and he began to soil.

The traumatic loss of his mother compounded the effects of Donald's earlier experience. He was offered non-intensive psychotherapy to help him to cope with the effects of that loss and, in particular, to help him to be aware of and bear his feelings. (Twice weekly seemed a manageable commitment for his father and aunt, who were willing to bring him despite some reservations.)

Donald was able to form a treatment relationship, although a prickly aggressive quality was characteristic of his mode of relating to me as it was to his teachers. The fear of closeness lay at the centre of his difficulties: it was a risk to love or be loved when both the inner and the outer world felt so precarious. This problem intensified around breaks in treatment and was coloured not only by the recent loss, but also by earlier repeated experiences of separation from both his parents. Furthermore, Donald had experienced marked fluctuations in his mother's capacity to care for him rather than been held in mind by a consistently responsive, available caretaker.

This account of Donald's treatment will show how his confusion, grief, and guilt over his mother's death were explored little by little, over time, often reappearing in different contexts, with different emphases, and were gradually worked through—or, where appropriate, accepted. In recognizing Donald's feelings, I served as a developmental object, enabling him to be aware of them himself. My helping him to bear his feelings facilitated the mourning process, enabling him to move on from the massive impact of his mother's loss. To do this, he had first to relinquish those aggressive defences against affectionate attachment which had been so reinforced at the time of mother's death. His struggles over attachment emerged within the relationship to me: I quickly became a transference object who would inevitably repudiate, reject, and abandon him, finally leaving him by dying, but Donald also sought in me a new developmental object, one who would accept and stay with him, and who could in the end survive both his anger and his love.

In our first session, it seemed important for me to say that we would spend time getting to know each other and that I would be around for a long, long time. In this response to his anxiety, I offered myself as a new object who would be unwaveringly "there". Such an approach contrasts with the classical approach, where it might be seen as a reassurance, blocking Donald's experience of anxiety within the transference. Given Donald's anxieties around attachment, however, it seems that it was precisely my creating a background of safety that provided the conditions in which the transference relationship could unfold.

At the end of his second session, Donald told me that his mother had died. Thereafter, there was much about his longing for mother and his fears that he had driven her away. He drew a train with a little boy in it going to Liverpool. He remembered being there with his mummy when he was 2 and being taken to a big shop with a magic grotto. In a following session, Donald made a magic wand. Asked what he would wish for with his wand, he wanted a kitten he could cuddle. I said that he had told me his mummy had died, and he might miss her cuddles. "I do", he replied, adding that she was in heaven and that he was going to make her a teddy bear. He described all the sewing that would need to be done. His aunt would take the bear to his mummy in heaven; he did not really know about heaven because he had not been to the graveyard. Momentarily overwhelmed by a sadness he could not express, he lay on the couch, saying he was tired. I said that sometimes, under the tiredness, he might have lots of sad and longing feelings that were very hard.

While still struggling with the loss of his mother, Donald knew that he would soon be leaving the warm familiarity of his nursery school and moving on to big school. A wish for safety and a sense of the precariousness of his life and attachments were evident. He asked me to draw some hearts, which he coloured in. As I drew, he said, "You are the apple of my eye". We both smiled, and I asked who had said that to him. It had been a friend of his mother's; Donald had liked him very much, but he did not see him a lot. When I remarked that this must be sad for him, Donald said that he was going to big school. I said it could be sad leaving people he liked and knew, and he agreed.

The hearts had been carefully coloured in, and he asked me to draw a baby one. I had to cut out the three big ones and the baby one, and he stuck them together. As we worked, I commented that Donald wanted to keep those he loved together. The little heart was firmly nestled between the big ones, which, according to Donald, represented Mummy, Daddy, and a friend. I said that the baby heart was kept very safe between the other ones and perhaps he sometimes wished he could feel that safe. Donald remained silent and then asked where I lived. When I took up his wish to know if I was nearby, he drew another little heart and gave it to me. I thanked him for it, remarking that maybe he was giving me a little piece of his heart and hoped I would look after it.

At the same time, Donald feared that as an anal, messy, poohy boy he had driven his mummy away, and that he might be unlovable. These fears would be played out increasingly in the transference. Donald needed to know whether I would still care for and keep him however messy he was. He drew a kitten with snot and pooh running out of its orifices, and he asked me to draw a cat with lots of little kittens. All had smiles on their faces, except for one, which he scribbled on, "the messy one". I verbalized that the messy one might be worried about not being loveable.

The concerns that Donald expressed within treatment were also being manifested in his school and home life. His nursery-school teacher told me that Donald had soiled himself twice in the nursery. He had spoken of missing his mother and hating his father. At home, he would crouch on the carpet and soil. There was certainly a provocative, aggressive component in the soiling, as well as an attempt to re-establish a relationship with a mothering object. It may also have been the result of a regression in the face of his many anxieties about past losses and the current imminent move to big school. With a good deal of support, father was able to handle these episodes sensitively and firmly, and they ceased fairly rapidly. That this was possible was due perhaps in part to treatment, in part to appropriate parental handling, and in great measure to Donald's own wish to enter his new school as a big (clean) boy.

It was not long before Donald realized that in many ways I was a disappointing person who never answered questions straight and was insufficiently, although consistently, available, while what he longed for was another mummy. Furthermore, I was given to saying things that he had absolutely no wish to hear. His highly ambivalent feelings were succinctly expressed when he asked me to make him a fortune-telling device. I was to write, "You are nice", "You are horrible", "I love you", and "Hello-and-good-bye".

His ambivalence, coupled with the impact of the loss of his mother, made for much anxiety and a sense of underlying desolation. During this period, he was restless and blinked a lot. One day, he brought a luridly coloured bear. It had a mechanical heart which lit up when pressed, while the bear played snatches of "There's No Place Like Home" and "Clementine". His attachment to the bear was clearly connected to feelings about his mother. Sitting very close to me, he said that he had dreamed of his mummy and that it had felt very real. I wondered if he had felt sad on waking, but it seemed that the dream was not so much a wish-fulfilment as a frightening drama in which he and Mummy were chased by monsters. Donald lay on the couch and demonstrated how the coffin-lid came down on them. I said how scary it must be to imagine that this was what had happened to Mummy and to feel that to be with Mummy meant that he, too, would be in a coffin.

In the fortnight leading to the first holiday break, Donald's underlying terror of separation and abandonment gathered apace. On the surface, he became increasingly angry with me. In a typical session he would be curled up under a chair, so that I could not see him, muttering, "Leave me alone". Or he attempted to defend against overwhelming feelings of being dropped and left by shouting that I was horrible and that coming to see me was boring.

At times, his feelings of being abandoned resulted in his testing me by putting himself somewhat at risk. Once, as he swung over the banisters, I caught hold of him, saying that I was going to keep him safe, noting how at times he could feel very unsafe. Donald shouted that I was not to handcuff him, and ran off, ending up in the small lobby between the hall and the front door. He informed me that this was his private place and I was to stay away. I agreed that I would not come into his private house unless he invited me in. I added that I knew he was angry with me because of the break and that he needed to know that I would not be angry back. Eventually, Donald was able to make his way to our room, where he used the furniture to make a house with an imaginary door that he could open and close. I noted how good it felt to be the one to decide who could come and visit, and he informed me that he would like a letter from "pooh-head". So I wrote saying that no matter how poohy and messy he felt, I was not going away for good, nor would I go away if he called me poohy and messy. Donald then offered to give me something if I opened my mouth: it was an imaginary piece of snot. I added that he was wanting to see if I would really accept a poohy, snotty Donald.

Donald made a house for himself and told me that mine was under the desk, next-door to his, and I took up his wish for me really to live close by so that despite the holiday we would not be far apart.

When we resumed in September, Donald's activities indicated that he had found the break hard and had had to cope with feelings of emotional starvation. He was compelled by an urge to glue and sellotape things together, which I took up as an expression of his need to find and secure a hold on me.

In a session soon after the break, he mumbled something about a little bird being hungry. It had not been fed because it said naughty things and poohed. I drew a bird, cut it out, and made it whisper into my ear. I said to Donald that the little bird was talking to the Viviane bird who wondered about these naughty things. Donald replied that it said things to grown-ups but did not mind if they got cross because it did not feel that it was a bad bird. I suggested that the bird perhaps pretended that he didn't care, but deep down, he did. I added that sometimes he believed he had made people go away. Donald then asked me to sellotape some things together, and I remarked that this was like making sure we would be securely tied together again.

Donald had many underlying questions about me. Was I reliable? Was I the same person as before the holiday? Did I really care for him? He was rather quiet, as if he needed to keep his distance in the face of all his uncertainties. In one session, as he sellotaped a penguin to a spaceship, he mumbled, "Oh pooh". I said that perhaps he felt that his mother had died and gone away because he was messy. Donald climbed onto the desk and said, "Mummy is dead, Daddy doesn't like me, aunty and uncle don't like me. I'm going to steal lots of stuff and money and buy things." He had poignantly described a movement away from the world of unreliable objects, with a concomitant sense of himself as unlovable, towards the consolation of inanimate things and food.

At the same time, there had been a quite striking move in terms of phase development. Whereas before the break his central concerns involved dyadic relationships, several of Donald's drawings now featured threes—three rainbows, three cars, etc. This betokened a beginning move to oedipal concerns which became more apparent over the following months. The timing of this move was interesting. Although this was his first overt step into oedipality in treatment, Donald may well have gained a foothold in the oedipal position prior to his mother's death. He would have wished to vanquish father and win mother. Yet he must also have been angered by his mother's inconsistency, and her death may have left him with a terrifying fear of what his death wishes could do to his objects. Certainly, it left him with the belief that loving feelings inevitably brought loss. All this may have curtailed any move towards resolution and forced a developmental retreat.

Donald's longing for a mummy and his wish to be my boy were now increasingly evident. His longing contained persisting elements of wishes for the pre-oedipal mother: in one session, he drew a boy, cut out the drawing, and asked me to write underneath, "Donald's boy for Viviane". I thanked him, remarking that it was as if I were being given the boy to look after and maybe Donald wanted me to look after him too. His oedipal wishes caused him great anxiety. He held on to his penis rather anxiously, while speaking of children who had girlfriends and boyfriends. I was at times subjected to phallic-like attacks: Donald prodded me and attempted to stick pins into my bottom. Castration fears and fears of damaging the other were quite prominent. Once when Donald was preoccupied with pencils being broken, I made a link to his fear that something might happen to his willy. Donald scoffed, but he did inform me that sometimes he had erections. It was then possible to say that there might be times when these made him worried.

After expressing the wish for closeness, Donald feared that I might die and he would be left. In one session, he drew a face which he covered with red squiggles, telling me it was spurting blood. He drew some bones and asked me if I knew what they looked like. He stabbed the drawing several times, saying, "Dead, dead, dead!" with much affect, then lay on the couch. I said that he was letting me know about his worries over what had happened to his mummy. "Yes, but I don't want to think about it", he replied firmly, and then he announced, "Pack-up time".

His anxieties became more overtly linked with sexual excitement and curiosity. Attempts to articulate his fears simply exacerbated his feeling of not being contained. I found it hard to know how to intervene in a way that did not increase his excitement and anxiety. There was much talk of "tits" and "bums". Periodically, the Lego box would go flying, or he would lie on the floor and scream if I so much as opened my mouth to speak. He became increasingly negative, and I found myself beginning to dread sessions and the obliterating onslaughts, but my continued presence in the face of these attacks and ability to survive them was living proof that Donald's worst fears had not come to pass.

This period marked a crucial point in his treatment. His earlier longings for his mother, now experienced in the transference, were inevitably linked with fears of abandonment and rejection, just as his mother had abandoned and rejected him, and fears that he might destroy me, just as he felt that he had destroyed his mother. In not abandoning or rejecting him, and perhaps above all, in surviving, I gave concrete proof that his transference expectations did not have to come to pass: in the relationship to me as a new object, he could discover the possibility of secure relating. In addition, within that relationship he could regain a level that he had only tentatively reached before, eventually negotiating oedipal conflicts directly in relation to me as the oedipal mother.

Meanwhile, this was a hard time for him. Alongside his libidinal wishes and fears were fantasies about the meaning of being dead and buried. His aunt took him to his mother's grave. Donald told me that the tombstone did not have her name on it yet. He explained that while the body is in the grave, the spirit goes to heaven. In one way, this explanation appeared to make sense to him, but a drawing of a little figure in a cage, unable to get out, suggested frightening thoughts of being trapped. And the notion of a spirit suggested the idea of ghosts. Donald drew a ghost in his cup, telling me that there were ghosts all around but they were friendly ones. We had to make masks and put them on. Donald switched off the lights, saying that we had to scare each other, actively trying to master his anxieties.

As we approached the second holiday, there was an intensification of his fear of losing me and being forgotten. He told me a joke: "Will you remember me in a week?"—I said I would. "Will you remember me in two weeks?"—I nodded. "Knock, knock." I duly replied, "Who's there?" "Doctor." "Doctor Who?" "Don't you know who I am? You said you would remember me." I linked this to his concern about whether I would remember him over Christmas. Donald stood very close to me. I said I would send him a card so he would know I was thinking about him, but his questioning "You will?" suggested that he was not wholly convinced. He was not able to say his customary good-bye as he left.

The concerns that Donald brought into treatment around the first and second holiday breaks gave a clear indication of developmental moves. At the time of the first break, he had been predominantly preoccupied with anal concerns, feeling abandoned as a messy, poohy child. By the second break, he had moved towards another developmental level. He had sought and found acceptance as a phallic boy, and his ongoing renegotiation of the oedipal phase was accompanied by some profound internal changes. He was increasingly able to mentalize, to think about and find verbal expression for his internal life.

On his return in the New Year, Donald said that his aunt had forgotten my name and referred to me as "thingy". Did I know the name of the caretaker, he asked? I said that he had done lots of thinking on whether people remembered each other and whether I would remember him despite our separation. In this and the next few sessions there were many games of hide-and-seek, which I linked to the separation and coming back together after the break.

Donald's concern over whether I would remember him was also connected with his own wish to remember his mummy. With great pleasure, he told me that he would be seeing a friend of his mummy's and they would make Plasticine models together, as they had done a few times when she was alive. He added that this would be a way of remembering his mummy. Memory seemed a way of keeping mother alive. Donald would sometimes remark that he looked like his mummy and once said that her spirit lived on in him. But to remember brought an acute longing for a replacement, and the idea of a replacement brought a renewed fear of loss. In one session, Donald wanted to know how old I was, and when I said "Old", he asked, "Does that mean you'll die soon?" I said that his mummy had been special to him and had died and perhaps he feared that if I was special I too would die. "Yes", was the unequivocal reply.

There was also a fear that his current oedipal strivings were dangerous. In play with the dolls, Donald tried to ensure that males and females were paired. If I tried to talk, he told me to shut up because it made him very angry. Whereas the oedipal wish usually involves the separation of the parental couple, Donald had already lost a member of the couple, hence his strong wish to keep the pairs bonded. In the end, I remarked that his dad was not part of a pair, and Donald could say that he might like a stepmother. When I took up his evident wish for me to marry his father and become his stepmother, he asked insistently if I had children, adding that he thought not. I said that he might be wondering if he could be special to me. This led to a rapid, loud protest, as he lay on the floor with much kicking and screaming.

Donald's search for love was allied to a worry about the feelings that threatened to overwhelm him. His brief verbal communications during this time were cryptic in the extreme, but the occasional mutter hinted at a preoccupation with body parts. Eventually, I remarked that he was telling me that he had some secrets and was not sure that he wanted to let me know them. "How did you know?", he asked. I told him that I was listening to what he said. Donald then made me a paper bracelet and tenderly slipped it over my hand, but shortly afterwards he hit me with a stick. I took up his wish to be special and kind to me, noting that this was all mixed up with his worrying thoughts about hurting me.

Oedipal wishes brought Donald's castration fears to the surface again. In the following session he sang, "Do your ears wobble and hang low?" My suggestion that boys might worry about their penises' wobbling and what could happen led to an outraged protest and a drawing of a large stupid me with huge hands, and a little angry Donald. I noted how hard it was to feel so small and angry next to this huge, dangerous lady.

From here on I was a horrible poohy lady whom he hated coming to see, and I had to take up his anxiety repeatedly. I was both threatening and unsatisfactory. Donald ensured that the whole clinic knew. He would leave our room and sit crouched by the radiator in the hall, plaintively saying, "I want something".

In one session when he managed to return to the room, we worked silently, drawing Mutant Hero Turtles. Eventually, Donald spoke sadly of his cat, Chippy, who had to be given away; and a family friend whom he had liked had died of a heart-attack. I pointed to a heart on his T-shirt and said that a little piece must have been hurt when these things happened. Donald replied that when his mother died the heart had a hole in its middle. He added that he would die because his heart did not work properly. This statement reflected his view that to grow was dangerous, if to reach adulthood meant dying.

As the first anniversary of his mother's death approached, he would attempt to climb on the window-sill. I would talk about remaining safe, whereupon he would run downstairs for a biscuit. Once, he attempted to open a locked cupboard, simply saying, "I want something". I said that he wanted something when he felt I could not give him what he needed. With much feeling, he said that he wanted his mummy and he wished his daddy had died instead. I acknowledged how hard and unfair it felt that he had lots of love to give his mummy and she was not there. In this phase, there was much splitting between his dead idealized mother and his denigrated father. Not only was daddy alive and mummy not, but daddy would not provide what was most wanted. Donald expressed all this graphically when he sang: "My daddy wouldn't buy me a bow–wow. I've got a little cat and I'm very fond of that, but I'd rather have a bow–wow–wow."

In the sessions prior to and following the third break (Easter), Donald became increasingly controlling. If I did anything slightly wrong, he would hurl abuse at me: "You stupid idiot!" Once, frustrated when neither of us was able to put a piece of Sellotape through a slot, he vented his rage by lying on the floor and shouting at me until he broke into bitter tears. He had frequent fluctuations of mood. We would be doing something together and then the next moment, without warning, he would burst into a rage. I felt I was treading on eggshells. At the last break, Donald's concern had been to know and test out whether I would remember him and whether I would be sufficiently invested in him to reclaim him. This third break saw a marked increase in his vulnerability and rage in the wake of his more conscious longing to be loved and his loving feelings.

Donald's father phoned me to say that Donald had been saying recently that he hated coming and felt that I did not really care for him. Shortly after this, I met with father. I tried to explain that Donald was now experiencing his worst fears of not being love-able, and I linked this to the disruptions in his early life, taking care to emphasize that now he was in a far more secure position. We talked about how father could explain to Donald that I was there to help him to understand his own feelings of hatred and his terror that he was not loveable. It was at this time that father openly voiced his own wish for a relationship and his anxieties about how best to manage this in a way that would not upset his son.

Whilst a terrified, aggressive, and frustrated negativity reigned in the treatment-room, outside it Donald was becoming relatively settled. His fears and longings were now concentrated within the transference and held in the therapeutic relationship, leaving him freer outside. Father continued to complain that at times Donald was hard to discipline and would fall into rages, but he was clearly no longer as exasperated as he had been. He also said that Donald seemed to be managing adequately at school.

Now when Donald continued to abuse me verbally and to say how much he hated coming, I consistently took up his wish to provoke me and his underlying fear that I would become tired of him and throw him out. But when I tried to talk, he would yell, "Shut up!" Eventually, I said that he often treated me horribly and called me names, and I wondered what that meant. I had figured that he was trying his hardest to make me dislike him, but deep down inside he really cared whether I liked him or not. I linked his wish to make me feel like rubbish to his underlying feelings of being worthless and in danger of being discarded, and it became more possible to address his feelings of distrust.

In this period, I also grew much firmer about what I allowed him to do in the treatment-room. I had to draw limits to safeguard a basic sense of safety. To have allowed Donald fully to enact his panic and rage in active destruction would have been to leave him in a state of disorganization with no internal possibility of reinstating containment. For this he still needed external support from me.

So the Lego box would be spirited out of the way before he could tip it up. I would repeatedly explain that doing just what he felt like doing left him feeling even more helpless and anxious. A typical session would have Donald calling me "Shit, shit, shit". I would take up both the provocation and his own feeling of being "shit". As the abuse continued, I would talk about his wanting to test me to see how far he could go and his fear that I would throw him out. On one such occasion, Donald answered: "But you won't throw me out." He then made a spaceship and threw it against the wall. I said that it was not a good idea for him to feel he could just keep throwing things, but that it did let me know how horrible and angry he felt inside when we talked about his fear of being thrown away. To my surprise, he responded by saying "Just one more time", and then he was able to stop.

During this period, there was another call from father, who clearly felt in need of a co-parent. He spoke of how Donald, if refused something, immediately felt unloved. I tried to support father in limit setting, suggesting ways in which he could explain to Donald that to be refused something material did not mean that Donald was unloved. "Incidentally", father remarked, "Donald has not objected to coming recently."

At the same time, father raised the question of how much longer Donald would need to come. Treatment, with all the attendant difficulties of arranging for Donald to be brought and fetched, and the small and slow changes, was beginning to feel burdensome. I said that whatever happened it was important that Donald work through this phase; he would need plenty of time to work towards an ending. Father, despite a degree of impatience to have done with the whole business, was nonetheless able to understand and accept this.

In the week leading up to our fourth break, Donald's hatred of me—the abandoning object—was fully vented, but he was able to make a shift towards tolerating his feelings. As usual, he told me to shut up and screamed that I was shit. I said that he was telling me how horrible he felt and was wondering if I was going to find him horrible too. I added that despite the fact that he was doing everything in his power to hate me, I wondered if he still wanted a postcard over the break. He nodded, and shortly after this drew he some noughts and crosses on his leg, representing hugs and kisses.

I said that I could see that he had lots of hugs and kisses to give and wanted some back, but sometimes he just felt hatred and then he worried that he would be hated back.

In the last session before the holiday, Donald was calm and contained. He noticed a small dictating machine and sang into it, "My daddy wouldn't buy me a bow–wow". I asked if he wanted a message. Donald nodded and lay close by me on the couch, covering up his ears. I wished him a good holiday, hoped that he would enjoy himself, and said that I would send him a card. Donald listened to the message with interest when it was played back. He told me to block my ears while he recorded a message. His message wished me a nice holiday and said that he would miss me. As I played it back, Donald giggled to cover his embarrassment. I remarked that it was a very big thing that he could let me know that he would miss me.

Treatment resumed in September. Donald did not protest at returning. Father again raised the question of termination. I was struck by the changes in Donald. He seemed altogether more able to manage himself. When frustrated in a task he would still mumble angrily or call me stupid, but he did not spiral into helpless rage. I would often remark on ways in which he had changed, and in this sense therapy acted as a support for his increased capacity to manage his affects. He related more easily, with less sense of outright hostility or prickly distrust. He felt somewhat safer in his attachments and had discovered the possibility of enjoyment. On our way downstairs, we passed a mirror. Several times I caught his eye in the mirror, and he would smile in silent complicity at this reflected picture of the two of us. Sometimes, with an easy, unexcited affection, he would take my hand and lead me into the room.

Donald still said he hated me and that I was a stupid idiot, but less vituperatively. He also said that he did not want to come any more, that there was not enough to do, that all we did was talk and it was boring. It was hard to disentangle how far this represented a continuing defensive rejection of me, which needed to be worked through, and how far it was a genuine wish. Certainly, father's wish for him to stop fed into Donald's reluctance to continue. I finally decided, given the overall altered affective balance, to agree that perhaps he was ready to stop. We talked of Christmas as a termination date, and I said that it was important that we say a proper good-bye and that he know that I would be here if ever he wanted to see me again. "Of course you will, you work here", replied the pragmatist. I expected a regression, a re-enactment of previous feelings at being left, but this did not occur. Perhaps Donald felt empowered by having been heard in his wish to stop coming. This might have been important for a child who, for much of his life, had been shunted from pillar to post.

But Donald continued to want to play hide-and-seek and then suddenly informed me that he did not want to stop. Asked why, he replied, "Where else can I play Robocop and do drawings and things?" I said I could see that he felt he would miss me and coming here. He lay on the couch, reiterating that he did not want to stop. I suggested he tell his dad, and father phoned to say that Donald wanted to continue. Father supposed that it had been more his own wish than Donald's that he stop. I was moved and intrigued by the developments, although it was not clear how far Donald's wish to continue represented a defence against fears of loss inevitably revived by our plan to finish, or how far the whole episode was a concrete expression of discarding and reclaiming the object in a passive into active defence.

Certainly, at this point Donald was able to move into a different type of relationship. An unashamed affection and, with it, a lessening of the intertwined aggression, became more and more evident. Always present, though, was the fear of a renewed loss. Donald announced that he might have a stepmother one day—but "It won't be you." He asked me, "Who is the first person to die—I don't mean in Jesus Christ's time, but you or me?" He decided: "You will probably die first, but not until I'm a teenager." I linked his question to his apprehension that feeling attached to me meant that he was in danger of something happening to me. I added that small children can feel that they have caused a parent to die. Donald told me that small children believe that a dead person will come alive again, but he knew that that was not true.

Donald decided that he wanted to continue until after Christmas, but thought that once a week would be enough and he would then be able to do other things after school. (This signalled a more secure foothold in latency.) It seemed important that he have a "weaning" period. I linked his wish to come once a week to our having a different sort of good-bye, when, instead of his being left abruptly, he could leave me, knowing that our ending was not a death.

In the final termination period, Donald made many drawings and we would develop stories to accompany them. The ghosts receded and their place was taken by figures towards whom one of the other characters would have very mixed feelings. Verbalization of this greater affective complexity interested him greatly. At school he was heard telling another child, "Maybe you can have a mixture of feelings". In sessions, I was taking up both his wish to be a bigger boy and leave me, and his sadness that we would be saying good-bye. His leaving was facilitated by father, who supported the idea that Donald could always come back to let me know how he was getting on.

The changes in Donald may be seen in the context of his developmental progress. He moved from a fantasy life coloured mainly by anal concerns, into the phallic and then the oedipal phase. At first he feared abandonment as a messy, poohy boy. His fantasies and related anxieties gradually moved into the oedipal realm where loving feelings were felt as dangerous. He experienced marked castration fears. At this stage, too, I was both a transference object and a new developmental object, the oedipal mother. The relationship to me enabled Donald to experience a phase that he had previously tentatively reached but from which he had had to retreat. I entered into Donald's developmental stream as someone with whom he could experience a different type of relationship with another outcome. Furthermore, I could survive and withstand the worst excesses of his fear and rage, and I could be loved, hated, and, finally, left in a different way. Donald's past could not be undone, but this new experience of secure relating could ultimately be internalized and new directions shaped.

Throughout Donald's treatment, I had to weave in and out of different types and levels of intervention. At times, my emphasis would be on links made to his past. At other times, I would remark on his feelings solely in relation to myself in the present. But whether I was interpreting with regard to the past, or reflecting with regard to the present, an important characteristic of my work with Donald was that much of it took place in displacement, through play and story telling. Through the medium of mutually created drawings and stories, a world of greater affective complexity, including mixed feelings, could gradually be delineated, verbalized, and elaborated. Finally, rather than intervene, I had to know when to leave well alone as Donald's appropriate forward development unfolded.

CHAPTER SEVEN

"Michael":
a journey from
the physical to the mental realm

Tessa Baradon

I n this chapter I discuss a particular aspect of the role of the analyst's mind in constructing the psychological world of the child patient.

The material is drawn from the case of "Michael" who, at 6 years of age, continued to express affect and ideas through his body and seemed blocked in his capacity for symbolic representation. The referral came from his headmistress, who regarded Michael as the "silliest boy in the school". He was unable to cope in the classroom or the playground and had no friends. Although his parents recognized some of his difficulties, throughout his treatment they remained conflicted about whether he needed help or had simply been born with a certain "character".

Michael was from an intact and closely knit family. His primary caretaker and attachment figure was the mother, whose investment in Michael was intense and highly ambivalent: an idealized closeness with him—gratifying but intrusive to both—alternated with rages in which loving ties were temporarily withdrawn, leaving him desolate and furious. At the age of 2 years, after his brother's birth, Michael was taken from his mother to spend three weeks with his father in their country of origin. In the parents' account, problems came to a head at this stage: thereafter, Michael remained a frightened, restless child, unable to separate or settle at nursery and school.

In the diagnostic interviews, I was struck by his enacted view of himself and his objects. On the one hand, he struck the pose of a rather grandiose, elderly European gentleman. He seemed to expect a shared omnipotence with me; for example, he presented himself as possessing magic (as he believed his mother did) and expected me to be able to read his mind. On the other hand, he presented at the Anna Freud Centre as an anal child who broke wind continuously, could not use the toilet, and wriggled his bottom to engage, excite, and provoke. His narcissistic neediness, which came across as an undiscriminating trust (in me, as in the receptionist he had just met), precluded an empathic acknowledgement of the other. There was a deficit of the ego functions expectable at his age, such as reality testing, the understanding of causality, and the capacity to use thought, language, and play in trial action.

Michael's analysis suggested that his confusing experiences of an adoring and raging mother had impinged on the process of self–other differentiation, so that often he did not distinguish between the contents of his mind and those of mother's. His experiences also seemed to have affected the construction of integrated and enduring representations of the mother and contributed to a split self representation wherein he experienced himself as both dangerously omnipotent and as a faecal mess. It is also possible that the abrupt loss of his caretakers and familiar environment at 2 years was beyond the toddler's capacity to mentalize—that is, to represent his own feelings and thoughts and those of others. He adapted by denying his longings and his panic, with an inhibition of the mental processes of thinking, linking, and explaining. The ability to give meaning to feeling states and behaviour brings structure and coherence to the child's internal world. Impaired as Michael was in this capacity, his inner world was characterized by chaos: boundaries were blurred, he was at the mercy of impulses, and his affect was largely unmodulated. All this increased his sense of confusion and fragmentation which was expressed in his behaviour and object relationships.

The analysis lasted only a year and a half, and was curtailed by Michael's parents' abrupt withdrawal of him when his functioning improved. During the analysis, there was a gradual move from the enactment of feelings and thoughts via his body to a capacity for mental representation. It was necessary for me to adapt the technique of the analysis to his level of mentalization. At first, interpretations of conflict, for example, aroused deep anxiety in Michael as he experienced my words rather concretely. At this stage, I spoke sparingly, focusing mainly on feelings and transactions in the here-and-now of the sessions. As Michael's mental processes developed, it became possible for me to use interpretations to address the inner confusion and Michael was able to use them, thus reducing his anxiety.

The following clinical material focuses on the relationship between *his* experience of himself and his objects and *my* experience and representations of him. I will attempt to highlight turning points in our interaction and show how these affected his processes of mentalization (Chapter 1).

Clinical material

The parents accepted Michael's need for analysis only some time after the assessment interviews, so the analysis did not begin until he was 7½ years old. In his early sessions, he engaged in numerous activities, in and out of the treatment room—all carried out with anxiety and excitement, and accompanied by outbursts of anger. He would often start with an attempt at structure through a board game, but quickly move to mess with Plasticine and glue. He would impulsively leave the room to tell the receptionist something incomprehensible, and then return in an equal rush to the treatment-room. This impulsiveness and rushing around seemed a physical expression of his lack of mental containment. Moreover, Michael seemed to expect me to lose him from my mind as he lost me from his, and it was his reinstatement in my mind, as much as his recovery of me, that seemed significant.

An immediate and strongly ambivalent transference was established. On the one hand, I was seen as a gratifying adult towards whom he was in turn trusting, cajoling, or bullying. Requesting that I provide the game of Monopoly, Michael stroked my cheek—"Please, please Tessa, can you get it?" But this relationship to me was non-discriminate: there was a category of objects called "ladies"—the receptionist, his escort, teachers, myself—to whom he turned to be soothed. On the other hand, when I did not produce the game, Michael would throw himself against the wall, head in hand, moaning "You make me so unhappy, you are not kind to me." I became the rejecting object, and he reacted with hate towards me. His over-familiarity in handling my body then took the form of hitting, spitting, screaming into my ear, or throwing himself at me.

My early response to Michael's neediness and anxiety was a maternal wish to comfort him. At the same time, I felt invaded, disregarded, and often anxious as the thrust and chaos in the sessions became overwhelming. For weeks, the theme of unsafety dominated the material and was expressed mainly in bodily terms. Michael was unable to go to the toilet until he was bursting, by which time the room was suffocatingly smelly. The sessions were frequently disrupted by violent tempers in which Michael lashed out at the frightening figure that I had become, partly because my attempts to consider and interpret his anxiety and rage were experienced as concrete attacks. Usually I could tolerate his uncontained outbursts, but at times, when his attacks were relentless, I felt as helpless as he did. Occasionally I tried to contain him physically, but this, too, was perceived as hostile, and he reacted with escalating attempts to prove that he was the stronger. In retrospect, I see that I was speaking to a mental capacity, a "part of his mind", that had not yet come into being—that of reflection.

A few months into treatment there was a session in which I was particularly provoked. I had to hold Michael's fists to stop him punching me. Michael went limp and sagged to the floor at my feet. At that moment, standing over him, I felt like the menacing bully of his fantasies, and I had a fleeting thought that I could manhandle this child. I was immediately shocked at the reaction Michael had managed to provoke in me, but mulling over the session later, I realized that in my attempts to contain the sessions I had been responding in a fragmented way to his chaotic behaviour. In doing so, I had lost any picture of the whole child. My interpretations were, therefore, less empathic and compassionate. I also understood that my thinking about Michael was losing ground to a "mindless" reactivity and that I was experiencing his violent, chaotic inner state. To counter this, and in order to contain the projections, I had to reinstate my own mental processes of reflection. For example, where I had found it difficult to remember the details of the sessions from one day to the next, I took a few moments to think about the previous session before collecting Michael from the waiting-room. In this way I was able to reconstruct a sense of continuity and to hold the child in mind—not only the little monster of recent months but also the vulnerabilities and pain that underpinned his outbursts. [Whereas with some patients it may be appropriate to come to a session without memory or desire (Bion, 1967), with patients like Michael who affect the analyst's capacity to remember and make links, I have found it necessary to prepare my mind, to remember.]

In parallel I adopted a change in technique. Since Michael seemed so confused and frightened by the contents of his mind and what he thought was in my mind, these became our focus. I acknowledged what I thought that he was feeling and the evidence on which I based my thinking. For example: "It seems to me that you are feeling upset now, because I can see you no longer want to play with the bricks." Sometimes I added what he may have thought I was feeling towards him: "Perhaps you think that I think you are a silly boy when the bricks fall down." Such "analyst-centred" interpretations, which recognize that the patient is more interested in what is going on in the analyst's mind than in his own (Steiner, 1994), seemed to allow Michael to feel understood and therefore more contained. Moreover, in my attempts to think and understand, I was doing for Michael what he could not do for himself. This created a holding environment, and gradually the outbursts were reduced.

For the first time, Michael began to use a toy as a vehicle for symbolic thinking, a mechanical duck which, when wound up, flapped around noisily. Michael delighted in activating this toy so that it would scamper precariously around the desk. For months, the duck served as the repository of Michael's awful feelings about himself as a messy, smelly, greedy "pooh". Our working through these concerns was bolstered by my ongoing demonstrations that I was prepared to stay with him—despite his smelliness—and to wait for him outside the toilet. We were also able to explore his representation of the denigrating, hating, abandoning other. When at some point later Michael expressed his wish to get inside me "to understand your systems", I responded to this as an expression of relative safety which enabled him to explore my feelings and thoughts about him, and I said to him that perhaps he was wanting to understand how I thought thoughts about him so that he could learn how to understand his thoughts about himself.

Gradually Michael was able to form some identification with my perception of him and his mental states and to incorporate this into his struggle between "big Michael"—no longer quite as omnipotent—and "little Michael"—no longer quite as debased and rejected. However, he could not be sure of the relationship between himself and the object. In part this was because of the distortion created by his inhibition of mentalization, and in part because of the distortion of fantasy and defence.

Our work increasingly focused on his ambivalence. In the first instance, I kept careful track for him of his alternating feelings towards me ("Yesterday you liked me, today you seem not to"), and through this Michael began to create an internal recognition of himself as holding an array of feelings towards me and towards others. Later I started to make the links between why he felt as he did on different occasions, introducing him to the concept of cause and effect. Pivotal to his anger and hatred were his feelings about separations—which, in his internal world, spelt hostile abandonment/destruction by the object. Noting his disruptive or withdrawn reactions to weekend breaks, I said that the very difficult question for him was how to remember that we were still friends when we did not meet. This introduced a piece of play that became a symbolic ritual of re-engagement.

The game of "Hot and Cold", whereby one partner leaves the room whilst the other hides something and then assists in its discovery through clues, was overdetermined for Michael and myself and pulled together many earlier threads of his analysis. Firstly there was the issue of one of us being outside the room. When I left the room, I had to trust that he would not wreck it, and hold on to the image of a child who could play as well as destroy. At first, I tensely monitored the noises of his movements behind the closed door, much as he listened out for reassuring noises of my presence in the corridor when I accompanied him to the toilet. For his part, it took some days before Michael could tolerate being the one to leave the room and wait outside: he was afraid that he would be left forever waiting in the corridor. As his reality testing improved and he grew more confident, I would be kept waiting for long minutes. I addressed symbolic meanings ("You want me to know how you feel when you have to wait for our session") but tended more to a playful guessing about what he was planning and doing—in essence, playing around, very simplistically, with thoughts.

Then there was the question of hiding places. Michael gradually used the game to explore my more hidden spaces, such as my desk drawers. Sometimes it was possible to address some instinctual wishes, particularly when these were put in terms of conflicts over growing up. When the game became over-exciting, with the pen thrust down my jumper, I had to go back to the setting of boundaries that differentiated his body, feelings, wishes, and thoughts from mine, before I could interpret Michael's fantasies.

Then came the game of "I Spy with my little Eye", through which we tackled the task of distinguishing between thought and reality. At first, Michael seemed confused between what was actually in our environment that both of us could "objectively" see, and the vivid thoughts that he had in his mind—for example, of a hamburger—which he seemed to expect me to be able to view with my inner eye. I spoke to him about the difference between what was in his mind and imagination, which I could know about only with his help, and what I could share with him through our seeing it together in the "outside" world. Later, Michael coined the term "I Spy with my little Thought" to distinguish the imagined from what he spied with his eye. In this way, we were also establishing an understanding of inner and outer worlds, and of that which is shared versus that which may be private.

Michael brought a variation on the Hot and Cold game whereby he hid a pen and left a trail of written clues to guide me in its discovery. In this, he was trying to anticipate how my mind would work, to find ways of pointing me in the direction he wanted, or to adjust his thinking to accommodate mine. There was an affective change in the transference as he experienced both privacy and mutuality. Consequently, breaks in the analysis became less fraught.

Although the analysis was progressing well, when Michael was under stress he would revert to provocation. Yet my inner responses to these provocative episodes were much changed. Of course, there were feelings of frustration or boredom—in the vein of "not again"—but on the whole my internal view of Michael remained consistent and integrated. For his part, Michael demonstrated a growing capacity to observe himself and me in relation to each other in a variety of moods, and to sustain a continuous sense of himself—still, in part, through my eyes—in differing feeling states. Consequently, there was a dramatic shift to more reality-anchored, latency-style activities such as playing chess and cards. Reports from home and school indicated similar gains in that Michael had established some close friendships, was part of the peer group, and was catching up on his school work. However, progress and regression depended in part on external circumstances.

Michael's parents viewed his progress favourably and decided to withdraw him from treatment—unfortunately, he knew about this long before I did. When I did, one of my main questions was whether enough capacity to mentalize had developed for Michael to sustain a sense of inner relatedness, so necessary for his psychological "capacity to be alone" (Winnicott, 1958). While I was now able to work with his anxiety about destroying the internal object with his rage, there was again a question as to how far he could use my consistent attention to uphold a view of himself.

I now present in more detail a session from the thirteenth month. It was the last session of a week in which two sessions had been cancelled (by mother and by me, as Michael and I had both been ill). Michael arrived ten minutes late and had a brief altercation with the receptionist before I fetched him from the waiting-room. After greeting him, I mentioned that we had not met for some time; he was in such a state of agitation that he almost fell down the stairs. Then he picked up the chess set from the top of the lockers in such a way that it half fell and was half thrown to the floor. The pieces scattered and the box was broken. Michael crawled under the couch to retrieve the pieces, and I stuck the box together. Our activities ran in parallel, and I was waiting to see how we would come together. Michael wanted to play chess. During the game, he was defensively bossy and controlling and easily felt put down. On the whole, my response was to be friendly and accommodating, and, in a limited way, I commented on what was going on at that moment. Initially, I did not verbalize the link between his behaviour and recent and future loss as I thought this would be intolerable and could provoke a counterproductive outburst. So we played, and while playing Michael passed wind. After the second time, he admitted doing so but denied that he needed the toilet, despite appearing in extreme discomfort. I then wondered whether he did not want to go to the toilet because of the horrible feeling that bits of him could get lost. Angrily, he retorted: "Of course not. You are stupid." After a pause, he asked: "Well, are you coming with me or not?"

I was again positioned in the corridor, and Michael left the toilet door ajar. While I waited for him my mind drifted. I was, I think, doing a mental checklist of my day in which Michael, of course, featured, but not as the sole focus of my preoccupation. After a few minutes I collected my thoughts and raised my eyes to check on him. I saw him peering at me from behind the toilet door. Obviously he had seen me deep in thought. I wondered whether he felt I had left him—dropped him from my mind—and I felt guilty about this and feared that he would regress. Yet I also thought that perhaps he would be able to tolerate my being with him in a more limited way. In the event, I did not offer an interpretation of abandonment but merely reflected what had occurred: "I was thinking and you were watching me." Then I added: "Perhaps you were wondering what I was thinking." Michael responded by throwing himself at me in a rough embrace.

The framework of this session was that of loss. Unable to mentalize when extremely anxious and upset, Michael's feelings about loss became concretized in the broken chess box, dispersed chess pieces, and his fear of bodily disintegration when defecating. The interaction in the corridor illustrates the shift from the physical to the mental realm in the expression of internal experience. Undoubtedly, my temporary lapse of concentration was overdetermined and contained some negativity—such as weariness and irritation at the resurgence of the "toilet monsters". Yet there was also the sense of a release of tension in that Michael had been able to use a therapeutic intervention and was safely ensconced in the toilet. I think my mental drifting had much in common with the mother of a toddler whose newly acquired toileting relieves her from peering into his nappy—that is, creates a space between them for separateness and independence—whilst he remains held in the framework of her mind. It is this that I was trying to convey to Michael when I chose to comment on his "watching me think" rather than interpreting his anxiety that I had forgotten him. It seems to me that he perceived a notion of being held in mind—that is, of not being lost forever in a void of anxiety and rage—and it was to this that he was responding with his tumbling embrace.

Discussion

Michael's tendency to collapse in the face of the unexpected highlights some of the key issues in his analysis. In the absence of a secure and differentiated sense of self, change threatened his sense of psychological continuity. His anxieties about abandonment and disintegration expressed the internal reality of a child whose mental process of self–other differentiation and consolidation was impaired. For this reason, the construction of the processes of mentalization lay in the interface between his internal world and mine, as it does between infant and mother in the normal course of development.

The developmental task of promoting the capacity for mentalization in Michael, before he could engage in a more interpretative style of analysis which relies on reflective and symbolic thinking, required a modification of analytic technique. What emerged as most productive was to verbalize for him the emotional resonance of our interactions in the here-and-now. The focus was on his emotional experience and my thinking about it, and his thinking about what he imagined my experience to be. In a sense, this mirrors the intersubjective interplay and communications of attunement between mother and infant in early development (Stern, 1985; Trevarthen, 1979), except that it was made conscious in order to contain the anxiety around hostility. In the process of establishing the "I think that you think that I think" (see, for example, Fonagy, Moran, & Target, 1993), Michael was introduced to the distinction between his mind and mine, and between external and internal realities—that is, real and imagined or pretend.

However, my ability to represent Michael for himself faltered under the onslaught of his defensive attacks, and for a while we were both lost in our unthinking responses. The main challenge in the countertransference was to resist the pressure to react "mindlessly" and to retain, from one session to the next, my own mental functions of reflecting, reasoning, and linking. My salvaging these from a collusion with his attacks and provocations facilitated a shift in my experience of being-with-Michael. A turning point in the analysis came with the restoration of my integrated and affectionate reality view of him. Thereafter, looking into my mind offered Michael a new experience of finding himself, whole and benign, in contrast to his infantile experience of looking into his mother's mind and finding either her preoccupation with herself or an unpredictable and split view of him. Through his experience of my subjective reality of him, Michael could gradually acquire the ability to construct a view of himself and his own mind which modified his mainly chaotic and frightening representations of himself and his objects. Rather than experiencing himself as faecally contaminated and helpless, enmeshed in devouring and attacking relationships with his objects, Michael came to see himself as separate, sometimes effective, and often likeable. With the developments of mentalization and representation, affects and ideas that were previously expressed by Michael through his body were translated from the physical to the symbolic realm. Language, play, playfulness, and humour came to take their rightful place, at least some of the time, in the expression of feelings, thoughts, wishes, beliefs.

Moreover, Michael's engagement with my affective attitudes towards him helped to transform his primitive self-experience into "reflective self-awareness" (Hobson, 1993, p. 215). The particular constellation of attitudes he evoked in me came into play with his evolving representation of me as a specific, differentiated, personal object—no longer one of the generalized "ladies" or the transference monster. In this context, the interaction in the corridor, in which there was a shift from inattentive to attentive in me, resonated with the understanding that one can be held generally, and then found specifically, in the other's mind.

Acknowledgements

My thanks to Professor Peter Fonagy, Audrey Gavshon, Anne-Marie Sandler, and Dr Mary Target for their comments and support.

PART III

Clinical and educational interventions in work with children

CHAPTER EIGHT

"Maya":
the interplay of nursery education and analysis in restoring a child to the path of normal development

Marie Zaphiriou Woods & Anat Gedulter-Trieman

T his chapter shows how education and analysis can work together to promote children's development. In exploring the border between therapy and education, Edgcumbe (1975) defines education as "the contribution of the environment to the development and maturation of the individual's personality, capacities, skills, and talents" (p. 133). While acknowledging that children's parents are their first and most important educators, she highlights the essential contribution of teachers, particularly in the areas of learning and socialization. A good teacher may provide a unique opportunity to form new and different relationships, with wide-reaching implications for development in all areas of the personality, especially for children from isolated and troubled families. Similarly, one of us [MZW] has shown how "Nursery provision . . . can encourage body management, enhance self-esteem, improve relationships, stimulate speech development and intellectual functioning in general, and so facilitate adjustment to the community at large" (Zaphiriou Woods, 1988, p. 295). Under-5s are particularly amenable to a teacher's influence because "their personalities are still in the early stages of structuring. At this age, benign external influences can contribute to the growth of positive self and object representations which can modify or counterbalance the pre-existing structures arising from less than satisfactory early experiences" (p. 295).

At the Anna Freud Centre Nursery, children are regularly observed and discussed, so that the range of experience provided by the nursery can be adjusted as sensitively as possible to their individual requirements. This is good educational practice informed by a psychoanalytic understanding of children's developmental needs. Many children respond to such fine-tuned care by spontaneously making up the developmental delays and distortions with which they came to the nursery. Some, however, manifest continuing difficulties, which may require additional sorts of intervention. These may range from work with the parents (another way in which the child's environment can be modified in that the parents' relationship with their children alters as they develop new ways of thinking about and understanding them) to intensive analytic help for the child, addressing internalized conflicts and developmental needs that cannot be met within the nursery setting.

"Maya" joined the nursery at the age of 3 years. Her father had died in an accident two years earlier, and her mother, a Spanish immigrant, desperately needed to return to work to provide for herself and her daughter. In the months following Maya's entry into the nursery, we became increasingly concerned about her development. She was impulsive, confused, aggressive to her peers, and had considerable difficulties in learning. Her language development was poor, and an assessment by a community speech therapist suggested a "mild to moderate" learning disability. While such a diagnosis certainly fitted with Maya's inaccessibility to the nursery's educational efforts, our observations suggested that her uneven development and cognitive difficulties were emotional rather than constitutional in origin. Exploratory talks with the mother were followed by a full diagnostic assessment which confirmed our suspicions. Analysis was recommended for the child, supplemented by weekly meetings with the mother.

Maya was in analysis for just sixteen months, during which time her behaviour and functioning greatly improved and she successfully negotiated the transition to primary school.

Historical context

Anna Freud always saw education and therapy as playing complementary roles. Her training as a teacher, and her experience in
caring for young children in difficult and deprived circumstances
during the First World War in Vienna, preceded her training as a
psychoanalyst. She treated her first child analytic cases in the
1920s. Her recognition that the immature superego was less structuralized and autonomous than the adult's, and that children were
therefore more amenable to environmental influence, led to a series
of psychoanalytically informed educational experiments and an
early emphasis on work with parents (see Young-Bruehl, 1988).

The Anna Freud Centre Nursery continues many traditions
started in the Jackson Nursery in Vienna in the late 1930s, and the
Hampstead War Nurseries in England during the Second World
War. In these earlier ventures, Anna Freud was already responding to the urgent needs of children growing up in disadvantaged
circumstances. She began the practice of using meticulous daily
observations to supplement psychoanalytic reconstruction as a
way of learning about early emotional development, modifying
theory and practice in accordance with her findings. For instance,
she found that when helping the child to separate from the mother,
to arrange for a gradual separation and to proffer substitute figures
brought great psychological and educational advantages (Freud &
Burlingham, 1943). Freud and Burlingham's care and study of
young children separated from their parents in wartime is of particular relevance to the case of Maya. Indeed, our observations of
her behaviour during her first months in the nursery bear a remarkable resemblance to the observations of 1- and 2-year-olds in
the Hampstead War Nurseries (Burlingham & Freud, 1944, particularly observations in Chapter II regarding such children's aggressive, jealous, and envious relationship to the other children, in
Chapter III regarding their strong possessive attachment to the
mother substitute, and in Chapter V regarding their denial of the
father's death). As we were to discover, Maya, like them, had been
subjected to unassimilable separations and losses.

The Hampstead Nursery School, now The Anna Freud Centre
Nursery, was set up in 1957. From 1966, its aim became "to serve

the children of under-privileged and disadvantaged families and to enquire into the reasons for their frequent failure to adapt, first to school, and later to the wider social community" (A. Freud, 1975, p. 127). The task of the nursery school was: "To fill the gaps left in the parental care, irrespective of whether these omissions were in the area of physical nurture, affectionate support or mental stimulation" (p. 128). In the same paper, Anna Freud wrote: "When the child's failures or distortions of development are so massive that they do not respond to the educational efforts of the nursery school, the therapeutic service of the Clinic is ready to take over and to provide child guidance, or mother guidance or child analytic treatment" (p. 132).

In the course of the 1960s and 1970s, diagnostic and developmental issues were increasingly refined. The diagnostic profile and developmental lines, formulated in 1962 and 1963, respectively, made it possible to assess children's development as dependent on the interaction of three factors: "endowment; environment; rate of structuralization and maturation within the personality" (A. Freud, 1976). It was recognized that the effects of any modification in the environment would be limited by the child's endowment and the extent to which difficulties had become internalized and structuralized.

Accordingly, when Maya was unable to make good the delays in development with which she arrived in the nursery, her developmental difficulties could be seen as rooted either in some sort of constitutional impairment (i.e. endowment) or in early emotional experiences whose impact on structuralization (i.e. ego and superego development and the building up of self and object representations) affected her capacity to make use of the educational provision. Careful monitoring within the nursery and the subsequent diagnostic assessment were crucial in ensuring that Maya (and her mother) received the help they needed.

Observations from the nursery: the referral

Maya began to visit the nursery with her mother in the months leading up to her third birthday. Maya was large and rather clumsy, but she had a beautiful and frequent smile. Her mother, Mrs A, impressed the nursery staff with her calm intelligence and her straightforward account of Mr A's tragic accident. She said that Maya remembered her father because they often looked at photographs showing him with her as a baby. However, she never showed her own feelings about father to Maya.

From the first visit, Mrs A was unequivocal in her support and encouragement of Maya's involvement with the adults and children and the activities on offer in the nursery. Maya responded shyly but good-naturedly; for instance, when the teacher taught her the names of the colours, she obligingly and smilingly repeated them. Generally, she spoke in broken Spanish interspersed with some English words. Fortunately, both teachers understood Spanish and so could clarify her communications.

Maya's gradual introduction to the nursery facilitated a smooth separation. When Mrs A began to leave her for brief periods, Maya protested briefly, but she easily accepted comfort and reassurance from her already familiar teachers. Within a fortnight, she was spending the whole day in the nursery without her mother. She seemed to be revelling in her new relationships with adults and children alike. When one teacher put this into words for her, saying, "I think you really like Nursery", she emphatically agreed: "Yes, boy [s]chool and girl [s]chool". She played with both girls and boys, fearlessly joining in with the older boys' rough play, where her substantial weight and strength were both an advantage and a disadvantage, in that crying children began to complain that she had hurt them by pushing, hitting, and kicking. Maya seemed blank and uncomprehending after these incidents, unable to say what had happened or to respond to the teacher's verbalizations, explanations, and admonishments.

At this point, we were hopeful that Maya's delay in socialization and lack of understanding would be spontaneously made up in the nursery as she became used to the company of other children and began to speak better English. Since she could also be gentle, polite, affectionate, and empathically caring—for instance, on more than one occasion fetching a tissue when she heard a child crying—we were not overly concerned. Rather, the teachers concentrated on building up a warm relationship with her and stimulating her language development. To reduce any confusion resulting from her bilingualism, they advised her mother to speak only Spanish to her, while at nursery they spoke only English. A voluntary helper was enlisted to work individually with her twice a week in order to stimulate her language and play, and to mediate between her and the other children.

The hoped-for improvements in Maya at the nursery did not take place. She regularly rejected and even attacked her helper, becoming frustrated and frustrating in any learning situation. There was a little progress in her language development, and her relationships with her peers deteriorated. After the settling-in period, there are few observations of her being gentle or caring to the other children; rather, frequent mention is made of her loud voice ("raw, harsh"), her unclear speech, her noisy play, and her "forceful", "stubborn", and "toddler-like" behaviour. Although Maya was capable of organized, absorbed play on her own (with dolls, dressing up, "reading" books), many comments show her to have been much "like a bull in a china shop", desperate to be included in the other children's games and activities, inadvertently stepping on their legs, knocking them off their chairs, oblivious to their spoken and unspoken communications, and unable to express clearly her own wishes and feelings.

In one observation, she places an imaginary baby in a pram and proudly draws attention to it, pointing and saying "Baby". The adults acknowledge the communication, but the children misinterpret it as a request that they get into the pram and play baby. They feel put upon and reject her, saying "No", pushing her and the pram away. Maya looks confused, pauses, and then persists, until one child briefly gets into the pram only to then play at being the baby running away from her mother. Maya enters the game, becoming the angry mother, hand on hip, leg bent at the knee, ordering her back. The other child loses interest.

This pattern becomes typical: Maya is often the outsider, playing on her own. One child tells her that another child is not her friend—"She hates you, everybody hates you." Maya looks bewildered, upset, shakes her head, and leans forward. She struggles unsuccessfully to say something, and the child continues, "I hate you too. I'm not your friend." The teacher intervenes, but the child gets in one final dig: "My mother says she doesn't like that girl Maya either."

Maya is frequently picked on by the other children, becoming the helpless victim for whom the adults must speak up. At times, she resorts to the only weapon she has and retaliates physically, again requiring adult intervention. At other times, she is the unprovoked aggressor, attacking suddenly and furtively, snatching, pushing, biting, pulling hair. After these incidents, she is usually speechless, dull-looking, sullen, occasionally openly defiant. On one rare occasion, when she manages to admit responsibility, saying, "Yes I bite her, I angry", she is misunderstood as saying "I hungry", and again thrown into confusion.

Being misunderstood and rejected and, in turn, misunderstanding and attacking, seemed part of Maya's daily experience of nursery, and we began to think about this repeating pattern as a communication about her inner world.

Her relationship to adults gave us further clues. She was in fact, "hungry" for adult attention, frequently sidling up to visitors and observers, sometimes even organizing them into age-appropriate play (e.g. a tea party). With her teachers, she was loving and extremely needy of physical affection. Despite her trying behaviour, they remained remarkably positive towards her, striving to satisfy her emotional needs while moderating her envious competitiveness—for example, at the lunch table when she found it hard to wait for her turn, or when she claimed one teacher's lap as soon as she saw that another child had claimed the other's. Repeatedly, they tried to help her to verbalize her feelings and wishes before acting on them. Maya seemed too frustrated, blocked, and conflicted to use such developmental help within the nursery. Instead, the negative side of her ambivalence occasionally burst out, even towards her teachers, in shows of affection that became heavy-handed and intrusive. On one occasion, she physically attacked and threatened a female observer whose only crime, as far as we could see, was that she had replaced a previous observer with whom Maya had struck up a brief friendship. Generally, the observers felt saddened and concerned rather than annoyed by her disruptive, unpredictable behaviour, which suggested that it had to do with threatened loss rather than deliberate provocation. It seemed that since the separation from her mother in the nursery, Maya had been struggling to manage the aggression and anxiety that at times quite overwhelmed her.

Two further observations are relevant here. She became panic-stricken when her foot got caught on the lowest rung of the climbing frame, screaming until a teacher came to her assistance and then appearing dazed and staring for a period until she gradually recovered. A few days later, she watched intently the general consternation when a new little girl was knocked over in the playground. She turned around and fell smack on her face, hurting herself and needing comforting.

We began to suspect that Maya's disorganization and panic indicated a "general sensitivity to traumatization" (Furman, 1986), stemming from her early unprocessed loss. Certainly, as soon as her command of English improved even slightly, she revealed her preoccupation with her father, whom she presented as very much alive. She announced that Daddy was waiting for her in the park, or driving the car. When confronted with reality by another child—"You don't have a Dad"—Maya ignored her. It seemed that Mrs A's religious beliefs (that his spirit was watching from the sky) and her need to keep father alive (through daily prayers and looking at photos) were playing into Maya's denial and confusion. In an informal contact with the nursery consultant [MZW], Mrs A was able to think of ways of addressing Maya's confusion and helping her to understand the painful reality of father's death. Some weeks after this, a little boy played dead in the nursery; Maya became quiet, clearly very anxious, speechlessly pointing him out to the teacher, who explained that he was only pretending. A few days later, she announced at group time: "My Daddy ha muerto and Mummy's coming." Whenever she heard the other children speaking of their parents, she loudly reassured herself: "I've got a Mummy."

In a subsequent conversation with the nursery consultant, Mrs A reported Maya's continuing confusion regarding the loss of her father. She repeatedly asked her mother, "But didn't he love me?" and "Do you love me?" In the face of such anxiety, it was not surprising that Mrs A reported that Maya was very good at home ("like a lamb"), contrasting this with her contrariness in all group situations. However, she often had nightmares, and her Spanish was actually poorer than her English. Mrs A readily accepted the nursery consultant's recommendation that Maya have an assessment with a view to analysis.

Maya's history

Maya's parents had been childless for some years before they came to England to work. Mrs A's pregnancy was therefore a surprise. Mr A, a warm, caring man, was particularly delighted and became closely involved in Maya's care from the beginning. Since he did shift work, he was often available to take over while Mrs A did her part-time secretarial job.

Despite a difficult labour and birth, Maya was a calm, happy baby. She moved from the breast to bottles and solids with no apparent difficulties, and slept well. She began crawling at 8 months and at 1 year was beginning to walk with help. It was at this point that Mr A had a serious accident at work. He was hospitalized and died some weeks later. During this period, Maya lost not only her father, but also to some extent her mother, who left her crying and protesting in the care of people with whom she was often unfamiliar, while Mrs A divided her time between hospital visits and work. She then took Maya to Spain to bury Mr A. Maya was very unsettled in this strange environment; she became acutely ill on the way home in the aeroplane and had to be hospitalized.

Back in London, Maya "lost interest" in crawling and walking and regressed to bottom-shuffling. She developed nightmares, needing to sleep in mother's bed. She could not bear to let mother out of her sight, clinging and crying inconsolably. These separation difficulties continued until the successful transition to nursery. However, toilet training proceeded without problems and was completed before Maya began walking again, at the age of 2 years. According to her mother, Maya was "disgusted" by her faeces.

At the time of the referral, Maya was independent and competent regarding her own bodily care, going to the toilet on her own, washing her hands and bathing herself. She enjoyed domestic tasks with her mother, such as cooking and cleaning. However, Mrs A was concerned about her eyesight, speech, and hearing and took her to see a series of specialists. She also took her to ballet classes to correct her clumsiness. A sight test showed that Maya was severely astigmatic, and she was prescribed glasses. The speech therapist, who had suggested that Maya had a mild to moderate learning disability, said that she could comprehend only one new concept at a time: "She cannot be bombarded with too much new information." He recommended a hearing test. We too had been concerned about Maya's hearing, but the test revealed that she could hear very well. This last result gave weight to our view that emotional trauma—*not* constitutional impairment—lay behind Maya's uneven development.

Diagnostic assessment

In the assessment interviews, Maya, aged 3½ years, was at her most friendly, cheerful, and responsive, obligingly performing the successive tasks of the psychological test, and carefully observing the gestures of the diagnostician in order to imitate them exactly. Despite her poor English, she performed within the average range in the intelligence test. However, the unstructured diagnostic interviews were more threatening, and Maya could not maintain her self-confident front; she rushed to the toilet three times in the first interview and visibly struggled to keep her preoccupations and conflicts at bay.

For the whole of the first interview, she managed not to touch the little daddy doll despite staring intently at him. She maintained that all the toy animals were friendly, though one in particular was found "yucky" and treated with some disgust. She drew a series of sad pictures (a man and successive girls), threatening that she would "tell mummy" when the diagnostician verbalized that the girl was sad. She claimed that the mummy was well and that everyone was happy. In a second interview, two days later, she could no longer conceal her intense preoccupation with her father. Although she initially described the father doll as a "silly daddy", he was cold and hungry and she ministered tenderly to all his physical needs, finally putting him to bed, with his arm hugging the little girl figure. She said, "My daddy, my daddy". After this he became "naughty", locking the girl in the cupboard and getting into trouble with the mummy and the grandparents. In her subsequent drawings, daddy was "not better" while mummy was "better".

Putting together all we knew about Maya, the diagnostician concluded that anal sadistic features dominated the picture, and that Maya's attempts at reaction formation, splitting, denial, and repression were not successful. Although the relationship with mother (and most adults) was kept uniformly positive, her aggression erupted in relation to her peers (and in her nightmares). The father representation was very ambivalently cathected, perhaps carrying some of the negative feelings that she dared not express in relation to her mother. Her fear of loss of the object and the object's love was extreme, and superego precursors had a punitive quality. Maya found herself in acute conflict between her unacceptable impulses and feelings on the one side, and total prohibition (external and internalized) on the other. It seemed safer to concentrate on pleasing her adult objects and not to think too much, with serious consequences for her language and cognitive development.

It was felt that analysis was required to help Maya to resolve her conflicts and to make up the delays and distortions in her development. Her mother also needed to be seen, because her intolerance of her own affective life, her difficulty in mourning her dead husband, and her externalizations onto Maya were interfering with Maya's development.

Work with mother

The analyst's weekly meetings with Mrs A revealed that the extremely high standards that she set for herself and her daughter were especially daunting because of her religious conviction that one was punished not just for one's actions but also for one's thoughts and feelings. With help, Mrs A was able to moderate her standards regarding Maya's eating, sleeping, anality, and achievements. Slowly, she was able to own her terrible disappointment in what she saw as Maya's social, physical, and academic failure and then to recognize her externalization of unwanted aspects of herself onto her daughter. She was also able to see that she wanted Maya to prove her to be a good mother and to deny any difficulties in their relationship. It was a while before she could trust the therapist enough to give a picture of its tense unhappy aspects: Maya did not listen and was extremely demanding, constantly interrupting Mrs A's attempts to work or, very occasionally, to see friends in the evening. Mrs A tried to satisfy Maya but felt trapped, and their interactions lacked pleasure.

The absence of a partner increased Mrs A's burden of responsibility for looking after Maya. Mrs A tried to ensure that Maya did not feel that anything was missing and could not tolerate any signs of loss or pain in her daughter. Once, when Maya was staring at a family (mother, father, and daughter) in church, Mrs A turned Maya's face to the priest, saying "If you don't listen, you won't be able to answer the priest's questions".

Mrs A gradually became able to talk of her painful sense of loss, envy, and unfairness. Once able to be in touch with these feelings, she could begin to understand and tolerate them in her daughter.

The analysis

The permissiveness of the analytic setting evoked a mixture of excitement, pleasure, and fear in Maya. Her anal aggressive wishes to mess and destroy erupted, conflicting with her internalized demands to be good, polite, and gentle. She explored the limits of what was allowed, throwing toys all over the room, messing with glue, and trying out forbidden things—for example, she was clear about "Don't stick your tongue out", but did so. She viciously tore apart a crayon box, telling herself, "Be gentle, be gentle". When she played with the little daddy doll, he was harshly punished and locked in the cupboard, and then he in turn meted out similar treatment to the little girl. The daddy and girl had "naughty", "baddie" roles, while the mummy doll and a toy lion were "good", albeit punitive.

Within a fortnight, Maya's toy box had become so messy that it was hard to find anything or even to fit it back in her locker at the end of sessions. Maya then refused to go upstairs to the consulting-room. She adopted a large teddy bear, Sally, from the waiting-room and sat on the stairs chatting incomprehensibly to her. When, after some two weeks, I [AG-T] verbalized her fear of uncontained mess and suggested that we tidy up her messy box together, Maya came upstairs again, but play was limited to putting everything back in its place.

Sorting the box was not enough, and Maya again refused to go to the consulting-room. I asked Sally–bear why she did not like to go upstairs. After an exchange with Sally, Maya explained: there was a lion in the room who wanted to punish the little girl; she was messy and nobody wanted her. I asked Maya to promise Sally that she was not about to punish the little girl for being messy, nor was she going to leave her for that. Maya explained this to Sally and asked me to repeat it "because Sally didn't understand". After I had said it again, Maya stood up and asked to go to the room, "Because you stay".

Over the next few months I experienced in the counter-transference Maya's intolerable feelings of helplessness and being in the dark, not knowing and not understanding. Maya totally excluded me, "reading" books to herself and chatting incomprehensibly. When I spoke, she pretended not to hear or commanded me to shut up. She was bossy and controlling, telling me what I should and shouldn't do. The list of prohibitions was endless: nothing was right.

In one session, I verbalized my own feelings of puzzlement and confusion. Maya looked triumphant as if finally *her* feelings could be labelled and understood. Using the books that Maya was looking at, which all contained stories of danger and rescue, I spoke of the characters' fear and helplessness. Maya listened carefully but told me to shut up when I spoke of their anger. After one such session, Maya slowly dragged herself on her bottom all the way downstairs. It seemed that she was re-enacting the traumatic period around the time of her father's illness and death, when she could not make sense of what was going on and no one was there to understand or listen to her, a period that culminated in her refusal to walk.

Gradually, Maya began to include me in the widening range of fantasy games that had become her main mode of communication. However, these too aroused conflict because the boundary between fantasy and reality was not established; "pretend" mode swiftly shifted to "psychic equivalent mode" (Fonagy & Target, 1996). Unbearable thoughts, frightening feelings, and unacceptable wishes could all magically come true and were not permitted even in play.

A split had to be made: Maya introduced a witch to carry her unacceptable feelings and wishes. Like her, the witch was jealous and possessive; she tried to harm Maya and the therapist and to spoil their games. The witch was also a punitive figure who wanted to kill Maya because she was a naughty girl. Maya turned into a helpless, sweet pussycat seeking my protection. I had to tell the witch that Maya was a sweet little girl, not a naughty, greedy, ugly one.

Maya's loyalty conflict intensified as the witch increasingly came to represent her mother and became the object of Maya's anger and death wishes. The witch deserved to be shot because she said that the little girl was bad and naughty. Maya became terrified that her expressed wishes and thoughts could come true and actually kill her mother, but she also feared that her mother would realize her growing attachment to me and so abandon her. In a desperate attempt at avoidance and concealment, she adamantly refused to come to the two early morning sessions to which mother brought her. She told mother that I hit her, shouted at her, and made her ears ache. A temporary solution was found until the loyalty conflict could be fully addressed: Mrs A left Maya in the nursery and the nursery teacher brought her to these sessions as well as to the midday ones. Without her mother, Maya greeted me with her usual big smile.

For months, Maya's fear that her omnipotent thoughts and wishes could come true dominated the analytic work. She directed mother-and-daughter games in which the roles were reversed: I had to be the girl clinging to her fed-up mother. I talked about her wish to control her mummy's feelings and her fear of rejection and loss when she and mummy were angry with each other. In the girl role, I repeatedly spoke about how lucky I was that my thoughts and feelings were not magic, could not come true, and were there-fore not dangerous.

Having lost one parent, Maya was of course terrified of losing her one remaining parent—her mother. One day, looking at a book about big animals eating smaller ones, Maya listed the people she could eat when she was cross with them. She added "Mummy too" and then panicked: "But then I won't have a daddy and a mummy." In time, she was able to tell me that she wanted to kill me, "but only here" (pointing to her head) "and here" (pointing to her heart), laughing with relief that feelings were only feelings and did not lead to the rejection, retaliation, and loss that she had always dreaded. It became increasingly possible to allow bad witchy feelings into our discourse and for me to link them to how bad the witch was feeling inside.

Maya's low self-esteem and damaged body image became a focus of the analytic work. Maya, as mummy, took me, the little girl, to see the doctor. Nothing was right. The girl needed glasses, her fingers were burnt, her hearing had to be tested, her speech needed to improve. Most important of all, the doctor had carefully to examine her head and heart to make sure that her thoughts and feelings were all right. I was often put in the role of doctor provid-ing the little girl with exclusive care and absolute cure; however, the little girl was not reassured and was often in pain as if needing punishment.

Maya's masturbation conflict emerged along with her fantasy that she had damaged her body (and lost her penis) and caused the death of her father. Her envy re-emerged in relation to the nursery children who had everything (a daddy, good eyes, a penis) and in the transference: the cat scratched my eyes, and the witch wanted to cut my hair and take my goodies. As these issues were worked on, there was a noticeable reduction in Maya's aggressive behav-iour in the nursery.

Maya's sense of damage and lack played into her learning dif-ficulties, and her mother became increasingly angry as well as concerned. She complained that she had tried "hundreds of times" to teach Maya to count 1, 2, 3, but she seemed unable to. I noted that Maya tended to count 5, 6, 8, 9, 10—but never 1, 2, 3. One day, Maya was staring out of the window and described a family who lived across the road—a mummy, a daddy, and a girl. I counted the three people (1, 2, 3), and Maya repeated this. On her return from the long summer break, she was happily counting 1, 2, 3.

The long summer break brought separation issues to the fore. Maya feared to lose and be lost by me, as she once had lost her father—and her mother, who had also "disappeared" and "forgotten" her during that terrible early period. Losing and finding became a theme in the analysis, and Maya took away with her a Playdoh egg to remind her of me. She managed to lose it on the plane to Spain, saying on her return that a nice man ("somebody else's daddy") had found it for her. Weekend breaks became very difficult, and one Monday she announced that she had lost her baby doll for the weekend. She turned passive into active, becoming very controlling; she refused to leave the room at the end of Friday's session and tried to reorganize sessions so that she could come on Saturday. When she was thwarted, her anger broke out: she kicked and shouted "I don't need you", "I don't love you", but then had to "make up" before leaving, flying around like a fairy to regain my love and admiration.

Maya's fear of abandonment was aggravated by her very low self-esteem, and this in turn was fed by her anal and masturbation conflicts. She felt herself to be so ugly, smelly, and disgusting that she could not be loved or kept in anyone's mind. Desperately, she externalized unwanted aspects of herself: the baby doll was smelly and "pooh–pooh", and my book was dirty and messy while hers was nice and clean. However, she remained deeply ashamed and humiliated both about her pooh–pooh thoughts and feelings and her actual faeces. For a period, I was called upon to show my acceptance of the latter by accompanying her to the toilet when she defecated, and gradually we were able to work through the conflicts that played into her denigrated self-image. As Maya became more positive about her feminine identity and self-image, she drew for the first time a beautiful, detailed picture of a woman's face.

At the end of that week, Maya refused to leave the room. I linked her difficulties in leaving to the coming weekend and then opened the door. Maya took a few steps out of the room and then asked if we could go back for just a second. We returned to the room, and Maya kissed the wall behind my chair. I suggested that maybe she could keep the room in her mind for the next few days. Maya's eyes lit up. She said, as if discovering something exciting, "Yes, I could keep the *room* in my mind. . . [*pointing to her head*] and I could keep *you* in my mind." After a few more steps, she stopped and added: "And you could keep me in your mind."

These steps towards mentalization were accompanied by greater object constancy and enabled Maya to deal with an important new step in her life: leaving nursery and starting at primary school. Maya's fantasies and fears about the forthcoming change became central in our work. With my help, she made a Plasticine school and some figures. She called one of them "Maya"—"not me, a pretend one"—and then stuck spots on her, altering the name to "Spotty Maya". Spotty Maya was an aggressive, greedy, and bossy little girl. Nobody wanted to be her friend. Rejections led to an escalation of her rough, demanding behaviour. Maya comforted her spotty counterpart: "Don't worry, I still like you." In time, I could verbalize that when Spotty Maya felt helpless and didn't know what was going to happen, she regressed to becoming bossy, rough, and controlling, alienating her peers in anticipation of their feared rejection of her. With the aid of her new, more benign introjects and nascent reflective self, Maya was able to help Spotty Maya to understand her feelings and to find more adaptive ways of relating to her peers.

There were, in fact, dramatic improvements in Maya's peer relationships during her last weeks at nursery. Observations show her able to share her toys and to cooperate in imaginary play. She was kind and gentle to the younger children. Her teachers supported these progressive moves, adjusting their expectations and reminding her that she was now one of the "big girls" in the nursery. They praised her achievements in many areas: her many creative activities, learning to ride a bike, helping them set the table for lunch. Maya, in turn, thrived on their appreciation and enjoyment of her and became a self-assured and responsible member of the nursery. Her understanding of English was good, and, though her spoken English was still sometimes difficult to understand, it was improving.

Maya's first term at primary school was the final term of her analysis, and her sessions were reduced to three times a week. The analytic work concentrated on helping Maya to settle at school and work through crucial separation issues. At first, Maya could not remember the names of the new children. It seemed that she was afraid of forgetting and being forgotten by her old friends in the nursery, and by me in particular. She organized a game in which "only in pretend" I came to live with her and her mother, or at least to stay over weekends. In one game, the mother was ill and I had to visit the girl at her house. In the transference, I was the idealized mother but also at times the oedipal father, a prince who had to save Snow White from the poisoned apple. Maya arranged for the wedding ceremony to be performed over and over again.

Although Maya's scripts all ended with my staying forever, she began to face the reality of the impending separation. It stimulated thoughts about her father's death, and Maya needed to reassure herself that, although it felt as though I was abandoning her, it was not because she (Maya) was bad, nor would I die; rather, I would stay alive and continue to remember her. Maya talked of other children and their fathers, saying that her father died because "he was very ill". With his ghost finally and fully out of the cupboard, Maya was able to reach a more integrated view of herself and her mother. She made up a story of a lady with the same name as her mother who was a lovely person but very bossy and shouting sometimes. During this period, she refused to pray to her father at night and asked Mrs A to bring her a new daddy, a real one.

Maya went on to make new friends in her new school. Her first report described her as a "very kind and thoughtful child", "keen to learn", but still needing adult encouragement. In a follow-up visit two months after the end of her analysis, Maya wanted to play schools but could not find Spotty Maya. When I made her a new figure, Maya looked at it and said, "This is me, Spotty Maya". She started to prepare spots to stick on the little girl but then stopped. She looked seriously at me and said, "I'm not so spotty any more". After a short pause she added, "Maybe sometimes, but only a few spots".

Discussion

Maya's first year seems to have been "good enough"; she was warmly and empathically cared for. However, the series of events triggered by her father's accident, and culminating in her own illness and hospitalization, was extremely traumatic for Maya. Her mother was not able to function as a much-needed auxiliary ego during this period, and Maya was helplessly overwhelmed with unmanageable and incomprehensible stimuli. The environmental impingements, and her mother's continuing difficulties in mediating and representing her experience, resulted in a serious interference in her development, affecting the unfolding of her still immature personality and ongoing structuralization. Maya's secure early months, together with the nursery school's investment and concern and her subsequent analysis, made it possible to restore her to the path of normal development before the window of time closed on the development of essential capacities.

We know that Maya gave up her attempts to walk following the traumatic period. Erna Furman (1974) notes that when a child's parent dies, in the case of toddlers, the ego functions and activities most interfered with are "those which still depend on the libidinization by the lost love object" (p. 44). The loss of her father left Maya narcissistically depleted and without her main partner in the joys of practising. Her ability to negotiate the rapprochement phase was then undermined by the bewildering changes and losses that followed, and her bereaved mother's continuing emotional unavailability. These experiences heightened her age-appropriate anxieties and conflicts, and these were in turn aggravated by her early toilet training. Her mother externalized unacceptable aspects of herself onto Maya whilst at the same time rigidly controlling and repudiating them. Margaret Mahler (1968) has written: "It is the mother's love of the toddler and the acceptance of his (her) ambivalence that enable the toddler to cathect his (her) self-representation with neutralised energy" (p. 222). We know from the analysis that Maya dealt with her mother's intolerance of anger and mess by splitting her ambivalence, vesting her self representation with unfused aggression, and thereby heightening her need to cling on to her mother. Mahler, Pine, and Bergman (1975, p. 80) have also noted that if a child is too preoccupied with the mother's presence, this can drain developmental energy which is then insufficient for the evolution of the many developing ego functions.

Nevertheless, Maya did begin walking again, albeit late, and at 3 years presented in the nursery as a good, polite child who was able to let her mother go, once she had built up substitute attachments with the nursery staff. It was really only after the separation from her mother that the full impact of her early experiences on her ego functioning became apparent. Although her problems in socialization, in communicating, and in learning arose in part from the conflicts described above, they were fundamentally rooted in her difficulties in thinking.

Peter Fonagy (1989) has shown how emergent ego structures can be inhibited when a parent cannot bear to think what is in the child's mind and the child in turn defensively disregards his perceptions of his parent's thoughts and feelings. Mrs A, a normally caring and conscientious mother, absented herself from her daughter at the time of her greatest need because she could not bear to know what she or her little daughter were feeling. In the months and years that followed Mr A's death, it would seem that even the reality of his loss had to be denied, along with any signs of longing or distress. The analysis showed that Maya's overwhelming experience of helplessness, chaos, and confusion was exacerbated by the absence of shared verbal and affective communication. It remained encapsulated and unprocessed, and the associated thoughts and feelings were felt to be very dangerous and magically endowed with the capacity to alienate and destroy. The restriction on free interchange (internal and external) interfered with her language development, and also her learning, because she feared to take in forbidden knowledge. Both in the nursery and in the first part of her analysis, the experience of not understanding and not being understood was compulsively repeated.

Fonagy and Target (1996b; Target & Fonagy, 1996) have shown how difficult it is for a child to develop a theory of mind in such unsafe circumstances and how the lack of such a development has serious implications for reality testing and social understanding. Maya's lack of a theory of mind impeded her progress along the line of development from egocentrism to socialization. The associated language delay aggravated her difficulties in the nursery. As

Kaplan-Solms and McLean (1995) have noted, children often reject a child who is unable to interact at their level. They stress the role of language acquisition in "the mastery of affects, the developing complexity of interpersonal relationships, the internalisation of prohibitions and injunctions and the elaboration of the internal world in fantasy and in play" (p. 189).

Despite the very good relationships that Maya was able to develop with the nursery staff, her internalized conflicts and structural delays prevented her from making full use of the developmental help available in the nursery. Analysis was necessary to provide Maya with a sufficiently safe setting in which to express the full range of her fearful, messy, angry feelings with someone who would "stay"—that is, contain and survive her projected feelings, not be destroyed, and not abandon, criticize, and reject her in the way she feared. The therapist's verbalization and understanding of her hitherto unthinkable impulses, thoughts, and feelings showed Maya that mental states could be thought about, and, in turn, she was able to internalize this new relationship and develop a reflective self. Through her pretend play, this new understanding could be extended while self and object representations were explored, analysed, and modified, and harsh superego precursors moderated and supplemented by benign introjects. Hitherto hidden capacities to think and to learn and to form mutual individuated relationships were released and developed. Only then was Maya able to use the stimulation, guidance, and support of the nursery and to manage a smooth transition to primary school.

Acknowledgements

An earlier version of this chapter was presented to the New York Freudian Society on 3 October 1997. We wish to acknowledge the contributions of The Anna Freud Centre Nursery staff, colleagues, and students and particularly Audrey Gavshon, who supervised the analysis.

CHAPTER NINE

"Leo": multiple interventions in the case of a very disturbed young boy with autistic features

Maria Grazia Cassola & Adriana Grotta

Having shown signs of difficulty from birth, "Leo" has always been kept under observation and has been under the care of a number of different NHS professionals. At the age of 5 years, displaying marked autistic features, he was taken into psychotherapy by a private therapist [AG].

The psychotherapy was developmental in nature. Leo lacked psychological structure and had never developed a differentiated sense of self and other; interpretative work would have been incomprehensible and irrelevant to him in the period of treatment recounted here. He has recently, aged 9, made important and unexpected developmental steps. We therefore describe the various different types of intervention used and discuss the factors that have promoted his development.

Leo is a good-looking boy with large blue eyes. In the past, he was unwilling to make eye contact; now, he increasingly uses his eyes to get in touch with others, although when eye contact becomes too intense he looks frightened and averts his eyes. A year ago, it was discovered that he was short-sighted and had a congenital cataract; he was happy to be given glasses.

He looks a bit awkward in his movements but is now much more coordinated than in the past, when he used to tip-toe and bump into everything. His speech used to be sophisticated and "adult-like", with a mechanical, stereotyped quality. Sometimes he used bizarre expressions, at others he remembered and repeated advertisements or short stories, apparently with no communicative aim. Now he can communicate adequately when he is not distressed. He smiles and his eyes light up when one says something he likes, but he tries to keep excessively intense feelings at bay.

Background and history

Mother has been working as a cleaning-lady for the last five years. Shy and reserved, she often appears anxious and presents slight obsessional features. Father works for the Post Office. He is fond of his son and can be very affectionate towards him. In the past, he used to overstimulate Leo by, for example, throwing him in the air, unable to find other ways to get in touch with him.

The parents moved to Northern Italy many years ago. They felt very lonely in the first years of their marriage, especially after Leo was born. Both welcomed the pregnancy; however, it proved difficult from the beginning, with many physical problems, which inevitably affected mother's state of mind.

Between the third and the fourth month, a partial detachment of the placenta occurred. At risk of a miscarriage, mother had to stay in hospital for seventeen days. Between the fifth and the sixth month, the pregnancy was again at risk when there was a leak of amniotic fluid. Mother was hospitalized from the twenty-fifth week until the thirty-third, when Leo was delivered by Caesarean section, weighing 1.87 kg. Severely premature, he was in an incubator for forty-one days.

Later, mother remembered how frightened and unsafe she felt during the pregnancy because of the doctors' warnings that she would probably lose the child, and because she was afraid that she could not produce a healthy child after all the threats of miscarriage. After the baby was born, she felt "scolded" by a nurse who remarked that another woman's premature baby was bigger than hers. When she was discharged, she was acutely distressed and guilty at leaving her baby in hospital, feeling that his eyes were accusing her.

Leo was discharged with the diagnosis, "dystrophic infant, small for date". He was breast-fed for three months; from the fourth month, the bottle was added. He did not feed well, and vomited repeatedly. Mother reported that he used to stare at her during breast-feeding and that he started smiling at three months. But she also remembered her baby's bodily stiffness and restlessness. He was always very agitated and screamed so loudly in the first months that she had to close the windows.

The difficulties increased when she started weaning Leo. He was very reluctant to eat and very slow. He would eat very few kinds of food. He refused to chew solids and often vomited when confronted with new food or in new situations. In his first year, he caught many colds, which caused his mother great anxiety: she was afraid of complications that could lead to his death. Her fear was reinforced by the paediatrician's warnings: she tried hard not to make Leo cry, because even crying seemed a potential danger.

Leo started to walk at 15 months. Mother, remembering his first steps, commented, "I put some little stones in his hands, so that he had the impression of being held by my fingers." Well after Leo could manage stairs himself, she continued to carry him, even when she was encumbered by shopping bags.

At first, Leo's speech appeared to be developing relatively normally. In the first year, he showed the expected vocalization and lallation; at 8 months, he pronounced "mama" and "papa". But, during the second year, language development stopped. At 2½ years he produced a continuous sound like a grunt or roar, and he screamed when anyone thwarted him.

It was very difficult for him to accept separation from mother: if she left, he screamed and cried inconsolably. He tiptoed, he refused to eat, he had no sense of danger, and he totally ignored other children. He seemed hardly aware that he had a body; he was negativistic and destructive and did not comply with any requests.

At 3, when he was sent to school for a few hours a day, he became clean and dry.

Educational interventions:
from the first contacts with the parents
to a child-tailored project

Leo was first referred to the local NHS Mother and Child Clinic when he was discharged from hospital at 1 month. The clinic offers psychological and paediatric guidance for normal infants and children, neurological and psychiatric assessment and help for a variety of disturbances, and social assistance for deprived families. The child neurologist in the paediatric ward had noted a general sensitivity (frequent "startles") and abnormal relational behaviour, such as difficulty in sustaining eye contact and a lack of response to physical holding. But the parents refused to accept the referral, although they continued to take him to the neuropsychiatrist every two months for medical check-ups.

At 2½ months, the doctor noted "slight anomalies of the motor functioning of the superior and inferior limbs". These were overcome by 4½ months, but at 7 months the baby still showed "a hypertonic style with motor activity not aimed at handling objects". Leo could not sit and had long muscular spasms. At 9 months, his posture was still hypertonic and he started to show a tendency to tiptoe. When distressed, he would become still; at times he screamed, but he never cried tears.

At 13 months, Leo, hyper-excited and "nervous", started to present sleep disturbances, which made mother anxious. She also began to worry about Leo's late motor development. But she again refused a referral to the Mother and Child Clinic. It seems that these parents were not ready to acknowledge their son's serious difficulties, because of their guilt and fear of having damaged him. But they did accept a referral when Leo was 2¼ years old. The paediatrician wrote: "Leo doesn't talk, he has not started sphincter control, is impatient and tyrannical."

A psychologist at the Mother and Child Clinic carried out a series of observations and described Leo as "a little despot" or "a little animal", unable to make eye contact or to comply with verbal requests. He avoided any bodily contact and had many "phobias": he could not touch grass, flowers, or fruit. He had no rules, and his behaviour seemed aimless; he looked like a "lost" child, rather than a fragmented one. On the basis of these symptoms, the psychologist suggested a diagnosis of "suspected autism".

The clinic suggested a therapeutic plan involving both child and family, consisting of: (a) educational therapy, once a week, with a language therapist and a psychomotor therapist working together with the mother–child couple; (b) parent guidance and support provided by the psychologist and the neuropsychiatrist, working together; (c) attendance at the nursery school, with a support teacher and an individualized programme. The parents agreed to this plan.

The educational therapy

The clinic team had to take into account the fact that it was impossible to separate the mother–child couple. The first aim of the educational therapists' work was to hook Leo into a relationship and to help him to sustain it through eye contact and physical holding. He was taught to carry out simple tasks and to observe some basic rules. He had to learn the main spatial concepts. The therapists noted that mother felt progressively more at ease as the work went on, and that she began to assimilate certain functions of guidance and stimulation. It was very important to her that, beyond the mental working-through of her relationship with her son, she could see "concretely" what to do with him. This allowed her to change her internal representations of him as an unmanageable child and of herself as an inadequate mother.

Parent guidance and support

During this same period, the psychologist and the neuropsychiatrist met the parental couple regularly at two- or four-weekly intervals. Later, the neuropsychiatrist alone would meet with both parents, and occasionally with the mother only. The main objective was to make the mother–child separation thinkable. Work focused on promoting awareness that Leo was a different person from his mother and on the role of the father as a reassuring person for his wife. After a few months, mother had a fairly severe depressive crisis, which was understood as a sign that she was starting to separate from Leo. A second aim was to offer the parents some educational guidance. They were helped to encourage Leo's autonomy (washing himself, dressing himself, feeding himself) and to explain the meaning of rules and limits.

Later, the neuropsychiatrist started to introduce the idea of psychotherapy and of a helper at home. The gradualness of these steps made it possible for the parents to accept the help that was offered: they were able to see it as a tool to improve their functioning as parents, rather than as a disqualification of their role. This required the working through both of their ambivalence and aggression and of their view of the psychotherapist and the helper as "rivals" or "good parents". They became more able to verbalize their experiences and their feelings, recovering, or perhaps acquiring *de novo*, the capacity to share and to criticize one another.

Nursery school and primary school

At 3½, after one year of educational therapy, Leo was placed in the nursery school, initially for a few hours in the morning. He had a special teacher who provided him with a one-to-one relationship in this wider context, with the aim of improving his language and starting the process of socialization.

There were big problems in separating from his mother at the beginning. These were gradually overcome, but difficulties in relating with his peers remained until the end of his first grade at primary school. Initially, the other children did not have any meaning for him: they seemed to be mainly obstacles in his way. When he was obliged to take into account the existence of his peers, as on the occasion of birthday parties at school, he became disruptive and very disturbed. Sometimes he was aggressive towards his teachers, as when they failed to maintain a special, privileged relationship with him. Any changes at school were unbearable, as at home. Leo felt menaced, he vomited, or he stopped eating. By the end of nursery school, Leo had consolidated his autonomy, he was able to respect the community rules, and he was able to learn when helped by an adult.

At primary school, he had a special teacher to help him to bear a one-to-one relationship in a school context and to accept the other children's presence in small groups. Adaptation to primary school was another big step for Leo. Initially, it seemed that he experienced the school as a great "chaos", especially in less structured situations (the garden, the refectory). Often, he showed deep anxiety, manifested in crying, screaming, fights, and attacks on objects and people. He would calm down only if someone restrained him physically. Again, he refused food.

But school gradually became a positive experience, providing Leo with incentives and with the means of satisfying his great curiosity. He was gratified not only by the adults' acknowledgement of his gains, but by the very process of learning and cognitive functioning. By the end of the first year, he often said he wanted "to do things well". During the second year, the anxiety attacks gradually disappeared. Apparently motiveless aggressive behaviour decreased, while aggression as an answer to frustration appeared and increased, as when he threw a chair at a girl who said that she didn't want to marry him. Leo was taught the normal programme.

During Leo's first year at primary school, a young male worker visited the home twice weekly, with the aim of working on the more fragile areas. He focused particularly on the development of play and motor activity, and on the acquisition of social and behavioural rules at home and outside (in the park, in a child library, in a playgroup). Leo immediately accepted this worker, who became very important to him and who helped him to reinforce his masculinity. Leo learnt to ride a bicycle and began to experience pleasure in his body: he is now freer, less rigid, and no longer becomes anxious if he gets dirty or falls in the grass.

Beginning the psychotherapy

The first time that I [AG] saw Leo, I was deeply impressed. At 5½, he showed some stereotypic autistic language and behaviour and bodily stiffness, but he did not give the impression of being "locked" in his world all the time. He came in and started to explore the room, talking in an incomprehensible way with a strange "French" accent. After a while, he repeated some pieces of what could have been a broadcast about Giotto and the painters of the fourteenth Century. He did not seem to be worried about the person in the room with him: it was he who adjusted the distance. Already in the first session he nevertheless noticed me: a couple of glances initiated the contact. At one point, he opened some imaginary boxes in his hands and uttered some metallic sounds, pronouncing incomprehensible words. Then I introduced myself: in turn, I opened a box with my hands and said "Doctor Adriana". Leo picked out a little car, a red Ford, which later became his favourite one. At the end of the session, in front of his father, he said: "There is a Ford, over there."

Starting from this first session, we can single out some lines to follow in the course of Leo's therapy. The story of our relationship is the first line. It is worth noting that I had a particular expectation of this boy: his mother had described him as a child who respected no limits and whom nobody could control. This imagined child was very different from the real one. From the beginning, Leo seemed to feel completely at ease in the room and gave the impression of regarding it as a space "right" for him: he wandered around it saying "Nice, nice!"

For a long time, I seemed to be experienced as an accessory of the room, like a lamp which could be switched on and off at will. Leo's relationship with me would develop through the mediation of inanimate objects, which he used from the beginning to facilitate and regulate contact with me. The first object that Leo noticed was a car: for a long time he would talk of this car, especially at the end of the session, and he was happy to find it again the following time. I thought that the little red car represented his hard and mechanical self, and also our growing relationship.

The second line that we are going to consider is the development of the ego. As soon as Leo felt safe enough in the relationship with me, and sure of being fully accepted in both his healthy and psychotic aspects, he could use my offered help. His ego gained strength through the acquisition of different functions: the capacity to foresee an event from the perception of signs, and the ability to use language to express his bodily needs (going to the toilet, drinking). Gradually, as his ego became more integrated, he became more reality-oriented.

At the beginning, I focused my work on his relationship to his body, which seemed unrelated to him. It was as though he received sensations from his body which he could not understand or even ascribe to himself. He seemed unaware of pain; sometimes, he seemed to lack a body image. When he wanted to reach something, he ignored any obstacle in his way. I always tried to understand and put into words his physical states. I helped him when he vomited after a fit of coughing, or took care of him when he bumped into the corner of the table, saying that what was hurting was his head and not the table. The most impressive incident happened after one year of therapy; Leo often remembers it. He was sitting on the couch looking at a little book and did not realize that he was falling back. He landed on the floor, remaining exactly in the same position, his legs still crossed and his arms not reaching out to protect himself. He bumped his head but remained frozen with wide-open eyes, not realizing what had happened. I ran towards him, lifted him, and started to stroke his head softly, trying at the same time to describe to him what had happened. This kind of work aimed to continue what the educational therapist had started when she taught him about the use of his body.

The development of the self representation is our third line. As I helped Leo to mentalize and to integrate what he had "concretely" learnt, he could gradually locate different sensations, including pleasurable ones. Starting from the mental representation of the body, Leo began gradually to build up a mental representation of the self.

Line one: object relations

At the beginning I had the impression that Leo used me like a part of himself: he picked up my availability and created me when he needed me, otherwise he blotted me out. Yet one month later, from behind the glass door of the waiting-room, he said loudly, "I'm here", showing a capacity for anticipation and sending a claim.

Time seemed immobile in his world, but the sessions followed one another regularly, twice a week, giving him a foreseeable frame which contributed to the structure of an internal rhythm.

The object whom he made disappear, saying "Nothing, nothing", was there again every Tuesday and Thursday, at the same time. After a year and a half, Leo seemed to have internalized the sequence of the sessions, when he said to me: "I'll see you on Thursday".

During one of our first sessions, Leo was attracted by one of the books on the shelves, *The Rescue of Patty, The Young Rabbit*, which was about a trip to the seaside made by a family of rabbits. Whilst they are on a pier looking at the sunset, Patty leans out and falls into the sea. Granny Rose, who is knitting a very long scarf, throws it down into the sea and saves her. At the beginning, Leo did not understand what was going on and said that Patty had plunged into the sea in order to save a shark. After reading the story many times, he said that Patty had thrown herself into the sea to save her teddy bear who was drowning, and that Granny, alert, had saved both. He was very interested in the multicoloured scarf, and he often asked me to draw it. Whilst he read and re-read the story, I accompanied him with some gestures. He gave sideways glances at me. On one of these occasions, when I pretended to embrace an invisible teddy bear, he suddenly stopped reading, extended his arms and said "I'm a scarecrow." It was clear that emotions that were too intense, related to situations that evoked an excessive closeness, were immediately rejected.

Instead, he was eager to accept interactions that were somewhat distanced through the use of an indirect medium—the telephone, letters, television. I often played the role of different characters who rang him, or of a famous TV showman, to whom he talked as if in the show. Sometimes I wrote him letters or postcards. In this first period, I did not have the right to an autonomous life, as is clear if we consider the way he played the goose game (a board game). After a very short time, when Leo limited himself to reading the numbers, he started to make his piece move; any attempt of mine to join in with my piece was promptly stopped. Later on, my piece was allowed to look at the game from the top of the box of felt-tip pens.

In the same period (February), Leo, trying to play volley with a little ball, personified two players whom he knew from a Japanese cartoon. He said: "Shiro and Mila, two hearts for the volley-ball!" In March, he chose a wooden car, whose two drivers were identical. He called them "Flick" and "Flack". One day, these two were caught in a storm and hid themselves inside the cardigan that I was wearing, saying: "Let's go here, in the cave, where there is no monster." (My name, Grotta, means "cave" in Italian.) In September, after the summer holidays, Leo talked about "Bob" and "Bobette", who met some "nervous monsters" in space.

In October, at last, my piece was allowed to come down onto the board and follow his, although without my having the right to throw the dice. At the same time, the two wooden men became "Olive" and "Popeye". Popeye always stopped a train which was about to collide with their car, and Olive was ready to supply him with cans of spinach. In December, Leo asked the therapist to write a letter to him, then started crying, because "Dear Leo" and "Doctor Adriana" were too distant—one at the top and the other at the bottom of the letter. He began to be aware of separateness, and for that reason he needed the illusion of our still being together; his interest in glue arose in this period.

One day in March, he said "I can't tell you 'bye-bye'", and then he played with the Plasticine, saying that red and green were stuck together. I explained his wish that we stay stuck together like the red and green Plasticine, but added that they could be separated and return to being "red" and "green". Saying that, I separated the colours, which said "bye-bye" to one another, and then I stuck them together again. Leo laughed.

In April, Leo said some sentences from a soap opera, "I can't lose you . . . I want to live with you . . . I was uprooted." He started to express feelings related to the consciousness of being separate. Just before the summer, my piece gained the right to play and to throw the dice. He defined my piece as "feminine", and his as "masculine". It did not matter who lost and who won.

After two years of therapy, competitions become more and more frequent in various games. Now Leo exulted when he won; he said nothing when he lost. One day, he met me on the stairs and said to his mother: "I let my friend who is never angry go in, then I go in." When in the room, he asked me: "Don't you ever get cross?" Me: "Yes, sometimes I get cross too." Leo: "But not with me." Me: "Because you have never made me angry." Leo: "I cannot." At this stage, the object seemed to be idealized.

Line two: ego development

Leo's therapy has included much "developmental help" to enable him to use language, memory, attention, and reasoning as tools for adaptation to reality and not only as defensive devices.

The first objective was to refer to a "centre" within Leo, the many unintegrated cognitive and affective bits of experiences that seemed to impinge upon him. These I tried to "collect" and put together. Particular attention was given to promoting the personal pronoun "I", which Leo used reliably after eight months of treatment.

Leo had an "order", which was necessary to him, rigid and very fragile at the same time. His obsessional reasoning and behaviour was, as Alvarez (1992) points out, the first possible order, a defensive device taking the place of a faulty structure. As to the affects, I had to be very cautious, so that Leo could slowly begin to assign them to a "self" and acknowledge and tolerate them.

I remember his totally defensive attitude at the beginning, whenever I mentioned an affect. Even if it was not attributed to him, this immediately provoked his "flight" and stiffening. I often chose to mime affects with my face, because I felt that it was not useful to verbalize them. This way of representing affects enabled Leo to "see" in the other something that he could not yet experience himself. He could then feel together with me, both of us being tuned in to the same experience. Gradually, after I had verbalized his wish to find a "new" language, good for both of us (music, a foreign language, a fantasy language), it became possible to name the affects.

After the Easter holiday separation, in the second year of therapy, Leo embraced a small teddy bear, saying, "There aren't any words", and put it down at once. A month later, he saw my disappointment when the card-house I was building fell down, and he said, "I'll comfort you." In the following session, he told the felt-tips box that I had become sad, but that I became happy again. Recently, he has started to define the moods of the characters he invents in his role-plays.

One important aim was to give a sense to his nonsense. Of course, this was possible only from time to time. I did not want to decode his bizarre expressions or pieces of behaviour but tried instead to offer him a meaning for them. As it was often impossible to find a meaning in his behaviour and speech, I had to create one for him. Sometimes he accepted this, and so it became a shared meaning. Mothers do this all the time with their infants. It helps to validate the psychological existence of the baby and to build up the ego structure (Loewald, 1960). For example, after five months of therapy, Leo threw a pack of cards in the air. I asked him: "Are you celebrating Carnival?" This struck him, and from that time on that gesture became "to make Carnival"—to relax, to take it easy.

After a while, Leo started to attribute his nonsense to the box of felt-tips, which was called "the big electric box". At this point, it was easier for me to make an alliance with his healthier side and ask that side for help in understanding what the box was saying, or simply to make some comments about it. The "big electric box" had become a room-mate, a bit crazy and a nuisance, whom we had to tolerate. Now I can tell Leo if I have not understood and that I would like him to repeat a sentence. Often Leo repeats it in a different and understandable way.

I have always tried to be an "ally" but not to collude with Leo. It has been very important to distinguish between the moments when his play, although solitary, was truly play with meaning for him and the moments when it changed into something "hypnotic", which cut him off from reality. When that happened, I tried to involve him in a communicative interaction. (This was probably different from what happened at home, where his mother, tired, let him play on his own for hours.)

For Leo, the distinction between reality and play gradually became clearer, but reality and wish, or reality and fantasy, still remained confused. Often he specified that he was pretending: then anything could happen without danger. Without such specification, there could be risks. When I put a little ball on my nose as he was reading something about a seal, he said impatiently: "Stop it! You are a doctor, not a seal!" Or he said to his father, who was pretending to be a thief: "Stop it! You are a daddy and not a robber! You haven't got a mask, and you aren't even in a bank!"

Reality, no longer an unpredictable and scary chaos, began to have a stable structure. The sense of time and space consolidated as a frame of reference. Events started to be foreseeable, and memory could be employed to recall and to link pieces of experience. From the beginning, I had picked up Leo's tendency to disintegrate when faced with the smallest change, as well as his fear of noises, even the softest ones. In one of the first sessions, he was terrified by the noise of the lavatory flushing on an upper floor. Widening his eyes, he said, "The glasses have burst!" I explained what had happened, and thereafter I used any opportunity not only to explain what was going on, but also to help him to anticipate events. For example, I told him that the noise of shoes in the corridor meant that someone was coming, so that, as Leo heard my footsteps in the corridor, he began to know that I was coming.

Reality is now less threatening and confusing: Leo can even put his different "worlds" in touch: home, school, his grandparents' village. Now he can tell me: "My dad sends his regards", or "What will my granny say when she sees me wearing glasses?" Me: "What do you think that she is going to say?" Leo: "Mamma mia! How they suit you!"

Line three: self representation

At the beginning, Leo seemed to have a very fragile self representation, ready to fade out in response to external changes, which he experienced as disintegrating factors. One of the first objects that he chose to represent his "self" was a collection of little wooden balls threaded on a stick, one on the top of the other, which he called "E.T".

Another image of himself he sketched (Fig. 1) after he read the story of Patty rescued from the sea. This is "Leo", the "living being"—a phrase he used to define people and animals—after one year of therapy. The face has no contours and is at the mercy of the waves. One year later, Leo could lean out of the window, finally contained (Fig. 2). His look was still sad, or sulky, unsmiling. Sometimes he denied that he could smile: once when I noted his smile, he replied "I can't do it" (although recently he has been able to accept being described as smiling and pleased). Ten months

FIG. 1   5 years, 11 months

FIG. 2   6 years, 11 months

FIG. 3   7 years, 8 months

FIG. 4   8 years, 4 months

later, he drew his family (Fig. 3) during an interview with the neuropsychiatrist. At the age of 8, he represented himself as complete, as in Figure 4, which was made during a session.

Besides this living Leo, there was another one, mechanical, robotlike, which soon emerged in his play. There was the toy already described, called E.T., and there was "Smurf" (a little blue dwarf) who tried to go and visit his terrestrial friends in the Lego house. Regularly something terrible happened: an earthquake or a violent explosion which threw Smurf onto the lamp where he scalded himself. These scenes made me think how much Leo must feel himself an alien; they seemed a representation of the psychic "catastrophe" in his infancy. It is noteworthy that Leo expressed early on his wish to repair the damage. At the beginning, he asked me to "mend everything"; later he made the fire brigade intervene, and eventually he himself became a fireman.

After two years of therapy, he frequently used to ask, "Are the teddy bears living beings?", and he began to ask me to draw faces with different expressions—happy, angry, surprised.

A bit later he started to express his worries about death; he often coped with these by making "dead corpses" return to life. In the same period, his parents reported two important steps: he had acquired a transitional object, a Panda bear, and an imaginary friend, "Jack the policeman", to whom he habitually ascribed any mischief. At the same time, he consolidated his image as a heroic rescuer: he would telephone the police, the fire brigade, and the ambulance and save the people in danger. At other times, he would say to me, if there was a strange noise: "Don't worry, I'm here!"

As his sense of identity became more stable, signs of gender identity appeared—that is the basic awareness of belonging to the masculine gender. As Popeye saving Olive, he would proudly exhibit his biceps. Sometimes he seemed to imitate his father or his educator, in order to be a "man". One day, he wanted to enact a story with me, in which he was a magician and I was a princess. The emotional climate was intense: he wore a pointed hat, which he filled up with shining stars. I was "sad and ill", and he had found a miraculous potion to heal me and so gained the right to marry me.

Thus, while the struggle for existence and for selfhood remained central, Leo did also show indications of phallic concerns, and even hints of dawning oedipal interests.

Discussion

Leo had a difficult start. Being premature, he probably had some constitutional fragility. He alternated between an extreme irritability, manifesting itself in poor tolerance of stimuli, and bodily stiffness. His depressed mother could not pick up the weak signals that her child was sending her (looks, smile, first words); she could not contain and comfort her baby when he was distressed. This made it difficult for her to meet Leo's needs; she conveyed her deep anxiety to him all the time.

At the beginning of Leo's second year, his development stopped. Confronted with complex developmental tasks, his precarious equilibrium broke down, his functioning deteriorated, and development became distorted. Leo did not talk, did not communicate in other ways, did not look for eye contact, and had no autonomy. He was able to walk, but he depended entirely on the physical presence of his mother. Mother and son were stuck in a symbiotic-like relationship, each providing support for the other. This kind of relationship excluded the possibility of the inclusion of the father as the third one.

We could hypothesize a developmental arrest coinciding with the practising sub-phase of the separation–individuation process (Mahler et al., 1975). Mother was anxious and overprotective because of her persisting fears of death and deep sense of guilt. She limited Leo physically and could not allow him to experience autonomous functioning. Leo, for his part, was not "strong" enough to struggle, and he gave up his attempts to differentiate self and object. At the end of the second year, the parents could no longer deny Leo's difficulties, since they could not understand or communicate with him; at this point, they accepted the help offered.

Methods used and choices made

The educational therapy, a "concrete" form of help, made it possible for the parents to modify their perception of Leo and to change their mental representation of him, abandoning that of the extraterrestrial child. This had a positive effect on their relationship with him. The work of the two therapists and Leo's attendance at school rendered it possible for mother and child to bear being physically separate. At the same time, the regular meetings with the neuropsychiatrist and the psychologist allowed the parents to function as a couple. The paternal imago gained consistency in mother's mind, allowing the beginning of triangulation.

Two different spaces were then offered, one to the child and one to the parents—the individual psychotherapy and the meetings with the neuropsychiatrist—which allowed Leo and his parents to work on separation. We consider these interventions as therapeutic: both offered "developmental help". Leo needed to strengthen his sense of self, to render the representations of self and other more stable, and to develop those ego functions that allow differentiation and integration. The psychotherapy gave him the chance to experience new perceptions, which gradually were attributed to something that Leo began to "know" as self.

The parents, for their part, needed to be helped to make the "normal and ordinary" parental function emerge (Alvarez, 1992). The whole family had to learn how to function in a healthier way. Work with the parents aimed at giving some order and structure to Leo's external world, and to lessen the distress and the loneliness of the couple. The therapist tried to facilitate their understanding of Leo's internal world, thus reducing their unrelatedness to him. The therapist and the neuropsychiatrist periodically exchanged information and compared and reflected upon their work. This provided a chance to think about the case in a more integrated way, which in turn helped the process of integration both in the parents and in the child.

We think that the main therapeutic factors were the setting, the function of reclamation, and developmental assistance. We define "setting" as all the distinctive external features of the treatment, such as the regularity in time and sameness in space, but also the certainty represented by the growing relationship between the child and the therapist, which soon formed a "secure base" (Bowlby, 1988). We define "reclamation" as the therapist's being creative enough to compel Leo to give up his autistic-like protective devices (Alvarez, 1992). But it also meant that she had in her mind the perspective of a healthier development for Leo, from which he could get the developmental elements he needed (Loewald, 1960). Developmental help aimed to "teach" Leo things that are absolutely normal for other children in order to enable him to orient himself in reality, and it was based from the beginning on an alliance with the healthier part of Leo, which included a great curiosity (Gavshon, 1987).

At present, Leo has resumed his development, and he has quickly advanced in terms of expectable developmental steps, but he still shows some psychotic functioning in situations that he cannot control or when there is no auxiliary ego available.

We started from an initial diagnosis of Pervasive Developmental Disorder (ICD–10: WHO, 1992), until the evolution of the clinical picture gave us a clearer view of Leo's mental functioning and internal structures. This made us modify our expectations along the way. Leo presented a relatively intact ego apparatus, but he

functioned in an unintegrated way, unable to give order and pre-
dictability to the internal and external world, to differentiate self
and object, or to build up secondary process thinking. When he
was offered opportunities for integration, he picked them up at
once.

Prognosis

Leo is now making some moves towards greater autonomy: he
tries to regulate the distance from people without running away or
attacking, he has begun to express some feelings verbally, and he
shows a great interest in his body and in the sensations coming
from it. Furthermore, he shows pleasure in ego functioning. The
issue of his identifications is still open: we wonder to what degree
he relies on ego identifications that have a structuring function,
strengthening the self representation and building up secondary
autonomy, and to what degree he depends on adhesive, "as if"
identifications, which have a defensive and protective function.
When Leo behaves like the psychotherapist, or repeats her sentences in exactly the way that she has pronounced them, we think
that in part he is trying to keep the illusion of oneness with her, and
in part he is using what he has "learnt" to orientate himself in the
world. His "repertoire" is now quite large, but he has not yet found
his own personal "style". He is a creative child, but he still needs to
learn how to use his creativity in the process of identity formation
and in the service of the ego. Although superficial identifications
still tend to prevail, Leo is now beginning to rely on some core ego
identifications, as he now has a "consistency" and he faces others
in a more assertive way. He is able to approach other people without a mediator, outside the protective umbrella that caring adults
have provided. Like most latency children, he has a basic awareness of his identity in terms of "I am the son of ____", "I live in
____", "I like this and I dislike that."
Cognitively, he knows that he is a boy, but he is struggling with
the meaning of this in terms of relationships. In the last two years
he has tended to play masculine roles, drawing inspiration from
TV programmes; he has kissed the girls in his class passionately on
the mouth and has promised to marry one of them. He has started

to discover and to explore his genitals, and to masturbate, fulfilling both those basic needs related to the capacity to experience his body in an active/passive way (which has an integrative effect), and more mature needs of a phallic nature. Clear oedipal fantasies, involving a triadic relationship, are not yet evident.

Leo has begun to experience himself within time, and he tries hard to recover his past, often asking his mother to tell the story of his birth and of his first years. He is also experiencing the possibility of integrating "Leo the newborn baby", "Leo the student", and "Leo who will be a husband or will work as a restorer".

Leo's aggression appears to be goal-directed more often; it can be used to reach mature aims. Still present, though lessening, is aggression as a response to anxiety derived from fears of intrusion and loss of boundaries, or as a rage response when he is forced to abandon his narcissistic grandiosity or his obsessional defences. We do not yet know where the process of integration of his healthy and psychotic parts will lead. At present, Leo continues to transform the latter, trying to include them in a net of meanings, or to control them by isolating them in a space similar to the "big electric box".

In conclusion, in spite of the initial diagnosis, we can now make a more favourable prognosis, given Leo's ongoing development. We wonder how much the process of resuming a "developmental path" has to be attributed to our intervention and how much to the developmental potential of Leo and his parents. We have to take into account a constitutional factor, as well as a developmental process that has been reactivated thanks to an early and wide-ranging intervention. We are strongly persuaded that these results are in large part due to the variety of interventions possible which allowed us to meet different needs at different times.

The handling of such disturbed children and their families needs great consistency and flexibility in all the people involved in the treatment. As Anne Alvarez has pointed out (personal communication), the involved professionals have to develop an attitude that promotes communication at all levels when approaching disorders such as these, which are of a communicative nature. In this view psychotherapy is a necessary complement to a wider intervention that enables it to be more effective.

REFERENCES

Ablon, S. (1993). The therapeutic action of play and affect in child analysis. In: S. Ablon, D. Brown, E. Khantzian, & J. Mack (Eds.), *Human Feelings: Explorations in Affect Development and Meaning.* Hillsdale, NJ: Analytic Press.

Ablon, S. (1994). "How can we know the dancer from the dance?" The analysis of a five year old girl. *Psychoanalytic Study of the Child, 49:* 315–327.

Abrams, S. (1993). The developmental dimensions of play during treatment: conceptual overview. In: *The Many Meanings of Play.* New Haven, CT: Yale University Press.

Ainsworth, M. D. S., Blehar, M. C., Waters, E., & Wall, S. (1978). *Patterns of Attachment: A Psychological Study of the Strange Situation.* Hillsdale, NJ: Erlbaum.

Alessandri, S. M. (1991). Play and social behaviours in maltreated preschoolers. *Development and Psychopathology, 3:* 191–206.

Alessandri, S. M. (1992). Mother–child interactional correlates of maltreated and nonmaltreated children's play behavior. *Development and Psychopathology, 4:* 257–270.

Alexander, F., & French, T. H. (1946). *Psychoanalytic Therapy.* New York: Ronald Press.

Alvarez, A. (1985). The problem of neutrality: some reflections on the psychoanalytic attitude in the treatment of borderline and psychotic children. *Journal of Child Psychotherapy, 17:* 87–103.

Alvarez, A. (1992). *Live Company.* London: Tavistock/Routledge.

Alvarez, A. (1996). Addressing the element of deficit in children with autism: psychotherapy which is both psychoanalytically and developmentally informed. *Clinical Child Psychology and Psychiatry, 1* (4): 525–537.

Balint, M. (1968). *The Basic Fault.* London: Tavistock.

Bartsch, K., & Wellman, H. M. (1989). Young children's attribution of action to beliefs and desires. *Child Development, 60*: 946–964.

Beebe, B., Lachmann, F., & Jaffe, J. (1997). Mother–infant interaction structures and presymbolic self and object representations. *Psychoanalytical Dialogues, 7*: 133–182.

Beeghly, M., & Cicchetti, D. (1994). Child maltreatment, attachment, and the self system: emergence of an internal state lexicon in toddlers at high social risk. *Development and Psychopathology, 6*: 5–30.

Belsky, J. (1993). Etiology of child maltreatment: a developmental—ecological analysis. *Psychological Bulletin, 114*: 413–434.

Belsky, J., Fish, M., & Isabella, R. (1991). Continuity and discontinuity in infant negative and positive emotionality: family antecedent and attachment consequences. *Developmental Psychology, 27*: 421–431.

Belsky, J., Rosenberger, K., & Crnic, C. (1995). The origins of attachment security: "classical" and contextual determinants. In S. Goldberg, R. Muir, & J. Kerr (Eds.), *John Bowlby's Attachment Theory: Historical, Clinical and Social Significance* (pp. 153–184). Hillsdale, NJ: Analytic Press.

Belsky, J., Rovine, M., & Taylor, D. G. (1984). The Pennsylvania Infant and Family Development Project. III: The origins of individual differences in infant–mother attachment: maternal and infant contributions. *Child Development, 55*: 718–728.

Benoit, D., & Parker, K. (1994). Stability and transmission of attachment across three generations. *Child Development, 65*: 1444–1457.

Bion, W. R. (1962). *Learning from Experience.* London: Heinemann.

Bion, W. R. (1967a). Notes on memory and desire. *Psychoanalytic Forum, 2*: 271–80.

Birch, M. (1997). In the land of counterpane: travels in the realm of play. *Psychoanalytic Study of the Child, 52*: 57–75.

Blair, R. J. R. (1995). A cognitive developmental approach to morality: investigating the psychopath. *Cognition, 57*: 1–29.

Bleiberg, E. (1984). Narcissistic disorders in children. *Bulletin of the Menninger Clinic, 48*: 501–517.

Bleiberg, E. (1994). Borderline disorders in children and adolescents: the concept, the diagnosis, and the controversies. *Bulletin of the Menninger Clinic, 58*: 169–196.

Bollas, C. (1979). The transformational object. In: G. Kohon (Ed.), *The*

British School of Psychoanalysis: The Independent Tradition. London: Free Association Books, 1986.

Bowlby, J. (1958). The nature of the child's tie to his mother. *International Journal of Psycho-Analysis, 39*: 350–373.

Bowlby, J. (1969). *Attachment and Loss, Vol. 1*. London: Hogarth Press and the Institute of Psycho-Analysis.

Bowlby, J. (1973). *Attachment and Loss, Vol. 2*. London: Hogarth Press and the Institute of Psycho-Analysis.

Bowlby, J. (1980). *Attachment and Loss, Vol. 3*. London: Hogarth Press and the Institute of Psycho-Analysis.

Bowlby, J. (1988). *A Secure Base: Clinical Applications of Attachment Theory*. London: Routledge.

Braten, S. (1987). Dialogic mind: the infant and the adult in proto-conversation. In: M. Carvallo (Ed.), *Nature, Cognition and Systems*. Dordrecht/Boston: D. Reidel.

Burgner, M., & Kennedy, H. (1980). Different types of sado-masochistic behaviour in children. *Dialogue, 4*: 49–59.

Burland, J. A. (1997). The role of working through in bringing about psychoanalytic change. *International Journal of Psycho-Analysis, 78*: 469–484.

Burlingham, D., & Freud, A. (1944). *Infants without Families*. London: George Allen and Unwin.

Casement, P. (1985). *On Learning from the Patient*. London: Tavistock.

Caston, J. (1995). Mannequins in the labyrinth and the couch–lab intersect. In: T. Shapiro & R. Emde (Eds.), *Research in Psychoanalysis: Process, Development, Outcome*. Madison, CT: International Universities Press (pp. 51–65).

Cath, S., Gurwitt, A., & Ross, J. (1982). *Father and Child*. Boston: Little, Brown.

Chused, J. (1992). The patient's perception of the analyst: the hidden transference. *Psychoanalytic Quarterly, 61*: 161–184.

Cicchetti, D., & Beeghly, M. (1987). Symbolic development in maltreated youngsters: an organizational perspective. In: D. Cicchetti & M. Beeghly (Eds.), *Atypical symbolic development. New Directions for Child Development Vol. 36* (pp. 5–29). San Francisco, CA: Jossey-Bass.

Cohen, J. (1997). Child and adolescent psychoanalysis: research, practice and theory. *International Journal of Psycho-Analysis, 78*: 499–520.

Collins, N. R., & Read, S. J. (1994). Representations of attachment: the structure and function of working models. In K. Bartholomew & D. Perlman (Eds.), *Advances in Personal Relationships, Vol. 5: Attachment Process in Adulthood* (pp. 53–90). London: Jessica Kingsley.

Cox, M., Owen, T., Henderson, V., & Margand, N. (1992). Prediction of infant–father and infant–mother attachment. *Developmental Psychology, 28*: 474–483.

Crittenden, P. M. (1988). Relationships at risk. In: J. Belsky & T. Nezworski (Eds.), *Clinical Implications of Attachment* (pp. 136–174). Hillsdale, NJ: Erlbaum.

Crittenden, P. M. (1994). Peering into the black box: An exploratory treatise on the development of self in young children. In: D. Cicchetti & S. L. Toth (Eds.), *Disorders and Dysfunctions of the Self. Rochester Symposium on Developmental Psychopathology, Vol. 5* (pp. 79–148). Rochester, NY: University Rochester Press.

Crittenden, P. M., Partridge, M. F., & Clausen, A. H. (1991). Family patterns of relationship in normative and dysfunctional families. *Development and Psychopathology, 3*: 491–513.

Daldin, H. (1992). Assaultive behaviour in the analysis of children. *Psychoanalytic Psychology, 9* (4): 477–488.

Daldin, H. (1994). Expanding the clinical utility of the concept of developmental help to engage the severely disturbed adult patient in a psychoanalytic process. *British Journal of Psychotherapy, 10* (4): 521–532.

Del Carmen, R., Pedersen, F., Huffman, L., & Bryan, Y. (1993). Dyadic distress management predicts security of attachment. *Infant Behavior and Development, 16*: 131–147.

Dennett, D. C. (1983). Styles of mental representation. In: *Proceedings of the Aristotelian Society* (pp. 213–226). London: Aristotelian Society.

Dias, M. G., & Harris, P. L. (1990). The influence of the imagination on reasoning by young children. *British Journal of Developmental Psychology, 8*: 305–318.

Dunn, J. (1996). The Emanuel Miller Memorial Lecture 1995. Children's relationships: bridging the divide between cognitive and social development. *Journal of Child Psychology and Psychiatry, 37*: 507–518.

Edgcumbe, R. (1971). A consideration of the meaning of certain types of aggressive behaviour. *British Journal of Medical Psychology, 44*: 373–378.

Edgcumbe, R. (1975). The border between therapy and education. *Psychoanalytic Study of the Child, 5*: 133–147.

Edgcumbe, R. (1995). The history of Anna Freud's thinking on developmental disturbances. *Bulletin of the Anna Freud Centre, 18*: 21–34.

Emde, R. (1980a). Toward a psychoanalytic theory of affect: Part 1. The organizational model and its propositions. In: S. I. Greenspan & G. H. Pollock (Eds.), *The Course of Life: Infancy and Early Childhood* (pp. 63–83). Washington, DC: DHSS.

Emde, R. (1980b). Toward a psychoanalytic theory of affect: Part II. Emerging models of emotional development in infancy. In: S. I. Greenspan & G. H. Pollock (Eds.), *The Course of Life: Infancy and Early Childhood* (pp. 85–112). Washington, DC: DHSS.

Emde, R. (1980c). Ways of thinking about new knowledge and further research from a developmental orientation. *Psychoanalysis and Contemporary Thought, 3*: 213–235.

Emde, R. (1981). Changing models of infancy and the nature of early development: remodelling the foundation. *Journal of the American Psychoanalytic Association, 29*: 179–219.

Emde, R. (1988). Development terminable and interminable. I. Innate and motivational factors from infancy. *International Journal of Psycho-Analysis, 69*: 23–42.

Emde, R. (1992). Individual meaning and increasing complexity: contributions of Sigmund Freud and Reni Spitz to Developmental Psychology. *Developmental Psychology, 28*: 347–359.

Emde, R. (1995). Epilogue: a beginning—research approaches and expanding horizons for psychoanalysis. In: T. Shapiro & R. Emde (Eds.), *Research in Psychoanalysis, Process, Development, Outcome* (pp. 411–424). Madison, CT: International Universities Press.

Emde, R., & Buchsbaum, H. (1990). "Didn't you hear my mommy?" Autonomy with connectedness in moral self-emergence. In: D. Cicchetti & M. Beeghly (Eds.), *The Self in Transition* (pp. 35–60). Chicago, IL: University of Chicago Press.

Etchegoyen, H. (1996). Interview with Horacio Etchegoyen by Leopold Nosek. *Newsletter of the International Psychoanalytic Association, 5* (1): 56–62.

Fabricius, J. (1995). "The missing father–interpretation and developmental help in the analysis of a parent." Paper presented at an Anna Freud Centre Wednesday Meeting.

Fairbairn, W. (1952). *Psycho-Analytic Studies of the Personality*. London: Tavistock/Routledge & Kegan Paul.

Fajardo, B. (1993). Conditions for the relevance of infant research to clinical psychoanalysis. *International Journal of Psycho-Analysis, 74*: 975–992.

Ferenczi, S. (1932). *Clinical Diary*, ed. by J. Dupont, trans. by M. Balint & N. Zarday Jackson. Cambridge, MA: Harvard University Press.

Field, T., Healey, B., Goldstein, S., Perry, S., & Bendell, D. (1988). Infants of depressed mothers show "depressed" behaviour even with nondepressed adults. *Child Development, 59*: 1569–1579.

Fonagy, P. (1989). On tolerating mental states: theory of mind in borderline personality. *Bulletin of the Anna Freud Centre, 12*: 91–115.

Fonagy, P., & Moran, G. (1991). Understanding psychic change in child analysis. *International Journal of Psycho-Analysis, 72*: 15–22.

Fonagy, P., Moran, G., Edgcumbe, R., Kennedy, H., & Target, M. (1993). The roles of mental representations and mental processes in therapeutic action. *Psychoanalytic Study of the Child, 48*: 9–48.

Fonagy, P., Moran, G., & Target, M. (1993). Aggression and the psychological self. *International Journal of Psycho-Analysis, 74*: 471–485.

Fonagy, P., Steele, H., Moran, G., Steele, M., & Higgitt, A. (1991). The capacity for understanding mental states: the reflective self in parent and child and its significance for security of attachment. *Infant Mental Health Journal, 13*: 200–217.

Fonagy, P., Steele, M., Steele, H., Leigh, T., Kennedy, R., Mattoon, G., & Target, M. (1995). Attachment, the reflective self, and borderline states: the predictive specificity of the Adult Attachment Interview and pathological emotional development. In: S. Goldberg, R. Muir, & J. Kerr (Eds.), *Attachment Theory: Social, Developmental and Clinical Perspectives* (pp. 233–278). New York: Analytic Press.

Fonagy, P., & Target, M. (1995). Towards understanding violence: the use of the body and the role of the father. *International Journal of Psycho-Analysis, 76*: 487–502.

Fonagy, P., & Target, M. (1996a). A contemporary psychoanalytical perspective: psychodynamic developmental therapy. In: E. Hibbs & P. Jensen (Eds.), *Psychosocial Treatments for Child and Adolescent Disorders*. Washington, DC: American Psychological Association.

Fonagy, P., & Target, M. (1996b). Playing with reality: I. Theory of mind and the normal development of psychic reality. *International Journal of Psycho-Analysis, 77*: 217–233.

Fonagy, P., & Target, M. (1997a). Attachment and reflective function: Their role in self-organization. *Development & Psychopathology, 9*: 679–700.

Fonagy, P., & Target, M. (1997b). Introduction to the recovered memory debate: an empirical and psychoanalytical perspective. In: J. Sandler & P. Fonagy (Eds.), *Recovered Memories of Abuse: True or False?* (pp.183–216). London: Karnac Books.

Fonagy, P., Target, M., Edgcumbe, R., Moran, G., & Miller, J. (in preparation) *The Hampstead Manual of Intensive and Non-Intensive Dynamic Psychotherapy with Children.* New York: Guilford Press.

Fonagy, P., Target, M., Steele, M., & Gerber, A. (1995). Psychoanalytic perspectives on developmental psychopathology. In: D. Cicchetti & D. Cohen (Eds.), *Developmental Psychopathology, Vol. 1: Theory and Methods* (pp. 504–554). New Haven, CT: Yale University Press.

Fox, N. A., Kimmerly, N. L., & Schafer, W. D. (1991). Attachment to mother/attachment to father: A meta-analysis. *Child Development, 62*: 210–225.

Freud, A. (1949). Aggression in relation to emotional development: normal and pathological. *Psychoanalytic Study of the Child, 3/4*: 37–42.

Freud, A. (1965). *Normality and Pathology in Childhood.* New York: International Universities. Press.

Freud, A. (1970). Problems of termination in child analysis. In: *The Writings of Anna Freud, Vol. 7* (pp. 3–21). New York: International Universities Press.

Freud, A. (1975). The Nursery School of the Hampstead Child-Therapy Clinic. *Psychoanalytic Study of the Child, Monograph Series, 5*: 127–132.

Freud, A. (1976). Psychopathology seen against the background of normal development. In: *Psychoanalytic Study of Normal Development* (pp. 82–95). London: Hogarth Press.

Freud, A. (1978). The principal task of child analysis. In: *The Writings of Anna Freud, Vol. 8.* New York: International Universities Press.

Freud, A., & Burlingham, D. (1943). *War and Children.* New York: Medical War Books.

Freud, S. (1900a). *The Interpretation of Dreams. S.E., 4–5.*

Freud, S. (1901b). *The Psychopathology of Everyday Life. S.E.,* 6.

Freud, S. (1905d). *Three Essays on the Theory of Sexuality. S.E.,* 7.

Freud, S. (1920g). *Beyond the Pleasure Principle. S.E.,* 1.

Freud, S. (1923b). *The Ego and the Id. S.E.,* 19.

Freud, S. (1933a). *New Introductory Lectures on Psycho-Analysis. S.E.,* 22.

Freud, S. (1940a [1938]). *An Outline of Psycho-Analysis. S.E.,* 23.

Freud, S. (1950 [1895]). A project for a scientific psychology. *S.E., 1.*

Furman, E. (1974). *A Child's Parent Dies.* New Haven, CT: Yale University Press.

Furman, E. (1982). Mothers have to be there to be left. *Psychoanalytic Study of the Child,* 37: 15–28.

Furman, E. (1985). On fusion, integration and feeling good. *Psychoanalytic Study of the Child,* 40: 81–110.

Furman, E. (1986). On trauma: when is the death of a parent traumatic? *Psychoanalytic Study of the Child,* 41: 191–208.

Furman, E. (1992). *Toddlers and Their Mothers.* Madison, CT: International Universities Press.

Furman, E. (1997). Introduction to the Panel on Manifestations of Sexuality in the Analysis of Children, co-sponsored by the Association for Child Psychoanalysis. Fortieth IPA Congress, Barcelona.

Furman, R. (1994a). Discussion of "Hostile destructive behaviour in the analytic situation". *Child Analysis,* 5: 102–108.

Furman, R. (1994b). Some aspects of the analyst–analysand relationship. *Child Analysis,* 6: 106–127.

Gabbard, G. O. (1989). On "doing nothing" in the psychoanalytic treatment of the refractory borderline patient. *International Journal of Psycho-Analysis,* 70: 527–534.

Garbarino, J., & Sherman, D. (1990). High-risk neighbourhoods and high-risk families: the human ecology of child maltreatment. *Child Development,* 51: 188–198.

Gavshon, A. (1987). Treatment of an atypical boy. *Psychoanalytic Study of the Child,* 42: 145–171.

George, C., Kaplan, N., & Main, M. (1995). *The Berkeley Adult Attachment Interview.* Berkeley, CA: Department of Psychology, University of California.

Gergely, G., & Csibra, G. (1996). "Understanding rational actions in infancy: teleological interpretations without mental attribution. Symposium on 'Early Perception of Social Contingencies'." Paper presented at the 10th Biennial International Conference on Infant Studies, Providence, RI.

Gergely, G., & Watson, J. (1996). The social biofeedback model of parental affect-mirroring. *International Journal of Psycho-Analysis*, 77: 1181–1212.

Gergely, G., Nadasdy, Z., Csibra, G., & Biro, S. (1995). Taking the intentional stance at 12 months of age. *Cognition, 56*: 165–193.

Glover, E. (1937). Symposium on the theory of therapeutic results in psychoanalysis. *International Journal of Psycho-Analysis. 18*: 125–132.

Goosens, F., & van IJzendoorn, M. (1990). Quality of infants' attachment to professional caregivers. *Child Development, 61*: 832–837.

Gopnik, A. (1993). How we know our minds: the illusion of first-person knowledge of intentionality. *Behavioral and Brain Sciences, 16*: 1–14, 29–113.

Gopnik, A., & Astington, J. W. (1988). Children's understanding of representational change and its relation to the understanding of false belief and the appearance–reality distinction. *Child Development, 59*: 26–37.

Green, A. (1995). "Has sexuality got anything to do with psychoanalysis?" Freud Birthday Lecture, University College London.

Greenacre, P. (1980). A historical sketch of the use and disuse of reconstruction. *Psychoanalytic Study of the Child, 35*: 35–40.

Greenson, R. (1967). *The Technique and Practice of Psycho-Analysis*. London: Hogarth.

Greenspan, S. (1997). *Developmentally Based Psychotherapy*. Madison, CT: International Universities Press.

Grossmann, K., Grossmann, K. E., Spangler, G., Suess, G., & Unzner, L. (1985). Maternal sensitivity and newborn orienting responses as related to quality of attachment in Northern Germany. In: I. Bretherton & E. Waters (Eds.), *Growing Points in Attachment Theory and Research. Monographs of the Society for Research in Child Development, 50* (1–2): 233–256.

Hamilton, C. (1994). *Continuity and Discontinuity of Attachment from Infancy through Adolescence*. Unpublished doctoral dissertation, University of California at Los Angeles.

Hamilton, V. (1987). Some problems in the clinical application of attachment theory. *Psychoanalytic Psychotherapy, 3*: 67–83.

Herman, J. (1992). *Trauma and Recovery*. New York: Basic Books.

Herzog, J. (1995). Finding the mother and the father in the analytic play-space: attributes of neurotic process and its subsequent analytic exploration. *Bulletin of the Anna Freud Centre, 18*: 261–277.

Hobson, P. (1993). Understanding persons: the role of affect. In: S. Baron-Cohen et al. (Eds.), *Understanding Other Minds* (pp. 204–227). Oxford: Oxford University Press.

Hobson, R. P. (1995). The intersubjective domain: approaches from developmental psychology. In: T. Shapiro & R. Emde (Eds.), *Research in Psychoanalysis: Process, Development, Outcome*. Madison, CT: International Universities Press.

Hoffer, W. (1981). *Early Development and Education of the Child*. New York: Aronson.

Hopkins, J. (1992). Psychoanalysis, interpretation, and science. In: J. Hopkins & A. Saville (Eds.), *Psychoanalysis, Mind and Art: Perspectives on Richard Wollheim* (pp. 3–34). Oxford: Blackwell.

Hopkins, J. (1996). From baby games to let's pretend: the achievement of playing. *Journal of the British Association of Psychotherapy, 31* (1, Part 2): 20–27.

Hurry, A. (1990). Bisexual conflict and paedophilic fantasies in the analysis of a late adolescent. *Journal of Child Psychotherapy, 16*: 5–28.

Hurry, A. (1994a). Hostile destructive behaviour in the analytic situation. *Child Analysis, 5*: 79–101.

Hurry, A. (1994b). Homosexuality, biology and the work of Richard Isay. *Journal of the British Association of Psychotherapy, 27*: 123–129.

Hurry, A., & Sandler, J. (1971). Coping with reality: the child's defences against the external world. *British Journal of Medical Psychology, 44*: 379–385.

Isaacs, S. (1934). Rebellious and defiant children. In: *Childhood and After* (pp. 23–35). London: Routledge & Kegan Paul.

Isabella, R. A. (1993). Origins of attachment: maternal interactive behaviour across the first year. *Child Development, 64*: 605–621.

Isabella, R. A., & Belsky, J. (1991). Interactional synchrony and the origins of infant–mother attachment: a replication study. *Child Development, 62*: 373–384.

Isabella, R. A., Belsky, J., & von Eye, A. (1989). Origins of infant–mother attachment: an examination of interactional synchrony during the infant's first year. *Developmental Psychology, 25*: 12–21.

Johnson-Laird, P. N., & Byrne, R. M. (1991). *Deduction*. Hillsdale, NJ: Erlbaum.

Johnson-Laird, P. N., & Byrne, R. M. (1993). Precis of deduction. *Behavioral & Brain Sciences, 16*: 323–380.

Kagan, J. (1982). *Psychological Research on the Human Infant: An Evaluative Summary.* New York: Wiley.

Kantrowitz, J. (1995). Outcome research in psychoanalysis: review and reconsiderations. In: T. Shapiro & R. Emde (Eds.), *Research in Psychoanalysis: Process, Development, Outcome* (pp. 313–328). Madison, CT: International Universities Press.

Kantrowitz, J. (1997). A different perspective on the therapeutic process: the impact of the patient on the analyst. *Journal of the American Psychoanalytic Association, 45* (1): 127–153.

Kaplan-Solms, K., & McLean, D. (1995). Differential diagnosis of language disorder in a child-analytic setting. *Bulletin of the Anna Freud Centre, 18*: 187–204.

Kennedy, H. (1971). Problems in reconstruction in child analysis. *Psychoanalytic Study of the Child, 26*: 386–402. New York: Quadrangle.

Kennedy, H. (1979). The role of insight in child analysis: a developmental viewpoint. *Journal of the American Psychoanalytic Association, 27* (suppl.): 9–28.

Kleeman, J. (1967). The peek-a-boo game, Part 1: its origins, meanings and related phenomena in the first year. *Psychoanalytic Study of the Child, 22*: 239–273.

Kleeman, J. (1973). The peek-a-boo game: its evolution and associated behaviour, especially bye-bye and shame expression during the second year. *Journal of the American Academy of Child and Adolescent Psychiatry, 12*: 1–23.

Klein, M. (1945). The Oedipus complex in the light of early anxieties. In: *The Writings of Melanie Klein* (pp. 370–419). London: Hogarth Press, 1975.

Klein, M. (1957). *Envy and Gratitude.* London: Tavistock.

Kohon, G. (Ed.) (1986a). *The British School of Psychoanalysis: The Independent Tradition.* London: Free Association Books.

Kohon, G. (1986b). Introduction. In: G. Kohon (Ed.), *The British School of Psychoanalysis: The Independent Tradition* (pp. 19–80). London: Free Association Books.

Lamb, M. E., Thompson, R. A., Gardner, W. P., Charnov, E. L., & Estes, D. (1984). Security of infantile attachment as assessed in the "strange situation": its study and biological interpretation. *Behavioral and Brain Sciences, 7*: 127–147.

Lanyado, M. (1990). Putting theory into practice: struggling with perversion and chaos in the analytic situation. *Journal of Child Psychotherapy, 17* (1): 25–40.

Lewontin, R., Rose, S., & Kamin, L. (1984). *Not in Our Genes: Biology, Ideology and Human Nature.* New York: Pantheon Books.

Lichtenberg, J. D. (1987). Infant studies and clinical work with adults. *Psychoanalytic Inquiry, 7:* 311–330.

Lieberman, A. F., & Pawl, J. H. (1990). Disorders of attachment and secure base behavior in the second year of life: conceptual issues and clinical intervention. In: M. T. Greenberg, D. Cicchetti, & E. M. Cummings (Eds.), *Attachment in the Preschool Years* (pp. 375–398). Chicago, IL: University of Chicago Press.

Lionells, M. (1995). The interpersonal self, uniqueness, will and intentionality. In: J. Fiscalini, C. H. Mann, & D. B. Stern (Eds.), *Handbook of Interpersonal Psychoanalysis* (pp. 31–61). Hillsdale, NJ: Analytic Press.

Loewald, H. W. (1960). On the therapeutic action of psychoanalysis, *International Journal of Psycho-Analysis, 41:* 16–33.

Londerville, S., & Main, M. (1981). Security of attachment, compliance, and maternal training methods in the second year of life. *Developmental Psychology, 17:* 238–299.

Lyons-Ruth, K. (1996). Attachment relationships among children with aggressive behavior problems: the role of disorganized early attachment patterns. *Journal of Consulting & Clinical Psychology, 64:* 32–40.

Lyons-Ruth, K., Alpern, L., & Repacholi, B. (1993). Disorganized infant attachment classification and maternal psychosocial problems as predictors of hostile–aggressive behavior in the preschool classroom. *Child Development, 64:* 572–585.

Mahler, M. (1968). *On Human Symbiosis and the Vicissitudes of Individuation, Vol. 1: Infantile Psychosis.* New York: International Universities Press.

Mahler, M., Pine, F., & Bergman, A. (1975). *The Psychological Birth of the Human Infant.* London: Hutchinson.

Main, M. (1991). Metacognitive knowledge, metacognitive monitoring, and singular (coherent) vs (incoherent) models of attachment: findings and directions for future research. In: J. S. P. Harris & C. Parkes (Eds.), *Attachment Across the Lifecycle.* New York: Routledge.

Main, M., & Goldwyn, R. (1994). *Adult Attachment Rating and Classifi-cation System, Version 6.0*. Unpublished manuscript, University of California at Berkeley.

Main, M., & Hesse, E. (1992). Disorganized/disoriented infant behav-iour in the Strange Situation, lapses in the monitoring of reasoning and discourse during the parent's Adult Attachment Interview, and dissociative states. In: M. Ammaniti & D. Stern (Eds.), *Attach-ment and Psychoanalysis*. Rome: Gius, Latereza & Figli.

Main, M., & Solomon, J. (1990). Procedures for identifying infants as disorganized/disoriented during the Ainsworth Strange Situa-tion. In D. C. M. Greenberg & E. M. Cummings (Eds.), *Attachment During the Preschool Years: Theory, Research and Intervention* (pp. 121–160). Chicago, IL: University of Chicago Press.

Malatesta, C. Z., Grigoryev, P., Lamb, C., Albin, M., & Culver, C. (1986). Emotional socialisation and expressive development in pre-term and full-term infants. *Child Development, 57*: 316–330.

Mayes, L., & Cohen, D. (1993). Playing and therapeutic action in child analysis. *International Journal of Psycho-Analysis, 74*: 1235–1244 .

Meltzoff, A. (1993). The role of imitation in understanding persons and developing a theory of mind. In: S. Baron-Cohen, H. Tager-Flusberg, & D. Cohen (Eds.), *Understanding Other Minds: Perspec-tives from Autism*. New York: Oxford University Press.

Meltzoff, A., & Moore, M. K. (1989). Imitation in newborn infants: exploring the range of gestures imitated and the underlying mechanisms. *Developmental Psychology, 25*: 954–962.

Morton, J. (1997). Cognitive perspectives on recovered memories. In J. Sandler & P. Fonagy (Eds.), *Recovered Memories of Abuse: True or False?* (pp. 39-69). London: Karnac Books.

Neisser, U. (1991). Two perceptually given aspects of the self and their development. *Development Review, 11*: 197–209.

Neubauer, P. (1994). The role of displacement in psychoanalysis. *Psy-choanalytic Study of the Child, 49*: 107–119.

Novick, J. (1989). How does infant research affect our clinical work with adolescents? In: S. Dowling & A. Rothstein (Eds.), *The Signifi-cance of Infant Observational Research for Clinical Work with Children, Adolescents and Adults* (pp. 27–39). Madison, CT: International Universities Press.

Novick, J. (1990). Comments on termination in child, adolescent and adult analysis. *Psychoanalytic Study of the Child, 45*: 419–436.

Novick, J., & Novick, K. (1996). *Fearful Symmetry. The Development and Treatment of Sadomasochism*. Northvale, NJ: Aronson.

Novick, K. (1990). Access to infancy: different ways of remembering. *International Journal of Psycho-Analysis, 71*: 335–349.

O'Connor, M., Sigman, M., & Kasasi, C. (1992). Attachment behavior of infants exposed prenatally to alcohol. *Developmental Psychopathology, 4*: 243–256.

Ogden, T. (1994). The analytic third: working with intersubjective clinical facts. *International Journal of Psycho-Analysis, 75*: 3-19.

Ornstein, A., & Ornstein, P. (1994). On the conceptualisation of clinical facts in psychoanalysis. *International Journal of Psycho-Analysis, 75*: 977–994.

Pally, R. (1997). Developments in neuroscience. I: How brain development is shaped by genetic and environmental factors. *International Journal of Psycho-Analysis, 78*: 587–593.

Parens, H. (1991). A view of the development of hostility in early life. *Journal of the American Psychoanalytic Association, 39*: 75–108.

Penman, A. (1995). "'There has never been anything like a Classical Child Analysis': clinical discussions with Anna Freud, 1970–71." Paper presented at the Anna Freud Centre pre-Colloquium meeting.

Perner, J., Leekam, S., & Wimmer, H. (1987). Three-year-olds' difficulty in understanding false belief: cognitive limitation, lack of knowledge, or pragmatic misunderstanding? *British Journal of Developmental Psychology, 5*: 125–137.

Perry, B., Pollard, R., Blakley, T., Baker, W., & Vigilante, D. (1995). Childhood trauma, the neurobiology of adaptation, and "use-dependent" development of the brain: how "states" becomes "traits". *Infant Mental Health Journal, 16* (4): 271–291.

Pine, F. (1994). Some impressions regarding conflict, defect and deficit. *Psychoanalytic Study of the Child, 49*: 222–240.

Radojevic, M. (1992). "Predicting quality of infant attachment to father at 15 months from pre-natal paternal representations of attachment: an Australian contribution." Paper presented at the 25th International Congress of Psychology, Brussels, Belgium.

Rayner, E. (1992). Matching, attunement and the psychoanalytic dialogue. *International Journal of Psycho-Analysis, 73*: 39–54.

Rose, S. (1995). The rise of neurogenetic determinism, *Nature, 373*: 380–382.

Rose, S. (1997). *Lifelines: Biology, Freedom, Determinism*. London: Allen Lane/Penguin.

Ruszczynki, S. (1998). The "Marital Triangle": towards "Triangular Space" in the intimate couple relationship. *Journal of the British Association of Psychotherapists, 34* (3): 33–47.

Sandbank, T. (1993). Psychoanalysis and maternal work—some parallels. *International Journal of Psycho-Analysis, 74*: 715- 727.

Sandler, A.-M. (1996). The psychoanalytic legacy of Anna Freud. *Psychoanalytic Study of the Child, 51*: 270–284.

Sandler, J. (1976). Countertransference and role responsiveness. *International Review of Psychoanalysis, 3*: 43–47.

Sandler, J. , & Sandler, A.-M. (1997). A psychoanalytic theory of repression and the unconscious. In: J. Sandler & P. Fonagy (Eds.), *Recovered Memories of Abuse: True or False?* (pp. 163–181). London: Karnac Books.

Sandler, J., & Joffe, W. (1967). The tendency to persistence in psychological function and development, with special reference to fixation and regression. *Bulletin of the Menninger Clinic, 31*: 257–271.

Sandler, J., & Joffe, W. (1969). Towards a basic psychoanalytic model. *International Journal of Psycho-Analysis, 50*: 79–90.

Sandler, J., Kennedy, H., & Tyson, R. (1980). *The Technique of Child Psychoanalysis. Discussions with Anna Freud*. Cambridge, MA: Harvard University Press.

Sandler, J., & Sandler, A-M. (1984). The past unconscious, the present unconscious and interpretation of the transference. *Psychoanalytic Inquiry, 4*: 367–399.

Schneider-Rosen, K., & Cicchetti, D. (1984). The relationship between affect and cognition in maltreated infants: quality of attachment and the development of visual self-recognition. *Child Development, 55*: 648–658.

Schneider-Rosen, K., & Cicchetti, D. (1991). Early self-knowledge and emotional development: visual self-recognition and affective reactions to mirror self-image in maltreated and non-maltreated toddlers. *Developmental Psychology, 27*: 481–488.

Settlage, C. (1993). Therapeutic process and developmental process in the restructuring of object and self constancy. *Journal of the American Psychoanalytic Association, 41*: 473–492.

Shafran, R. (1995). Infancy. In: J. Fiscalini, C. H. Mann, & D. B. Stern

(Eds.), *Handbook of Interpersonal Psychoanalysis* (pp. 235–251). Hillsdale, NJ: Analytic Press.

Shapiro, T., & Emde, R. (Eds.) (1995). *Research in Psychoanalysis*. Madison, CT: International Universities Press.

Shengold, L. (1988). *Halo in the Sky: Observations on Anality and Defence*. New York: Guilford Press.

Slade, A. (1994). Making meaning and making believe: their role in clinical process. In: A. Slade & D. Wolf (Eds.), *Children at Play: Clinical and Developmental Approaches to Meaning and Representation* (pp. 81–107). New York/London: Oxford University Press.

Slade, A., Belsky, J., Aber, L., & Phelps, J. L. (in press). Maternal representations of their toddlers: links to adult attachment and observed mothering. *Developmental Psychology*.

Spangler, G., & Grossman, K. E. (1993). Biobehavioral organization in securely and insecurely attached infants. *Child Development, 64*: 1439–1450.

Spence, D. P. (1982). *Narrative Truth and Historical Truth. Meaning and Interpretation in Psychoanalysis*. New York/London: Norton.

Spence, D. P. (1984). *The Freudian Metaphor*. New York: Norton.

Sprince, M. (1971). An adolescent boy's battle against recovery: the analysis of an adolescent whose ongoing pre-oedipal tie to the mother aroused massive treatment resistance and a terror of health. *Psychoanalytic Study of the Child, 26*: 453–482.

Sroufe, L. A. (1990). An organizational perspective on the self. In: D. Cicchetti & M. Beeghly (Eds.), *The Self in Transition: Infancy to Childhood* (pp. 281–307). Chicago, IL: University of Chicago Press.

Steele, H., Steele, M., & Fonagy, P. (1996). Associations among attachment classifications of mothers, fathers, and their infants: evidence for a relationship-specific perspective. *Child Development, 67*: 541–555.

Stein, A. (1994). An observational study of mothers with eating disorders and their infants. *Journal of Child Psychology and Psychiatry and Allied Disciplines, 35* (4): 733–748.

Steiner, J. (1994). Patient-centred and analyst-centred interpretations: some implications of containment and countertransference. *Psychoanalytic Inquiry, 14*: 406–422.

Stern, D. N. (1985). *The Interpersonal World of the Infant: A View from Psychoanalysis and Developmental Psychology*. New York: Basic Books.

Stern, D. N. (1994). One way to build a clinically relevant baby. *Infant Mental Health Journal, 15*: 36–54.

Stewart, H. (1989). Technique at the basic fault/regression. *International Journal of Psycho-Analysis, 70*: 221–230.

Strachey, J. (1934). The nature of the therapeutic action of psychoanalysis. *International Journal of Psycho-Analysis, 15*: 127–159.

Sullivan, H. S. (1953). *The Interpersonal Theory of Psychiatry.* New York: Norton.

Tähkä, V. (1993). *Mind and Its Treatment.* Madison, CT: International Universities Press.

Target, M., & Fonagy, P. (1996). Playing with reality. II: The development of psychic reality from a theoretical perspective. *International Journal of Psycho-Analysis, 77*: 459–479.

Tonnesmann, M. (1980). Adolescent re-enactment, trauma and reconstruction. *Journal of Child Psychotherapy, 6*: 23–44.

Trevarthen, C. (1979). Communication and cooperation in early infancy: a description of primary intersubjectivity. In: M. Bullowa (Ed.), *Before Speech: The Beginning of Interpersonal Communication* (pp. 321–347). Cambridge: Cambridge University Press.

Trevarthen, C., & Marwick, H. (1986). Signs of motivation for speech in infants, and the nature of a mother's support for development of language. In B. Lindblom & R. Zetterstrom (Eds.), *Precursors of Early Speech.* Basingstoke: Macmillan.

Tronick, E. (1989). Emotions and emotional communication in infants. *American Psychologist, 44*: 112–119.

Tronick, E., & Cohn, J. F. (1989). Infant–mother face-to-face interaction: age and gender differences in coordination and the occurrence of miscoordination. *Child Development, 60*: 85–92.

van den Boom, D. (1990). Preventive intervention and the quality of mother–infant interaction and infant exploration in irritable infants. In: W. Koops et al. (Eds.), *Developmental Psychology Behind the Dikes* (pp. 249–270). Amsterdam: Eburon.

van den Boom, D. (1995). Do first-year intervention effects endure? Follow-up during toddlerhood of a sample of Dutch irritable infants. *Child Development, 66*: 1798–1816.

van IJzendoorn, M. H. (1995). Adult attachment representations, parental responsiveness, and infant attachment: a meta-analysis on the predictive validity of the Adult Attachment Interview. *Psychological Bulletin, 117*: 387–403.

van IJzendoorn, M. H., Goldberg, S., Kroonenberg, P. M., & Frenkel, O. J. (1992). The relative effects of maternal and child problems on the quality of attachment: a meta-analysis of attachment in clinical samples. *Child Development, 59*: 147–156.

Ward, M. J., & Carlson, E. A. (1995). Associations among Adult Attachment representations, maternal sensitivity, and infant–mother attachment in a sample of adolescent mothers. *Child Development, 66*: 69–79.

Waters, E., Merrick, S., Albersheim, L., Treboux, D., & Crowell, J. (1995, May). "From the strange situation to the Adult Attachment Interview: a 20-year longitudinal study of attachment security in infancy and early adulthood." Paper presented at the Society for Research in Child Development, Indianapolis.

Weiss, J. (1995). Empirical studies of the psychoanalytic process. In: T. Shapiro & R. Emde (Eds.), *Research in Psychoanalysis: Process, Development, Outcome* (pp. 7–29). Madison, CT: International Universities Press.

WHO (1992). *ICD–10 Classification of Mental and Behavioural Disorders: Clinical Descriptions and Diagnostic Guidelines*. Geneva.

Willock, B. (1990). From acting out to interactive play. *International Journal of Psycho-Analysis, 71*: 321–334.

Winnicott, D. W. (1947). Hate in the counter-transference. *International Journal of Psycho-Analysis* (1949), *30*: 69–74.

Winnicott, D. W. (1958). The capacity to be alone. In: *The Maturational Processes and the Facilitating Environment*. London: Hogarth Press, 1965. [Reprinted London: Karnac Books, 1990.]

Winnicott, D. W. (1960). Ego distortion in terms of true and false self. In: *The Maturational Processes and the Facilitating Environment* (pp. 140–152). London: Hogarth, 1965. [Reprinted London: Karnac Books, 1990.]

Winnicott, D. W. (1963). Dependence in infant-care, in child-care, and in the psycho-analytic setting. In: *The Maturational Processes and the Facilitating Environment* (pp. 249–259). London: Hogarth Press, 1965. [Reprinted London: Karnac Books, 1990.]

Winnicott, D. W. (1965). *The Maturational Processes and the Facilitating Environment*. London: Hogarth Press. [Reprinted London: Karnac Books, 1990.]

Winnicott, D. W. (1967). Mirror-role of mother and family in child development. In: P. Lomas (Ed.), *The Predicament of the Family: A*

Psycho-Analytical Symposium (pp. 26–33). London: Hogarth. Also in *Playing and Reality*. London: Tavistock, 1971.

Winnicott, D. W. (1971). *Playing and Reality*. London: Tavistock.

Wolff, P. H. (1996). The irrelevance of infant observations for psycho-analysis. *Journal of the American Psychoanalytic Association, 44*: 369–392.

Wollheim, R. (1995). *The Mind and Its Depths*. Cambridge, MA: Harvard University Press.

Yanof, J. (1996). Language, communication and transference in child analysis. 1. Selective mutism: the medium is the message. 2. Is child analysis really analysis? *Journal of the American Psychoanalytic Association, 44*: 79–116.

Young-Bruehl, E. (1988). *Anna Freud*, London: Macmillan.

Zahn-Waxler, C., Kochanska, G., Krupnick, J., & McKnew, D. (1990). Patterns of guilt in children of depressed and well mothers. *Developmental Psychology, 26*: 51–59.

Zahn-Waxler, C., Radke-Yarrow, M., Wagner, E., & Chapman, M. (1992). Development of concern for others. *Developmental Psychology, 28*: 126–136.

Zaphiriou Woods, M. (1988). Developmental help: interventions in the Nursery School. *Bulletin of the Anna Freud Centre, 11*: 295–305.

Zeanah, C. H., Benoit, D., Barton, M., Regan, C., Hirshberg, L. M., & Lipsitt, L. P. (1993). Representations of attachment in mothers and their one-year-old infants. *Journal of the American Academy of Child and Adolescent Psychiatry, 32*: 278–286.

INDEX